AMERICAN
DEMOCRACY &
THE VATICAN:
POPULATION
GROWTH & NATIONAL
SECURITY

AMERICAN
DEMOCRACY &
THE VATICAN:
POPULATION
GROWTH & NATIONAL
SECURITY

BY STEPHEN D. MUMFORD

HUMANIST PRESS

AMHERST, NEW YORK 14226

Chapter one, "Population Growth and Global Security: Toward an American Strategic Commitment," copyright © 1980 by Stephen D. Mumford.

Chapter three, "Abortion: A National Security Issue," copyright © 1982 by C. V. Mosby Co., reprinted with permission from the *American Journal of Obstetrics and Gynecology*, in which it first appeared.

Library of Congress Catalog Card Number: 84-72500

ISBN 0-931779-00-6 Hardcover
ISBN 0-931779-01-4 Paperback

Printed in the United States of America.

This book is dedicated to U.S. Navy Lt. Cdr. Albert Schaufelberger III, who understood the relationship between overpopulation and war and who gave his life in El Salvador, May 25, 1983, and to four other men of courage: Father Arthur McCormack, journalist Bill Moyers, former CIA Director William Colby, and LTC John G. Wilcox.

Contents

Foreword

Rapid population growth and a thermonuclear holocaust are recognized as the two major threats to modern civilization. Progress in reducing the threat of each has been remarkably slow. This might be expected in the case of the threat of nuclear war, considering the background of national interests and suspicions, especially among the superpowers. The lack of progress regarding population growth control is more puzzling.

The World Fertility Survey, the largest social science study ever conducted, has demonstrated that most women in developing countries with high population growth rates are having more children than they desire. An unfortunate symptom of this is the growing problem of child abandonment in these countries.

The 1984 United Nations International Conference on Population in Mexico City clearly defined the need for family-planning services, both as a basic human right and as a prerequisite to socio-economic development. The conference also recognized the threat to global security of failure to control population growth. One would think that the solution to rapid population growth is a straightforward public health matter of delivery of effective fertility control methods to the couples who desire such information. Some large populations, including China and Kerala State in India, have dramatically reduced birth rates in spite of low levels of economic development. Why is progress so slow in other parts of the developing world? Is any one method of fertility control essential to reach a population growth rate of one percent or less? Wherein lies the main obstruction to population growth control? How can it be overcome?

We are indebted to Dr. Stephen Mumford for his forthright analysis that provides answers to these critical questions. It is time that these issues are confronted and brought into open debate. There exists an urgent social responsibility to encourage such open and thoughtful debate.

ELTON KESSEL, M.D.

Preface

This book deals with the national and global security implications of world population growth and urges that this growth problem be redefined in terms different from the customary approaches. The solutions—modern methods of contraception, abortion, sterilization, expanding opportunities for women, sex education, and the like—are in fact gravely threatening the survival of the Vatican, at least its political dimension. According to Father Andrew Greeley, the Vatican leaders are concerned not so much with the religious dimensions of the Church as with its vast worldwide political power. The greater the number of their communicants, the greater the power of this hierarchy. These prelates, recognizing their jeopardy, have placed the religious dimension of the Church at risk in order to prevail politically.

The United States National Security Council, on the other hand, in 1979 and 1980, determined that world population growth seriously threatens the security of all nations including our own. Thus the dimensions of the conflict are defined.

The political Catholic Church (the Vatican) is pitted against the national security interests of the United States. Clearly, to ignore the population problem will be to invite severe consequences and, ultimately, a complete loss of our national security.

Thus threatened, the Vatican is resorting to desperate and bold measures in America. Four years ago, it went to great lengths to assist in the election of an American president, using the infrastructure created by the Catholic bishops' 1975 Pastoral Plan for Pro-Life Activities (often referred to as the Pastoral Plan of Action; *see*, appendix two), purportedly created to combat legalized abortion. The Reagan administration has been overwhelmingly the most Catholic in American history, and its agenda has been essentially the Vatican agenda.

About 4 percent of the U.S. population is Irish Roman Catholic. Mr. Reagan's father, like the leadership of the Catholic Church in America, was an Irish Roman Catholic, and his brother is a devout Catholic. No one doubts the president's close ties to the Catholic Church.

In any administration, the appointments most relevant to the population growth-security issue are national security advisor, secretary of state, director of the Central Intelligence Agency, attorney-general (responsible for illegal immigration control), and secretary of Health and Human Services (who sets the national example for provision of comprehensive family planning services).

Mr. Reagan has appointed three national security advisors— Richard Allen, William Clark, and James McFarland. All are Irish Catholic. His two secretaries of state have been Alexander Haig, an Irish Catholic, and George Schultz, a Catholic of German extraction. His CIA director is William Casey, an Irish Roman Catholic, as is his attorney-general, William French Smith. HHS Secretary Margaret Heckler is also Irish Roman Catholic.

In a nation in which only 4 percent of the population is Irish Catholic, this causes no small concern. Any scientist computing mathematical probabilities will agree that the odds of this arrangement happening by chance are nil. Now that it has become apparent that the agenda of the Reagan administration and the Vatican are essentially the same, concern has turned into alarm.

In his book, *American Freedom and Catholic Power*, published some thirty-five years ago, the Reverend Paul Blanshard discussed what theoretically could happen to American democracy if the Catholic Church conducted itself as it has in most other countries in recent history, manipulating governments at will.

Blanshard's book was labeled heretical and rabidly anti-Catholic. Librarians were ordered to remove it from their shelves. It was kept secretly in desk drawers. How tragic—for both non-Catholic and Catholic Americans.

Nowhere is it clearer that the best interests of the Vatican have superseded those of the United States than in matters concerning the population growth-national security issue. Many knowledgeable Americans, including Catholics, agree with another Irish Catholic American, a former secretary of defense and World Bank president, Robert McNamara, who believes that world population growth is a greater threat to U.S. security than thermonuclear war.

Of great importance is the fact that, like McNamara, most Catholic Americans do not subscribe to the Vatican position on population growth control. Catholic Americans use the same contraceptive methods and have abortions at the same rates as non-Catholic Americans, and they have the same desired family sizes. Furthermore, most American Catholics deeply disagree with the Vatican on the need for population growth control.

However, there is a cadre of devout Catholics, which, out of deep religious conviction, follow the dictates of the Vatican, without question. There is a smaller group of laypersons, less religious, that carry out orders for the rewards of power and privilege.

They have been joined by certain non-Catholics—fundamentalist Christians, Mormons, and Orothodox Jews—who are genuinely opposed to abortion, legal or not, although they are definitely in the minority among anti-abortionists (less than 30 percent of the activists). Other non-Catholic laypersons, such as Senator Helms and Congressman Levin, have joined the Vatican effort because they derive enormous power from the Vatican. *Nevertheless, it is undeniable that the energy, organization, and direction of the anti-abortion, anti-family-planning, anti-population-growth-control movement in the United States comes from the hierarchy of the Roman Catholic Church.*

The fears of the Reverend Mr. Blanshard are now being realized. The president, in a speech in Hoboken, New Jersey, on July 26, 1984, stated that he was following the leadership of Pope John Paul II in determining U.S. foreign policy in Central America in the latest efforts to save Vatican-backed oppressive governments from popular uprisings. The White House position paper prepared for the World Population Conference in Mexico City (*see*, appendix three) is the same as the Vatican policy on abortion, family planning, and population growth control.

The threat of the Vatican to democracy is overwhelmingly apparent in Pope Pius IX's Syllabus of Errors (*see*, appendix four), as binding today as when it was promulgated more than one hundred years ago. According to the Roman Catholic Encyclopedia, "all Catholics are bound to accept the syllabus." Today, before being ordained, every Catholic priest is required to swear to support the eighty articles of the syllabus. Priests who are American citizens have taken an oath to support a philosophy diametrically opposed to and condemning the principles of the Constitution of the United States and the Bill of Rights.

American Catholics are certain to pay a terrible price for this intrusion upon American sovereignty. In 1969, the so-called Soccer War was fought between El Salvador and Honduras. This was the first war ever directly attributed to overpopulation, a determination made by the Organization of American States. The war was prompted by massive illegal immigration from grossly overpopulated El Salvador into Honduras. Fifteen years later, the overpopulation problem continues to be all but ignored in El Salvador because the Vatican demands that it be ignored. The population today is growing at the incredible rate of 2.6 percent per year, and the country has a doubling time of *twenty-seven years!* The results of this continued growth have been general chaos, the illegal immigration of more than 20 percent of Salvadorans to the United States, a breakdown in social order, and destruction of the economic, social, and political structures of the country.

This is the kind of chaos that the United States has in store if we allow continued illegal immigration of tens of millions of Catholic Latin Americans and others into the United States. This approach to assuming control over the most powerful nation on earth appears to be what the Vatican has in mind, since it represents the only significant opposition to illegal immigration control.

The public trust in *all* American Catholics is imminently threatened by this refusal of the Vatican to respect American sovereignty. As soon as American non-Catholics sense that this trust has been broken by a significant number of Catholics who owe their first loyalty to the Vatican, public trust in Catholics in general will be destroyed, albeit undeservedly. If the Vatican proceeds with this infringement on U.S. sovereignty, a violent reaction is already predictable. Unfortunately, all of us will pay for the Vatican's struggle for power.

On September 12, 1984, Bill Moyers appeared with Dan Rather on the CBS evening news. His commentary referred to the alliance between the Roman Catholic bishops and Protestant fundamentalists. He discussed the threat of the separation of church and state issue, which has been renewed by the 1984 presidential campaign, and placed in the strongest terms the seriousness of this threat to America:

> *We have an alternative to civil war in this country—a holy civil war at that—and that is the Constitution.*

El Salvador and China offer us the best examples of the option Americans will have *if we continue to allow a government other than our own democratically representative one to determine U.S. foreign and domestic policy on population growth control activities.* Either an insecure nation in social, economic, and political chaos or a highly regimented one devoid of many cherished freedoms may be our future. Neither option should be acceptable to Americans. Population growth control is the only alternative.

This book is devoted to a complete discussion of the population growth-national security threat, and each issue set forth in the foregoing pages is discussed in depth.

STEPHEN D. MUMFORD

Introduction

There are two major issues of our time: the security threat of overpopulation and the threat of nuclear war. For the past several years,
the nuclear war threat has been the most widely discussed topic in
America, while overpopulation has received very little attention.
Recently, General Maxwell Taylor made a strong plea for the recognition of this problem in an editorial appearing in newspapers throughout this country. There was hardly any response. His book, *Precarious
Security*, published eight years ago, which made the same statement,
likewise prompted virtually no public debate. Why? The answer to this
question is the subject of this book. Chapter one makes the case that
overpopulation is the single greatest threat to national and global
security.

The great influx of illegal aliens is an imminent national security
threat. The reason why it is not being addressed is the subject of
chapter two.

Abortion is a serious national security issue. The logic behind this
statement is presented in chapter three. Not surprisingly, there has
been scarcely any public attention given to seeing abortion in this
context.

The Catholic Church intentionally or otherwise is thwarting
several social justice movements in the United States, including the
environmental, abortion, family planning, ERA, and illegal immigration control movements, because they are threatening the power of
the Vatican. Chapter four discusses why.

Chapter five presents the case for an American confrontation with the Vatican. It points out that Reagan's is the most Catholic administration in American history and why Catholics and non-Catholics alike should be deeply concerned.

Chapter one was prepared in collaboration with the Georgetown University Center for Strategic Studies. When the university blocked its publication because of its frank discussion of the seldom recognized role of the Roman Catholic Church, it was brought out as a monograph by the International Fertility Research Program in 1980 and distributed by the Population Action Council. It was subsequently published by *The Humanist* magazine in 1981. The next four chapters appeared in *The Humanist* as well: chapter two in 1981, chapter three in 1982, and chapters four and five in 1983. However, chapter three was originally carried in the *American Journal of Obstetrics and Gynecology* in 1982.

Unfortunately, all of the material in these chapters remains current, and, for this reason, it appears in this text in the original form. There were high hopes for changes in the American Church regarding population-related issues when, in 1979, the U.S. National Security Council determined that world population growth is a serious national security threat. We had expected more effective responses to these chapters from the growing numbers of Catholics working for changes within their Church. Except for a few bright spots, the responses have been disappointing and suggest that there will be but little change initiated from within the American Catholic Church. Chapter six offers specific examples of what American Catholics are saying in regard to the material in chapters one through five.

These first five chapters represent the *effects* of the Church on population growth control issues. Upon receipt of the shocking reactions such as those offered in chapter six, it became apparent that study of the foundation and inner workings of the Church was necessary to understand the background and *causes* of the obstruction by the Church. The remaining chapters are a product of this study.

Chapter seven takes a close look at the origins of power of the Vatican in America and shows why this power is threatened by population growth control. Chapter eight reveals the Vatican vitiation of the American population growth control establishment. Censorship has been the key to Vatican successes in America, including those thwarting population growth control. Chapter nine offers examples that have occurred early in 1984. Chapter ten summarizes the seriousness of the Vatican influence on U.S. policy making. The Reagan agenda appears identical to the Vatican agenda, and there is evidence that this is not by accident. It is clear that the Latinizing of American democracy is well underway. Chapter eleven defines why true American conservatives should be outraged by this Vatican influence on the government.

Milestones in the development of the current population growth threat to U.S. security are: (1) development of the ethic, "You should never criticize another person's religion," over the past two hundred years; (2) the ecumenical movement; (3) the Vatican's furthering and implementation of effective censorship of the American press regarding criticism of Vatican actions; (4) stress on the abortion issue; and (5) the creation of the Moral Majority by the Catholic Church to allow political mobilization under the cloak of American Protestant fundamentalism. These most important junctures are discussed and documented throughout the book.

This study finds that the implications of Vatican interference in the American democratic process for Catholics and non-Catholics alike during the next thirty years are most serious. The population growth control problem involves Vatican politics and must be discussed in these terms. At this point, it is clearly the most relevant discussion. The solution to the world population problem rests in considerable measure in the hands of the American press, which must break the improper actual and assumed censorship furthered by the Vatican in regard to its activities.

Two important points should be stressed and remembered as the reader studies the following pages.

The first is that a crucial distinction is made between the Catholic laity and their religion and the Vatican hierarchy and its economic and political power structure. The arguments presented here are solely concerned with the latter—a sovereign political entity whose wealth exceeds that of most nations on earth and whose power, because of its carefully maintained two-thousand-year-old hierarchical structure which allows for no dissent and its unique ability to act without territorial and other constraints faced by most nations, is enormous. There is virtually no difference between Catholics and non-Catholics in regard to desire for and use of contraception and frequency of obtaining abortions. The Church is capitalized in these pages for good reason—the subject is the Vatican hierarchy and the use of its power to influence other sovereign governments; the subject is not an individual's religion or his or her private practice thereof.

The second important point is that Protestant Americans have traditionally been unopposed to family planning and that the Vatican's cooptation of a segment of "Protestant" America is a political union. Many good conservatives and Protestants, such as Senator Barry Goldwater, have condemned the Moral Majority and its allies with good reason—they see it as a radical group with political objectives inimical to the United States and its Constitution. The Vatican is using this "fundamentalist" group, set up according to the blueprint prepared by the Vatican for organizing Catholic and non-Catholic groups for political purposes—the Bishops' Pastoral Plan for Pro-Life Activities (appendix two)—as an opening wedge to further its political ends in the United States. The Moral Majority and the Vatican are allies, and they are more than that. As has been the case in other such "religious" unions of the past, the Vatican has the most to gain.

Removal of Vatican politics from the worldwide population growth control effort will vastly enhance the prospects for successfully dealing with the overpopulation problem.

1.

Population Growth and Global Security: Toward an American Strategic Commitment

Prefatory Note

As the year 2000 approaches, the nightmares of overpopulation, widespread famine and disease, and an exhaustive depletion of our natural resources are quickly becoming realities. The Center for Strategic and International Studies's population studies program, long cognizant of these dangers, has been involved in a project addressing some sensitive and complex political questions surrounding international population growth control efforts. We are convinced that global population growth issues should be concerns of national security decision makers and we are perplexed by the government's deliberateness in not acknowledging this basic relationship.

With this fifth CSIS Note published within the framework of the Population Policy Roundtable, Dr. Stephen Mumford has written a monograph certain to incite controversy. CSIS clearly does not subscribe to every position taken it it; however, by placing demographic growth, global security, and American strategic interests on the same continuum, the author has produced a unique analysis of the population problem. He attacks the problem by highlighting three crucial areas for consideration: the relationship between population growth control and national security issues, the role of American leadership in resolving the problem, and the barriers to effective action—most notably, the anachronistic tenets of the Roman Catholic Church with regard to abortion and contraception. Dr. Mumford stresses the need for global cooperation and commitment if the problem is to be arrested, and he urges the United States to assume the responsibility of leading other countries in the fight to control population growth.

The recently published *Global 2000 Report to the President* concurs with many of Dr. Mumford's conclusions. It recognizes the "progressive degradation and impoverishment of the earth's natural resource base" and the need for international cooperation. And like Dr. Mumford's monograph, the *Global 2000 Report* realizes the political impact that an uncontrolled population growth would have on the relationship between industrialized nations and less developed countries (LDCs) where the greatest growth rates occur. In this modern political system of interdependence, the fates of both industrialized nations and LDCs are inextricably linked.

Dr. Mumford has held the position of scientist at the International Fertility Research Program (IFRP) since 1977, where he is primarily responsible for the development of surgical contraception research strategies. He has a degree in agriculture from the University of Kentucky and was later commissioned in the Army Medical Service Corps, leaving active duty with the rank of captain. During a tour of duty in Asia, he first recognized the linkage between political stability and population pressures. He obtained his doctorate in population studies from the University of Texas. Dr. Mumford is the author of *Population Growth Control: The Next Move is America's* (New York: Philosophical Library, Inc., 1977) and has written several other books and articles on the biomedical and social aspects of family planning. In 1978, he testified before the House Select Committee on Population on the topic of world population growth as a national security threat.

There is indisputable need to re-examine current population policies and to investigate alternative solutions to this potentially devastating problem.

Georges A. Fauriol
Population Studies
Third World Program
Center for Strategic and International Studies
Georgetown University
August 1980

Introduction

In the past three decades, a new threat to international and domestic security has emerged: uncontrolled world population movements, compounded by a global natural resource interdependence. If current growth rates continue, the inevitability of widespread social and political instability by the year 2000 makes population growth the most serious threat—a threat more often recognized than acknowledged.

Widespread acknowledgment and a corresponding political, moral, and economic commitment are essential if this strategic threat to world peace is to be countered. Yet, although some of our nation's finest minds have acknowledged the profound security implications of population growth over the past six years, they remain no more than a handful. Key factors delaying the appropriate commitment are the desire to avoid: (1) thinking about the gravity of the world predicament; (2) the issues of abortion and teenage childbearing; (3) confrontation with pronatalistic organizations; and, most significant, (4) confrontation with the hierarchy of the Roman Catholic Church.

The Catholic Church has exerted great influence on U.S. policy in population matters as a result of its intimidation of elected officials and the built-in reverence most Americans have for an ecclesiastical hierarchy. The teachings of the Church and its hierarchy's insistence that these teachings be followed have resulted in an unintentional suppression of the substantial knowledge about the consequences of overpopulation. The main source of energy, organization, and direction for the anti-abortion movement in the United States and the movement to frustrate enforcement of U.S. immigration laws is the Roman Catholic Church. Ultimately, either humankind or nature will sharply limit population growth—preferably, it will be humankind.

The current world population growth control effort is essentially ineffective. If we are to reverse this trend, the United States must overcome the formidable obstacle that the Catholic hierarchy presents and accept a new leadership role. I suggest that the United States is the only nation capable of successfully surmounting this obstacle.

Redefining National Security

Americans would like to forget that their national security is the foundation for the freedoms and privileges that they cherish. Freedom of political activity, of personal expression, and of the press cannot be realized in the absence of national security. But what do we mean by that? Two decades ago, Arnold Wolfers characterized national security as an ambiguous symbol fraught with semantic and definitional problems. The last quarter of the twentieth century has brought home the realization that threats can no longer be defined solely in terms of armies and the sophistication of their military hardware. It has become increasingly apparent that to the long-standing interest in military affairs and a defense policy must be added topics that affect national security in less obvious but increasingly important ways: energy resources, availability of industrial raw materials, the diffusion of military technology, chronic unemployment, and food production. In this rapidly changing environment, one overwhelming factor underlying these issues remains: global population growth.

Two of the most significant changes in history have occurred since 1945. The first is a drastic decrease in worldwide death rates without a concomitant decrease in birth rates. The second is the sharply increased dependence of affluent nations upon the less affluent nations as suppliers of industrial raw materials.

The world added a fourth billion to its population in a mere fifteen years (1960–1975), and from 1976 to 2000 it will add an additional 2.5 billion. To avert catastrophic food shortages, world food production must increase by 43 percent in the next two decades.[1] This will not occur automatically. Many agriculturists believe a 20 percent increase in food production is a more realistic hope—one percent per year. If we have only a 20 percent increase in food production in the next twenty years, we will have a shortfall equal to the total food requirements of one billion people—one-third of the world's presently underfed developing world population beyond the existing (1980) shortfall. The International Food Policy Research Institute predicts that even by 1990 the world food deficit will be 120 to 140 million metric tons per year[2]—the total food requirements of 660 to 770 million people calculated using the current Indian average of 400 pounds of grain per capita per year. The realistic possibility that hunger may cause widespread disruption of social organization makes world population growth a serious security issue.

Ninety percent of the world's population growth occurs in the developing world, where growth rates are 2 percent or more per year.[3] It is in the countries of the developing world that the disparity between food production and population growth is the greatest. Hunger-induced social disorganization will cause some nations to lose their domestic stability and internal cohesion. As the security of a nation slips away, surrounding nations will have to be concerned not only with their own diminishing per capita food production but also with the migration of hungry people from neighboring countries. Alternatively, a weakened social fabric may easily result in incremental decreases in food supplies. A catastrophic spiral is thereby set in motion.

Witness Cambodia. Initially, the Pol Pot government deliberately took steps to destroy the existing social organization. Fewer crops were planted, harvested, and distributed; the result was great hunger. Continuing civil strife further reduced food production, and hunger became more widespread. Then, hunger itself hastened social disorganization; both contributed to increased civil strife and damaged the infrastructure of the agricultural system. With each growing season, fewer and fewer crops were planted and hunger increased. Seed stocks were eaten, and fuel needed for food production became less available;

draft animals and breeding stocks were slaughtered. By 1979, only a small portion of the food produced just five years earlier was harvested. Social organization has been completely shattered. The millions of deaths due to starvation and the large number of violent deaths are direct results of the destruction of social organization. Hunger did not initiate the devastation in Cambodia, but it has obviously exacerbated its impact.

One of the most significant changes in history is the sharply increased dependence of affluent, developed nations upon the less affluent, developing nations for a steady supply of industrialized raw materials. Modern industry requires steady supplies of aluminum, chromium, copper, iron, lead, manganese, nickel, phosphorus, potassium, sulfur, tin, tungsten, and zinc. Out of thirty-six basic raw materials, the United States is now self-sufficient in only ten and is dependent upon foreign sources for increasing percentages of the other twenty-six.[4] In 1979, the U.S. Bureau of Mines released the following figures, which show just how dependent America has become:

> Ninety-nine percent of all platinum comes from South Africa, U.S.S.R., and Canada; 90 percent of all cobalt from Zaire, Zambia, Canada, and Morocco; 78 percent of all manganese from South Africa, Gabon, Brazil, and Australia; 70 percent of all chromium from U.S.S.R., South Africa, Rhodesia (Zimbabwe), and the Philippines; 65 percent of all tin from Malaysia, U.S.S.R., China, and Italy; and 64 percent of all bauxite from Australia, Jamaica, Guinea, and Surinam.[5]

In addition, the importance of an uninterrupted supply of petroleum has become evident to all.

It is obvious that political instability in raw-material exporting countries will affect their ability to satisfy the increasing demands of the developed world. Accessibility to these resources can no longer be assumed. A sharp reduction in the flow of essential industrial raw materials to the developed world will have a devastating effect on its industrial systems. Furthermore, the battle is on among the industrialized nations to establish adequate strategic raw material reserves.

The European nations have shown much more concern for securing supplies of strategic materials. West Germany is the leader of the movement with respect to volume, but France has also been quietly stockpiling raw materials since 1975. Emphasis is placed on secrecy. A sharp decline in the import of an essential material can have a devastating effect. For example, a West German government-sponsored report recently noted that a 30 percent decline in chrome imports over one year could cut the country's entire gross national product by 25 percent because of repercussions in the automobile, aircraft, and defense industries, which depend upon the metal to strengthen steel, among other things.[6]

The United States, in the face of sharp reductions in imports of essential industrial raw materials, could realistically expect an urban unemployment/underemployment rate of 30 to 40 percent (rates typical in the developing world today).[7] An unemployment/underemployment rate of this magnitude in American cities, where expectations are high, would impose a direct threat to the nation's stability.

There are two complicating factors. The first is the threat to U.S. agricultural production capacities. American agriculture enjoys its high productivity, in great part, as a result of the considerable industrial input into the agricultural system. For example, a single farm in the Midwest depends on thousands of chemicals, tools, and pieces of machinery to bring a single crop to the marketplace. Input from the industrial sector is made at every step in the process, from the preparation of hybrid seed to the packaging of the product for supermarket shelves. There are approximately four industrial laborers working to support a single farmer.[8] If our industrial system is severely damaged by the curtailment of raw material imports, our highly industrialized agricultural system would be severely damaged and agricultural production would drop sharply; just how sharply is difficult to predict, but shorter food supplies in the United States would be inevitable.

The second complicating factor is a potential massive influx of illegal immigrants into the United States. A crude estimate is that the number of illegal immigrants during the next twenty years could reach 161 million (see chapter two). The "boat people" of Indochina are just the first glimmer of what is to come. Even today the boat people of Haiti are landing in southern Florida where more than 25,000 already reside; one-half of this number landing in 1980 alone. More than 110,000 illegal aliens from Cuba, over one percent of the population of that island, were deposited on Florida shores in a seven-week period beginning April 1980.[9]

This great migration is bound to have a profound impact on the American socioeconomic environment and is already being felt among the weakest links of our society: the minorities. Managing the domestic impact while minimizing the problems caused by the influx of other migrants will require a considerable investment. Even at the low cost of $1,000 each, the apprehension, detention, processing, and deportation of some 161 million illegal aliens could in theory reach an astounding $161 billion. In these pressures lie the dangers of widespread terrorism, crime against persons and property at a higher rate than now believed possible, and, ultimately, societal disintegration. In comparison, the possibility of a conventional armed attack from the Soviet

Union becomes a threat of lesser importance.

Acknowledging the Problem: American Leadership

An acknowledgment that world population growth is a serious threat to the security of all nations, including the United States, is essential if the population problem is to be dealt with successfully. Massive assistance in a population control effort should not be just at the expense of the people of the developing world; rather, it is in everyone's self-interest to achieve mutual benefits.

Norman Borlaug, father of the green revolution, never looked to his revolution as the solution to the food problem. Rather, he felt that it would buy perhaps an additional fifteen or twenty years, during which the brakes could be applied to population growth.[10] The year 1968 marked the beginning of his revolution. Twelve of those years have now passed, and we have essentially wasted this purchase. In fact, the total impact of the deliberate attempts of governments, excluding China, to achieve population growth control has postponed the scenario described above for only a matter of months. To gain twelve months, population growth control efforts would have to prevent eighty million births—a number that has taken us more than ten years to achieve.[11] Obviously, the present approach is just not working.

Reason dictates that we do not attempt to manage this problem with less than an adequate commitment, and only after world population growth is acknowledged by the United States and other countries to be a serious security threat will adequate allocations be forthcoming and a solution attainable. The United States made the political, moral, and economic commitment to win World War II. Today, it allocates more than one-fourth of its defense budget each year specifically to counter the Russian threat.[12] Arresting population growth requires an enormous effort and a highly complex solution. The exact cost is unknown, but costs comparable to those expended by the United States and the U.S.S.R. to counter the perceived threats to their respective national security cannot be discounted.

The United States has as much at stake as any other nation if the current laissez faire approach to the solution of this extremely complex problem continues. Most countries, expecting the United States to be the leader, have delegated responsibility to us. If the United States does not accept the challenge, the year 2000 will find a world with a billion or more people than it would have had otherwise.

In general, the United States should adopt laws and policies similar to or similar in effect to those of Hong Kong, Singapore, and the People's Republic of China. Unfortunately, few, if any, nations will follow these governments in the elimination of pronatalist laws and policies and in the institution of antinatalist ones. However, many countries would follow the United States if it boldly instituted these changes.

Pronatalist forces, who encourage births, must be stopped. We must adopt the antinatalist policies that we are suggesting for rapidly growing developing countries. All government policies and laws encouraging childbirth must be changed. All tax incentives for having children must be eliminated, as well as any remaining welfare incentives. Teenage childbearing must be eliminated, and childbearing before the mid-twenties strongly discouraged to lengthen the time between generations. Childless and one-child families must be encouraged.

Leadership is unquestionably the most important component of the world population growth control effort; providing resources or research and development is of far less importance. At this juncture, the United Nations is in no position to provide this leadership. The United Nations possesses neither the influence nor the organizational capacity to do so, nor could leadership be delegated or acquired in some way. We must acknowledge that the United States, with its growing dependence on developing countries, industrialized agriculture, and vulnerability to massive illegal immigration, is as much in jeopardy as any other country. Without this American commitment, the attempt to control population growth will continue to founder, no matter how extensive the research or how great the expenditure.

Taking a Stand

Why has there not been an appropriate government response to global population pressures? Perhaps acknowledgment of the issue must be much more widespread before action by leaders can be expected. An extensive search of the literature indicates that one of the first persons to go on record in this regard was World Population Society founder Dr. Charles Cargill. Cargill emphasized the relationship between national security and population at the first annual meeting of the World Population Society in February 1974 and repeated the point to many groups, including the House Select Committee on Population in 1978.

In 1976, former Assistant Secretary of State George W. Ball referred to demographic pressures in his book, *Diplomacy for a Crowded World*. In April 1977, World Bank President Robert McNamara underlined the importance of the problem in an address to the Massachusetts Institute of Technology. About this same time, former director of the Central Intelligence Agency William Colby made the same avowal in a television news interview and has since reiterated his belief that world population growth is the most serious threat to U.S. security.[13] Lester Brown, ecologist and president of the Worldwatch Institute, has emphasized the salience of population growth factors in his treatise, "Redefining National Security." In December 1977, Dr. Zbigniew Brzezinski, national security advisor, referred to these pressures in a press briefing. The same year, former HEW Deputy Assistant Secretary Dr. Louis Hellman recognized the problem in a statement entitled "The U.S. Role in Resolving the World Population Problem," prepared at the request of President Carter.[14] In February 1978, Ambassador Marshall Green, then coordinator of population affairs, U.S. Department of State, outlined its significance in testimony before the House Select Committee on Population. Retired Army General Maxwell Taylor acknowledged the threat before the same committee in April 1978. In July 1978, former Ohio Governor John J. Gilligan, at that time director of the Agency for International Development (AID), declared world population growth to be a national security threat before the National Press Club. More recently in December 1979, the president's twenty-member Commission on World Hunger did give some recognition to the threat in their final report.[15] Ambassador Richard Benedick, coordinator of population affairs at the State Department, has made a forceful plea for greater efforts to deal with these threats in an address to the Members of Congress for Peace through Law.

The people listed above represent many careers and political persuasions. This is but a small group of individuals. Ironically enough, there is a conspicuous absence of demographers, the recognized population experts who tend to lead American thought on matters of population. No perceptible government action has yet occurred as a result of these statements. To date, not a single major organization in America has come out and supported these tough positions. Why aren't more individuals and institutions more courageous in doing so?

Barriers to Effective Action

1. *Desire to avoid the issue of abortion.* Abortion is an issue that only extremists are comfortable in discussing; there is little room for the middle-of-the-roaders; neutrality invites the enmity of both extremes. To avoid the conflict and the loss of friends, we avoid the subject altogether. Yet, we recognize that no contraceptive method is fail-proof; in fact, some methods, such as rhythm or contraceptive foam, fail quite often. We also recognize that many people do not use a method when

they should and some do not have access to a reliable method. Thus, we correctly suspect that any serious population growth control effort will necessarily include great numbers of abortions.

No matter how unfortunate or distasteful, abortion is instrumental in promoting a serious population growth control effort and will remain so for at least another twenty years. Even today, abortion plays a most significant role. Each year there are seventy to ninety million more births than deaths, and each year there are an estimated forty to fifty million or more induced abortions, one-half of which are performed illegally.[16] An abortion followed by use of a moderately effective contraceptive method prevents, on the average, approximately one birth. The world's growth rate would be roughly 50 percent greater if there were no abortions. Had there been no abortions over the past thirty years, starvation would probably be far more widespread, and our world far more chaotic.

Had birth control been promoted with the same vigor as death control (as advocated by some since the 1940s)[17] from World War II until today, abortion would not need to be encouraged. Now we have no choice but to encourage this procedure. Thus, if we acknowledge that world population growth is a serious threat to the security of all nations, to the security of all persons, and to the survival of all persons, then we will be forced to deal with an issue we prefer to avoid.

2. *Desire to avoid the issue of teenage childbearing.* In the United States, each year there are approximately one million teenage pregnancies (ages ten to nineteen), accounting for about one out of every four pregnancies. About 300,000 of these pregnancies result in induced abortions, 100,000 result in hasty marriages, and 600,000 result in births.[18] These births cost American taxpayers $8.3 billion every year,[19] an amount greater than the national budget for over one-half of the nations of the world.[20] This is an average of $13,833 for each birth, and is only the direct cost, that is, cash support payments, food stamps, social services, free medical services; the indirect costs are not included in this figure. For example, children raised by teenage parents—little more than children themselves—are far more inclined to become delinquents and criminals and are disproportionately represented in our penal institution population.

Thus far, Americans have failed to compensate for this recent explosion in the number of fertile, sexually active, unwed teenagers. There is but one reason—the lack of courage to deal with four volatile issues: universal sex education; availability and promotion of contraceptives for teenagers; availability and promotion of abortion; and infringement on total reproductive freedom. Therefore, we must unreservedly confront each of these issues before we can deal successfully with the teenage pregnancy problem. The global problems of overpopulation are critical enough without the added pressures of unwanted pregnancies straining the world's limited resources. Furthermore, the welfare of these accidental births places an overwhelming and unnecessary financial drain on the nation's domestic economy. Taxpayers should not have to bear the monetary burden for teenagers emotionally and financially unprepared to assume the responsibilities of sexual freedom and subsequent accidental pregnancies. Sex education and the full availability of and accessibility to contraception and abortion are essential if the problem is to be solved. Furthermore, we must adopt the posture that teenagers should not have the freedom to reproduce unless they can handle all direct and indirect costs, and, of course, none can.

3. *Desire to avoid confrontation with pronatalist organizations.* Pronatalist means encouraging births either intentionally or unintentionally. There are many pronatalist organizations in the United States, many of which are unintentionally pronatalist. An organization providing goods or services for a family on a schedule that is not based on cost per child is pronatalist. It is providing these goods or services free to children of larger families at the expense of smaller families, removing the economic disincentive to have children. Most medical insurance companies and some hotel chains can thus be regarded as pronatalist. If an insurance company, or an employer in its group medical insurance package, requires all employees to share in the costs of childbearing for those who have children during their employment under that package, then that company or employer should be viewed as pronatalist.

The most influential and effective of the pronatalist institutions are the religious institutions. Virtually all religious groups in the United States are pronatalist to some degree. The degree, of course, is determined by their activities to encourage births, ranging from giving prizes each Mother's Day to the mother with the greatest number of children, to asserting that having many children is an ecclesiastical duty. Significantly, religious groups have always held a special place in the United States. Freedom of religion has been a value treasured since the birth of our nation.

The Role of the Roman Catholic Church Hierarchy

Many of the thoughts in this section are a consequence of a reading of Father Andrew Greeley's recent book, *The Making of the Popes 1978: The Politics of Intrigue in the Vatican* (Kansas City: Andrews and McMeel, Inc., 1979). Few Americans, Catholic or non-Catholic, have an understanding of the political intrigue that reigns within the

Catholic hierarchy, particularly among that small group of older Italian elite headquartered in Rome. In many ways, we Americans have placed our future in their hands. I would suggest that Father Greeley's book should be considered required reading by every American concerned about the national security of the United States.

The Catholic Church holds a very special place among the pronatalist religious groups and deserves to be discussed separately for several reasons. It is the most influential social institution in the world today and is the best organized religious group, possessing a sophisticated infrastructure, and is highly responsive to the chain of command. In the United States, it is the largest religious group and clearly the most influential.[21] The Church's teachings on contraception, abortion, and sterilization influence the world's policies, either with intent or de facto.[22] The Church's teachings and the hierarchy's insistence that they be followed is resulting in an unintentional suppression of a vast knowledge of the consequences of overpopulation: that ultimately either man or nature will sharply limit population and that abortion, contraception, and sterilization must be used by every at-risk fertile couple on earth if global peace and security is to be maintained.

While the Catholic Church is no longer influential with its followers in the United States, in matters of reproduction,[23] it is, nevertheless, a powerful political force. Ironically, it is upon the policymakers that the Church's influence is the greatest. It openly expounds that it no longer honors the concept of the separation of church and state in the United States.[24] It frankly admits its involvement in the political process and its financial support of selected candidates.[25] The Church maintains its political power through the forewarning of our nation's elected officials by either using or threatening to use its vast resources (funds, communication network, and so forth) and its organization against them.[26] Nowhere is the Catholic hierarchy's refusal to honor the concept of separation of church and state more obvious than in matters of population growth control.

What has made this tolerance for Catholic influence on U.S. public policy concerns particularly perplexing is that the leadership of the Catholic Church in America owes its allegiance to the leadership in Vatican City, the seat of the Church's central government, or Curia.[27] Thus, the leaders of the Church in Vatican City are orchestrating this interference in American political affairs. One can suggest that, in effect, a foreign government or a foreign power is interfering with U.S. governmental affairs. Such interference is only one side of the issue.

Causing even greater concern is the recognized difficulty in changing the Church's stand on contraception, abortion, and population growth control. When Pope John XXIII came to power in 1958, there were fifty-two members of the College of Cardinals, twelve of whom were in their eighties. In 1962, Pope John XXIII called the Ecumenical Council Vatican II amid signs that the teachings of the Church on these matters of contraception, abortion, and population growth control were about to change. Unfortunately, he died before the second of the four sessions commenced. Even before his death, there had been considerable controvesy between the progressives (including Pope John) and the ultraconservatives. Pope Paul VI then came to power, giving the edge to the ultraconservative faction. Pope Paul with the assistance (solicited or unsolicited) of Curial reactionaries, including Cardinal Alfredo Ottaviani, and operating in an information vacuum, solidified his political position on this matter. First, in the selection of new cardinals and bishops to replace those who died, he ranked the candidates by their attitudes toward contraception, abortion, and population control, selecting the most conservative (almost a single-issue selection, as we say in American politics).[28] Second, to dilute the power of the moderates, the Pope expanded the size of the College of Cardinals to an all-time high of 145 in 1973. The number entitled to participate in papal elections was limited to 120.[29] Thus, he ensured that the ultraconservative faction would be selecting the next pope, as well as some others in the future. Certainly no moderation on fertility matters occurred during Pope Paul's reign.

Pope John Paul I lived just long enough to demonstrate to the world that Pope Paul's political maneuvers were successful. Pope John Paul II wasted no time confirming that Pope Paul's strategy had successfully extended beyond the election of his successor. During Pope John Paul II's visits to the Western Hemisphere, he made it painfully clear that he intends no changes in population control policy. In the words of the Irish writer-diplomat, Conor Cruise O'Brien, "Where Pope Paul was cautiously and colorlessly conservative, Pope John Paul II is a crusading traditionalist. . . ."[30]

The power struggle within the Catholic Church over the past twenty years has made it apparent, even to the casual observer, that abortion, contraception, and population growth control are political issues within the Catholic Church leadership, *not* moral issues. It is sometimes difficult to believe that the leadership of the Church may regard these as moral issues. The vast majority of Catholic theologians were dismayed by Pope Paul's continued insistence in his encyclical *Humanae Vitae* that contraception, abortion, and population growth control are immoral. One need only read the paper "Catholic Perspectives on Population Issues" by Francis X. Murphy, C.S.S.R., and Joseph F. Erhart (Population Reference Bureau, Washington, D.C., 1975)[31], in which the overwhelming support (clearly a majority) for changing the Catholic Church's teachings on contraception, abortion, and population growth control by theologians, clergy, and lay leaders alike is thoroughly documented, to see just how widespread this overwhelmingly negative response to *Humanae Vitae* was among theologians and lay leaders. From the preceding observations, it is safe to suggest that the men who are leaders of the Catholic Church in America have more in common with their colleagues of the Italian Curia than they do with the mainstream of American Catholics.

Few American Catholics probably believe that it is God's will to bring hundreds of millions (or more likely billions) of children into the world in the next few decades, only to have them suffer for a few months or a few years and perish—an inevitable prospect under current teachings of birth control. It is estimated that 365 million people were chronically undernourished when *Humanae Vitae* was issued in 1968.[32] According to the Food and Agriculture Organization (FAO), in over sixty developing countries, growth in agricultural production did not match population growth during the years 1970 to 1977.[33] The World Food Council estimated that in 1979 the number of people who were severely undernourished had grown to 450 million and that of people with some degree of malnutrition to 1.3 billion.[34]

In 1978, according to UNICEF, thirty million children under age five starved to death.[35] In 1978, 134 million children were born and 22 percent of this number died from starvation. The simple reality is that we are bringing more children into the world than we can provide for. At current rates (thirty million per year), 900 million children will be born and will die of starvation in the next thirty years alone. This is a most crushing thought. Even worse, the rate is certain to climb far above thirty million tragic deaths per year even under the best circumstances.

The Vatican leadership of the Church not only is irresponsible for having thwarted unilateral, bilateral, and multilateral efforts to slow population growth for almost thirty years but also for not having led the population growth control effort. As the world's largest and most influential social organization, the Church could have been the single most important force in preventing the great human tragedy we are just beginning to witness.[36]

The Vatican's current position on population matters has undermined and possibly negated most of the positive contributions it has made in global development in the past two thousand years. An NBC white paper on illegal immigration from Mexico aired March 28, 1980, was most revealing in this regard. In this program, a Catholic priest asked a Mexican couple, who were in the United States illegally, how many children they had. Nine was the response. Exlaimed the priest, "Oh! How wonderful!" It is not wonderful. It is tragic for Mexico and its people, and it has profound implications for the United States and the Western Hemisphere. Such attitudes on the part of a powerful institution make one search for other motives.

The Roman Catholic Church has been a source of considerable pressure in the United States, supporting lax immigration policies. Its support of illegal Mexican immigration cannot be completely accounted for by the Church's desire to build a political power base, as some have suggested.[37] The March 1980 NBC program demonstrated that the bishops and priests were motivated by an intense feeling of guilt derived from the Church's absolute insistence that everyone bring more children into the world than our earth can provide for. There is obviously a built-in contradiction resulting in efforts to accept, perhaps increase, the illegal flow of Mexicans into the United States. The Church is suggesting that millions ignore U.S. immigration policies and our relations with Mexico. Certainly nothing has contributed more to the poverty, the despair, and the human suffering of Mexico than the definite encouragement of large families among Mexicans. But, as the NBC program queried, can or should the United States be expected to pay the price?

It is apparent that the influence of the ultraconservative wing of the Catholic Church is shaping opposition to effective population control policies. My own analysis suggests that these ultraconservatives fear any policy that would undermine the Church's claim to infallibility. Any reversals of traditional, accepted Catholic doctrine might blasphemously imply a previous oversight or misconception on the part of the Catholic Church. Certainly the Church is aware that a population program can only be marginally successful if abortion and sterilization services are not widely available and their use encouraged; nevertheless, the Catholic Church inflexibly adheres to its antiquated tenets. On these issues, confrontation with the Catholic Church has not only affected the tenor of the domestic debate but it has also influenced the range of our foreign assistance programs. I would suggest that the Church has perhaps blocked a productive consideration of global population pressures as a threat to U.S national security.

Looking into the Future

Failure to acknowledge that population growth threatens persons and nations calls attention to a number of somber scenarios. Those few aspects discussed below provide some indication of the profound challenges we can expect, from family to federal government. Our procrastination in confronting the problem will probably be expensive and the price will increase with each year of continued delay.

There could be great impingement on our personal life-style. As we procrastinate, the degree of regimentation that we will encounter as the demand for food, fuel, and other resources outstrips shrinking supplies will grow rapidly. This continued delay brings us closer and closer to a society similar to George Orwell's *1984*. The People's Republic of China is a highly regimented society regulated in order to manage effectively a population that had outstripped the resources of the land. To maintain social organization—and to avoid chaos in China—very strict regimentation had to be imposed to derive maximum benefit from scarce resources. Our refusal to respond to the threat of overpopulation is bringing us dangerously close to such a highly regimented society because our resource base is shrinking. The longer we procrastinate, the more strict and the more extensive will be the regimentation.

The great influx of aliens attempting illegal immigration will have a profound impact on American life. The requirement of carrying a national identification card at all times will be imposed. Anti-terrorist activities may force a sharp retreat in the promotion of civil rights. An increased police/domestic military presence to counter terrorist and other criminal activities by underemployed illegal aliens will be more evident. An expansion in our Coast Guard service is most likely. Money spent to halt, apprehend, and deport illegal aliens will be one of the largest expenditures in the U.S. budget. The money spent will include the estimated $161 billion that will be needed over the next twenty years for apprehension, detention, processing, and deportation of the estimated 161 million illegal aliens discussed earlier.

As conditions deteriorate in the United States in the coming decades, American Catholics and non-Catholics alike will look for targets upon which to lay blame for the decline. Some will remember the compassion shown by Pope John XXIII in the late 1950s and early 1960s and the widespread belief among Catholic theologians, clergy, and lay leaders that contraception, abortion, and population growth control were necessary and moral. Some will question why the leadership of the American Catholic Church did not argue for change in the Church's teachings on these matters. Some will realize that the teachings of the Church, reaffirmed in 1968, were inconsistent with peace, prosperity, or even the continued security of Americans.

The American military establishment will undergo profound changes. For example, its size may drastically increase in response to increasing global insecurity. Soldiers will be asked to fight to ensure the continued supply of materials essential to the survival of Americans and to maintain domestic order.

This is but a sample of the consequences due to our refusal to acknowledge population growth as a security threat. This acknowledgment must occur before an adequate political, economic, and moral commitment will be forthcoming. As our supplies of resources shrink, as social disorganization increases, and as we become concerned with mere survival, the freedoms that Americans have enjoyed for so long will vanish one by one.

Conclusion

This essay has not described a world population growth control program. Presently no one knows the specifics of a successful program; no one has ever seriously outlined the appropriate financial commitment (admittedly an expensive one). There is a frightening lack of respect for the world population problem. Likewise, there is no clear respect for an appropriate response. I would suggest that we are talking about a Marshall Plan or something similar to our space program. Ultimately, it could run in the $30 billion per year range.

The ease with which people assume that the future will be a simple extension of the past, despite the two significant historical changes of unprecedented world population growth and increased American political and economic dependence upon the developing world, may be the single greatest danger that we face in the coming decades. We simply cannot make this assumption. At a minimum, our national leaders should address the issue; it needs to become a key item in our national policy agenda.

The inevitability of widespread social and political chaos in the face of continued unprecedented 2 percent growth for the next two decades makes population growth the single greatest threat to world peace. Strategically, acknowledgment of this new threat is a must if an adequate political, moral, and economic commitment to action is to be forthcoming. The effective opposition to population growth control activities by the Catholic hierarchy has clearly been the single greatest deterrent. This is a political issue that needs to be overcome, hopefully with the help of Catholics themselves. It is fair to say that, using the teachings of the Church, the Vatican has effectively thwarted the development of and successful implementation of population policies worldwide with the exception of the People's Republic of China. Because of its global geopolitical presence, its economic capabilities, and the strength of its democratic institutions, the only nation capable of successfully addressing that barrier is the United States.

In the face of continued inaction, the scenarios described earlier will become a reality. We should prefer a massive effort that later proves to be unnecessary (but yet had the worldwide side effects of improved food production, nutritional status, maternal and child health, literacy, advancement of women's rights, environment, and security) to a lesser effort that later proves to be totally inadequate.

In order to avert this demographic disaster, strong decisive leadership is the key. What is needed is a highly influential and respected organization that can elicit unwavering commitments from other countries and command whatever resources deemed necessary to achieve its final goal. The United States alone has the capacity to marshal these commitments and, more importantly, it has the tremendous organizational skills needed for this massive effort. This effort may require ten million full-time employees or more, with a U.S. component of several hundred thousand. The first step, however, must be a dedicated commitment by the United States acted upon immediately.

At present, no such institution exists nor would any combination of those existing suffice. Only the creation of a NASA-type agency, modeled on a military organization, and with a wartime sense of urgency, will be adequate. Selection of this organization will not solve the problem, but it will identify an efficient organizational framework most able to effect a solution.

Notes

1. From a statement by S. T. Keel, senior vice-president of the International Minerals and Chemical Corporation, in *World Development Letter* (December 17, 1979), 2:24:96.

2. From the *World Development Letter* (July 2, 1979), 2:13:50.

3. Using the 1979 World Population Estimates prepared by the Environmental Fund, the current annual increase in the developed world (North America, Europe, Japan, U.S.S.R., and Oceania) is 8 million as opposed to the annual increase of 74.56 million in the developing world (Latin America, Africa, and Asia excluding Japan) or 9.7 percent and 90.3 percent respectively. Using the same data source, the rates of growth for the two were found to be 0.7 percent and 2.26 percent respectively.

4. A. W. Schmidt, speech presented at the Allegheny Cenference on Community Development, June 12, 1978. *The Other Side* (January 1980), 18:1.

5. From the *World Development Letter* (February 12, 1979), 2:3:12.

6. A. Spence, "European Nations Move on Two Fronts to Secure Supplies of Strategic Materials," *Wall Street Journal* (September 9, 1979).

7. The International Labor Office estimates that 40 percent of the workforce of 700 million people in the developing world outside China and other communist countries are unemployed or underemployed. This estimate combines both urban and rural areas. About 33 million are unemployed and the rest are underemployed and seek additional work either because they work only a few hours per day or too few days per year. Jean van der Tak, Carl Haub, and Elaine Murphy, "Our Population Predicament: A New Look," *Population Bulletin* (December 1979), 34:5:21.

8. From a bulletin devoted to the industrialization of American agriculture. "The Food and Fiber System—How It Works," Economic Research Service, U.S. Department of Agriculture, Agricultural Information Bulletin No. 383 (March 1975), pp. 1–3.

9. W. L. Chaze, "In the Last Days of Cuban Boatlift," *U.S. News and World Report* (June 16, 1980), p. 29.

10. L. R. Brown, "Population and Affluence: Growing Pressures on World Food Resources," *Population Bulletin* (1973), 29:2:10.

11. This estimate of the number of births prevented by organized family planning programs was calculated in the following manner. If we assume that the world population growth rate has declined 0.4 percent—2.3 percent to 1.9 percent—if we assume than one-half of this decline is due to organized programs, a generous assumption, and if we assume that this decline has been in full effect for the past decade, also a generous assumption, then, using the 1975 population of 4.0 billion as a base, 8 million births would have been prevented each year for ten years, for a total of 80 million births prevented. Since the annual growth of the world population is 80 million, this means that all organized efforts to date have only bought us twelve additional months to solve the problem. This estimate shows just how small is the effect of existing programs but, more importantly, it shows us how far we have to go.

12. From 1978 to 1980, the average defense budget has exceeded $120 billion, and more than $30 billion has been allocated specifically to counter the perceived Russian threat. (From the Budget of the United States, p. 89, Superintendent of Documents, Government Printing Office, Washington, D.C., 1979.)

13. From an article entitled "Population" in the *Cincinnati Enquirer* (August 13, 1978) that referred to a statement made by Mr. Colby in testimony before a congressional committee a few days earlier.

14. Dr. Louis Hellman, deputy assistant secretary for population affairs, Department of Health, Education, and Welfare, "The U.S. Role in Resolving the World Population Problem," submitted to the president upon request, January 1977. *The Other Side* (July 1978), 13:1.

15. The report predicts that a major shortage of food could occur in the next twenty years—with disastrous effects for the U.S. Commission Chairman Sol Linowitz, in his accompanying letter to the president, stated that, "A hungry world is an unstable world." The report goes on to say, "The most potentially explosive force in the world today is the frustrated desire of poor people to attain a decent standard of living. The anger, despair, and often hatred that result represent a real and persistent threat to international order."

16. T. M. King, "Abortion and Abortifacients," *The Draper Fund Report* (Summer 1978), 6:27.

17. *See*, G. I. Burch and E. Pendell, *Human Breeding and Survival: Population Roads to Peace or War* (New York: Penguin Books, Inc., 1947).

18. From a fundraising letter prepared for Mary Tyler Moore's signature by the Population Institute, Washington, D.C., 1979.

19. The estimate was made by Stanford Research Institute and reported in the *Washington Post* (May 12, 1979), p. 10.

20. *The World Almanac* and *Book of Facts* (New York: Newspaper Enterprise Association, Inc., 1979), pp. 513–599.

21. This is in spite of the fact that (according to Greeley), after Vatican Council II: "Colorless administrators were appointed to critical positions instead of leaders with broad vision—most notably in the United States [to punish the American Church for supporting Vatical Council II] where, according to one historian, the hierarchy has never been as undistinguished ss it is now" (p. 98).

22. There are three exceptions: People's Republic of China, Singapore, and Hong Kong. All communist countries, including the Soviet Union, except China, are being influenced by these teachings (*see*, A. C. White, "A Long Campaign," *People* [1980], 7:1:21.

23. Traditional large family of American Catholics is no longer the norm. *Family Planning Perspectives* (July/August 1978), 10:4:241. From C. F. Westoff and E. F. Jones,

"The End of 'Catholic' Fertility" (paper presented at the annual meeting of the Population Association of America, Atlanta, April 12–15, 1978).

24. From E. Willis, "Abortion Rights: Overruling Pro-Fascist," *The Village Voice* (February 4, 1980), p. 7:

> [In] Judge John F. Dooling's 328-page decision striking down the Hyde Amendment. . . . He demonstrates that the purpose of the Hyde Amendment was never to save the taxpayers' money, keep the government neutral on a delicate moral issue, or distinguish between "necessary" and so-called "convenience" abortions. The amendment, says Dooling bluntly, was a ploy by anti-abortion congressmen frustrated in their attempt to pass a constitutional amendment that would override the Supreme Court's 1973 pro-abortion decision; its purpose was quite simply to circumvent the Court's ruling and prevent as many abortions as possible. Dooling, a practicing Catholic, makes short work of the anti-abortionists' pretensions to being a spontaneous grassroots movement that owes its political victories to sheer moral appeal. He confirms that right-to-life's main source of energy, organization, and direction has been the Catholic Church and describes in detail how the movement uses one-issue voting to put pressure on legislators, candidates, and the party organizations that nominate them—a tactic that gains its influence far out of proportion to its numbers. After quoting various Christian and Jewish theologians' differing opinions on abortion and the question of fetal personhood, Dooling argues that the anti-abortionists' absolutist view is not based on any moral or religious censensus but reflects a sectarian position that "is not genuinely argued; it is adamantly asserted. . . . The Hyde Amendment," he concludes, "is religiously motivated legislation that imposes a particular theological viewpoint, violating dissenters' First Amendment rights."

25. A fundraising letter from the Fund to Defeat the Abortion Candidates, a project of LIFE-PAC, The Anti-Abortion Political Action Committee, Washington, D.C. (an arm of the Catholic Church), received in March 1980, signed by Father Vincent Tanzola, S.J., containing a color photograph of the pope and a quote, shows how open the Church has been in its political activities. The following excerpts illuminate this point:

> For years Catholics have helped to lead the fight against legalized abortions, but we must face the facts, our fight is far from over. For years our efforts have focused on national leaders in national elections and Amendments to the U.S. Constitution. . . . Local and statewide races are our target. Our goals are very simple and very direct. We plan on cutting the pipeline for all state funds being used to buy the death of unborn children. We'll do this by voting abortionist legislators, county officials, and other key elected persons out of our local and state government. . . . And we've proven we can do it—LIFE-PAC is the oldest pro-life political action committee, and we have been successful in 82 percent of the races we have worked in. . . . Most recently, LIFE-PAC scored a major victory by helping elect a solid pro-life candidate to the Governorship of Louisiana. . . . Now we have the chance to duplicate our efforts in about five hundred specifically targeted local and statewide races. We can defeat abortion candidates and elect pro-life representatives. . . . Please help LIFE-PAC do our special work. Please hear the words of our beloved Pope John Paul II . . . and put an end to abortion by helping to elect pro-life candidates to office.

26. In 1976, Representative Daniel Flood (D–Pennsylvania), a Catholic, spoke eloquently against the first anti-abortion amendment attached to a Medicaid bill. Three weeks later, Flood reversed his position and has been a leader of anti-abortion members since. "My bishop got to me," Flood told a colleague.

"It's the holy wars all over again," said Representative William Clay (D–Missouri), a Catholic from a heavily Catholic district. "I'm here to represent the citizens of the United States, not the Catholic Church. A priest in St. Louis told people it would be a sin to vote for me."

Representative Frank Thompson (D–New Jersey), a Catholic: "But then the good father speaks from the pulpit. He has the Knights of Columbus, the Altar and Rosary Society, and the PTA approaching their fellow parishioners with petitions and postcards. I think many of them feel coerced into signing."

V. Glaser, "Right-to-Vote? Abortion Advocacy Brings Added Pressures to Catholic Congressmen," *Charlotte Observer* (August 1978), C-1:27.

27. Father Greeley defines the Roman Curia as "the Church's Central Administration Civil Service, internationalized at the top level but still mostly Italian at lower levels" (p. 251), and the Italian Curia "not all of whose members are Italian, is that informal group of churchmen who generally support the policy and the perspective of the more conservative Italian Cardinals residing in Rome. Usually when people speak of the Curia, they mean the Italian Curia" (p. 252). The following passages are most illuminating:

(a) On quest for power: "The Curia leaders are still ruthless in their quest for power, absolutely unforgiving to their enemies, and not very trustworthy to their friends" (p. 40).

(b) On the Birth Control Commission: "Only a few members of the commission dissented, but those were Curialists like Cardinal Ottaviani. . . . Ottaviani and his colleagues began to orchestrate a backstairs campaign against the commission decision, complete with articles in magazines and newspapers, letters from the bishops around the world, and protests from carefully chosen 'Catholic married couples' " (p. 45). (The Italian Curialists censored information going to the pope.)

28. Also from Father Greeley: "*Humanae Vitae* was the catalyst. After that, it's been all downhill, and everyone in the Church, from parish priest-sociologist on up to would-be Cardinals and Cardinals, has been judged by his response to that encyclical" (p. 84). "The birth control problem was not even open for discussion among Catholic theologians, and loyalty to the decision was a sine qua non for promotion. In some cases, it seemed the only criterion" (p. 100).

29. F. A. Foy (editor), *1978 Catholic Almanac* (Huntington, IN: Our Sunday Visitor, Inc., 1978), p. 198.

30. C. C. O'Brien, "The Pope and the Unwanted Child," *People* (1980), 7:1:24.

31. This thirty-one-page monograph is essential for a full understanding of the Church's "unresolvable moral dilemma." It discusses the fact that the "Catholic Church still influences a considerable proportion of the world's thinking." It demonstrates the Church's clear understanding of the "catastrophic threat of overpopulation" and "the projected apocalyptic possibility of a doubling of the world's population." A thorough history is provided, excluding most of the internal political aspects, of course. Some examples of the interference in the activities of the United Nations agencies (WHO, FAO, UNICEF, UNESCO) regarding family planning and population policy research that completely thwarted efforts for two critical decades, and continues somewhat less effectively today, are provided. Most important, the overwhelming support (clearly a majority) for changing the Church's teaching on contraception, abortion, and population growth control by theologians, clergy, and lay leaders alike is thoroughly documented.

32. Based on FAO estimates. Van der Tak, et al., *op. cit.*, p. 25.

33. "World Hunger and Malnutrition Continue: Slow Progress in Carrying Out World Food Conference Objectives," report to the Congress of the United States, Comptroller General, ID-80-12 (January 1980), p. 49.

34. Ibid., p. 22.

35. From an address by Robert S. McNamara, president of the World Bank, to the Board of Governors, Belgrade, Yugoslavia (October 2, 1979).

36. A four-year study by a group of Roman Catholic theologians documents the scholarly justifications for marked "refinements" in traditional Catholic teachings on contraception, sterilization, and other aspects of sexuality. The report, published by Paulist Press under the title *Human Sexuality, New Directions in American Catholic Thought*, was commissioned by the prestigious Catholic Theological Society of America, a group of ordained and lay scholars. The theologians traced evidence from biblical scriptures, official Church statements, and documents covering centuries of tradition and theology as well as contemporary knowledge in the empirical sciences. On the basis of these analyses, they concluded that sexual contact should be "conducive to creative growth and integration." The chapter on pastoral guidelines states:

> The attitude, therefore, of "leaving it all in the hands of God and accepting whatever he sends" is both simplistic and morally irresponsible. Responsible parenthood demands readiness to acknowledge that there are situations and conditions where it would be irresponsible and hence *immoral* to beget children. [emphasis added]

"Theologians Urge 'Refinements' in Catholic Teachings on Sex," Planned Parenthood, *World Population Washington Memo* (July 15, 1977), p. 4.

37. M. H. Mothersill, *Population Portents* (Indianapolis: Mothersill, 1963), p. 73.

2.

Illegal Immigration, National Security, and the Church

Illegal immigration has received considerable press coverage but little systematic evaluation, given the magnitude of the problem and the seriousness of its implications. This report constitutes a long-range projection of the impact of illegal immigration on the size of the U.S. population, an examination of national security implications of the implacable massive immigration into our country, and a forum for public discussion of the group most effectively opposing attempts to deal with this threat to our security.

The Next Twenty Years

This crude estimate of the number of aliens who will attempt illegal entry into the United States over the next twenty years was based on: Population Reference Bureau projections for the year 2000; current per capita income (World Bank Atlas, 1975), for determining relative ability to immigrate; geographic location and apparent difficulty in reaching the United States; expected relative deterioration in living conditions in country of origin; ease of finding refuge; and ease of assimilation.

Six assumptions were made:

- The higher the growth rate in the country of origin, the greater the desire to migrate.
- The higher the current per capita income in the country of origin,

the greater the proportion able to afford to migrate.
• Geography is critical. A border or a short sea voyage to U.S. shores greatly facilitates immigration to this country; it is obviously easier to reach the United States from London, England, than from Kolar, India.
• Conditions in some affluent countries deficient in food, fuel, and industrial raw materials will deteriorate more quickly than in others.
• Immigration into the United States is more feasible for those with relatives or friends already here, and, in turn, for those from nations with large numbers of legal immigrants present in the United States.
• The greater the immigrant's ease in adapting to the community, language, and culture, the more encouraged a prospective immigrant will be.

The following method was used for the estimate.

Each country was considered with respect to each of the six parameters and each of the assumptions. With the exception of the population and per-capita-income estimates, the parameters were subjectively estimated and the countries ranked. The proportion expected to immigrate was estimated and multiplied by the projected population to determine the estimated number that will immigrate.

Two affluent countries, Japan and West Germany, were chosen to standardize all countries except Mexico and the Caribbean islands, which are special cases. Mexico shares 1,933 miles of its border with the United States and thus has inexpensive and easy access to this country by air, land, and sea. One-fourth to one-third of its labor force is currently in this country, a labor force that will increase by 136 percent over the next twenty years. Mexico is already terribly over-populated, and its population is expected to grow from its current 70 million to a catastrophic 134.4 million by the year 2000. The majority of Mexicans have family or friends in the United States, legally or illegally, providing ample opportunity for refuge. The Catholic Church actively encourages illegal Mexican immigration.[1] Spanish is widely spoken in the United States, and a considerable Mexican presence in many areas of our country enhances assimilation.

The Caribbean island countries on the whole are already grossly overpopulated and will be simply unable to absorb the 15 million people the region is expected to add in the next twenty years. Though Mexico has certain geographic advantages, the Caribbean countries are in a similar situation. Their nationals enjoy an ease of entry into the United States and of dropping out of sight there not enjoyed by people in other parts of the world.

Japan and West Germany are used as a standard because, although very overpopulated, at their current standard of living, their citizens are affluent and highly educated. Both are heavy importers of food (more than one-third of their supply) and essentially dependent upon other nations for industrial raw materials and energy. As world food, energy, and raw material supplies grow tighter, these two countries will be particularly hard pressed. However, their people are very prosperous and many are fluent in English. They have been a significant source of legal immigration and have developed large numbers of close personal relationships with individual Americans, so they can be expected to produce a maximum number of immigrants to the United States. (The United Kingdom and Italy are in similar positions.)[2] It is estimated that, at a minimum, 10 percent of the populations of Japan and West Germany are expected to *attempt* to immigrate at least once during the next twenty years. Some will no doubt make several attempts.

All other estimates of attempts were made in this manner. China and North Korea (comprising one-quarter of humanity) were excluded because the relationships between these countries and the United States with respect to the coming two decades are not sufficiently established or predictable to permit this.

The total estimate for the twenty-year period is 161.57 million (*see,* Table I, p. 26) or an average of 8.08 million per year. It is predicted that an average of 2 million will arrive by land across the Mexican border (not much more than the numbers of the past few years), 1 million by sea, 1 million by land via the Canadian border (having traveled to Canada itself mostly by plane), and 4 million by air.

This is a conservative estimate, admittedly crude and susceptible to considerable refinement given the resources. However, given the implications of even such an estimated immigration, some idea of the magnitude of the problem we will face becomes clear. This great illegal immigration is already underway. It is a near certainty that the 10 million mark has already been passed and the 15 million mark is being rapidly approached, if not already exceeded.

The recent study by Daniel R. Vining of the University of Pennsylvania suggests that, in the past ten years, 10.5 million more people arrived by air than left by air.[3] If we assume that all 400,000 annual legal immigrants arrived by air, then 6.5 million visitors have remained illegally in that decade and are still with us.

The same study found that, of the 500 million annual border crossings, 17 million people (3 percent) arrived in the United States by air, about 5 million (1 percent) by sea, and 478 million (96 percent) by land. Furthermore, E. P. Kraly, in a recent report in *American Demographics*, states that nonimmigrant admissions increased from 4.4 million in 1970 to over 8 million in 1977. This group includes tourists, business visitors, foreign students, exchange visitors, temporary workers, and trainees.[4] My estimate of 8.08 million attempts at an illegal

TABLE I

Estimate of the Number of Aliens Who Will Attempt Illegal Entry Into the United States Over the Next Twenty Years

	Estimated Percentage of Attempted Illegal Immigration to United States by Year 2000	Population Projection for Year 2000 (millions)	Estimated Number Who Will Attempt Illegal Immigration to United States by Year 2000 (millions)
MEXICO	30.0	134.4	40.32
CENTRAL AMERICA	10.0	37.6	3.76
CARIBBEAN	20.0	44.0	8.8
SOUTH AMERICA			
Brazil	5.0	207.5	10.38
Colombia	5.0	44.3	2.22
Venezuela	7.0	23.1	1.62
Peru	4.0	30.9	1.29
Argentina, Chile, Uruguay	5.0	52.0	2.60
Other Countries	2.0	31.8	0.64
EUROPE			
West Germany	10.0	66.5	6.65
United Kingdom	10.0	62.3	6.23
Italy	10.0	61.7	6.17
France	7.0	61.9	4.33
Spain	4.0	45.1	1.80
Other Noncommunist European Countries	8.0	82.8	6.62
Other Communist European Countries	1.5	159.9	2.40
SOVIET UNION	1.0	314.0	3.14
SOUTHWEST ASIA			
Saudi Arabia	20.0	12.9	2.58
Bahrain, Kuwait, Oman, Qatar, United Arab Emirates	20.0	5.8	1.16
Israel	10.0	5.5	0.55
Other Countries	1.0	141.8	1.42
CENTRAL SOUTH ASIA			
Iran	5.0	67.0	3.35
India	1.0	1051.4	10.51
Remainder	0.5	374.6	1.87
SOUTHEAST ASIA			
Philippines	4.0	86.3	3.45
Malaysia	4.0	22.0	0.88
Remainder	0.5	474.7	2.37
EAST ASIA			
Japan	10.0	132.7	13.27
Hong Kong	10.0	5.8	0.58
South Korea	5.0	52.3	2.62
Taiwan	5.0	22.0	1.10
Other Countries (including China and North Korea)*	—	—	—
NORTHERN AFRICA			
Egypt	3.0	64.0	1.92
Other	1.5	126.0	1.89
OTHER AFRICAN COUNTRIES	0.5	625.0	3.13
TOTAL			161.57

*Since the relationship between these countries and the United States with respect to the coming decades is not completely established, there is no basis for an estimate.

SOURCE OF DATA: Data used to estimate the percentage who will attempt illegal immigration include the per capita GNP, which was obtained from the 1976 World Population Data Sheet of the Population Reference Bureau, and percent increase in the labor force by the year 2000 was obtained from the World Population Estimates Sheet, published by the Environmental Fund.

Population projections for year 2000 were obtained from the 1976 World Population Data Sheet of the Population Reference Bureau.

entry per year (4 million by air, 3 million ultimately by land, and 1 million by sea) is completely fathomable in light of the current border-crossing rates for each of the modes of entry, the level of apparent illegal entry by air over the past decade, and the current level of recorded nonimmigrant admissions.

The cost of apprehension, retention, processing, and deportation of these 161 million people would be staggering. Even at an average of only $1,000 each, which is unrealistically low, the total cost would be $161 billion.

Figure I (p. 28) shows the enormous impact of the projected massive influx of illegal aliens on U.S. population size in just twenty years. Arrests have averaged about 1 million annually for several years and are indicated by the dark shaded area. Given the sharp Immigration and Naturalization Service (INS) budget cut slated by the Reagan Administration, the number of these apprehensions is likely to drop considerably. With the estimated 10 million illegals currently in the country and the estimated 161 million who will attempt immigration in the next twenty years minus the projected 20 million arrests, the total number in twenty years is estimated to be 151 million, or about three times the population increase of 48 million projected by the U.S. Census Bureau as a result of natural increase and legal immigration.

The Vatican Alternative to Family Planning and Abortion

Our government is addressing itself to dealing effectively with this problem of illegal immigration. The remainder of this chapter will discuss how and why these efforts are systematically negated by the posture of the Roman Catholic Church leadership, which has organized opposition to an adequate response to halt the invasion of illegal aliens. If the Church were to withdraw from this political arena, most remaining opposition would be vitiated.

During Pope John Paul II's visit to the United States in October 1979, he campaigned for the right of illegal aliens to migrate at will to the United States. He made his stand on this issue clear to American politicians and labor unions, the American Catholic hierarchy, the news media, and other sectors. It is estimated that over 90 percent of all illegal aliens coming into the United States are Roman Catholics. The Church does not recognize national boundaries and national sovereignty. There is but one world—a Catholic world—and it has no boundaries.

The Church created and maintains a nationwide network of centers devoted to locating and assisting illegal aliens to circumvent the immigration laws of the land. These centers have been described

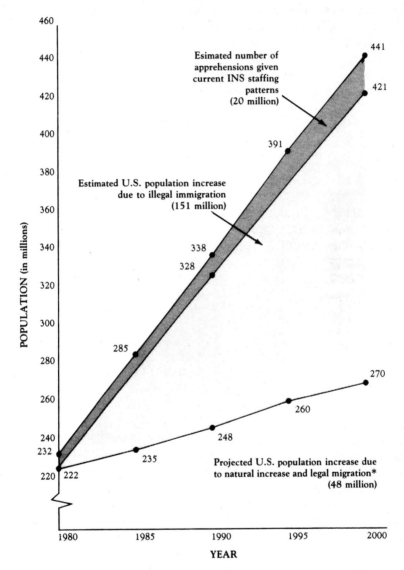

FIGURE I

Estimate of the Effect of Illegal Immigration on U.S. Population Growth to the Year 2000, Assuming Current Policies Continue

Esimated number of apprehensions given current INS staffing patterns (20 million)

Estimated U.S. population increase due to illegal immigration (151 million)

Projected U.S. population increase due to natural increase and legal migration* (48 million)

POPULATION (in millions)

460
441
440
421
420
400
391
380
360
340
338
328
320
300
285
280
270
260
260
248
240
232
235
220 | 222

1980   1985   1990   1995   2000

YEAR

*U.S. Bureau of the Census Medium Projections

NOTE 1: The estimate of the number of illegal aliens expected is shown as a straight line increase of 8.08 million per year (average derived from Table I). However, this increase will most likely approximate an exponential growth curve.

NOTE 2: Estimate does not include the substantial number of children expected to be born of illegal aliens in the United States.

in widely distributed pamphlets and have been advertised on Spanish language radio stations. In one such spot announcement aired on a station in our nation's capital, our former director of the Immigration and Naturalization Service urged illegal aliens to use these centers. One lengthy handbook in Spanish, *El Otro Lado*, a guide for illegal aliens, states that assistance can be obtained from a Church in any Catholic diocese, thus suggesting that all Catholic Churches participate in the network. The handbook lists names, addresses, and telephone numbers of centers in twenty-nine states and includes the Catholic Welfare Bureau in Los Angeles, the U.S. Catholic Conference in Washington, D.C., the Archdiocese of New Orleans, the Catholic Resettlement Council of Cleveland, and Catholic Services for Immigrants in San Antonio. (The list appears on pages 25–29 of the original Spanish text.)

The handbook advises that, "Private lawyers usually cost a lot, but a lawyer from Legal Aid can help you at no charge. There are Legal Aid offices throughout the United States. Most cities have more than one office. Some are noted here. You can find the addresses of Legal Aid by looking through all the letter *L* in your telephone directory." (This list appears on pages 29–32 of the original Spanish text.) The services of the U.S. taxpayer-supported Legal Aid Program are used by illegal aliens to fight deportation. In the United States it is a felony to aid or harbor an illegal alien. Thus the hierarchy is promoting disobedience of the laws of the land. (Copies of the handbook can be obtained for fifty cents from: New Mexico People and Energy, Box 4726, Albuquerque, NM 87196.)

There are other ways in which the Church is being obstructionist. Political pressure tactics similar to those seen in the case of abortion and family planning are used by the Church to intimidate politicians into ensuring that the United States accommodates illegal aliens to the greatest extent tolerable to its citizens. Public opinion polls have consistently expressed the consensus of this citizenry that illegal immigration is hazardous to the country's economy and must be halted. This group includes the vast majority of American Catholics. It appears that the American Catholic hierarchy is almost completely unsupported by Catholic laypersons on this issue.

The Church lends its support to elected officials who favor its position on illegal immigration and opposes those who work to curb it. Church manipulation of appointed officials and ranking bureaucrats has probably had an even greater obstructionist effect. A decade of observing these activities, particularly since the initiation in 1975 of a national network of centers, leads me to the same conclusion reached by Federal Judge John Dooling in his 328-page decision striking down the Hyde Amendment regarding the right-to-life movement: "It is they [the Roman Catholic Church] who have vitalized the movement, given it organization and direction, and used ecclesiastical channels of communication in its support."

Latin American nations, prohibited by the Church from undertaking effective family planning programs, are seriously overpopulated and will, with few exceptions, double their populations in the next eighteen to thirty years. Already tens of millions of Latin American poor live without hope in conditions of human misery and hunger, and it is the children who are affected most acutely.

This great human disaster is witnessed by the Church, even by the pope himself, and the only alternative consistent with Church dogma is to move the tens of millions to North America.

The recent Presidential Commission on Immigration Reform was led by one of America's most prominent Roman Catholic priests, whose public statements have clearly shown his excellent grasp of the disastrous implications of our continuing failure to deal with illegal immigration. Yet his commission's report recommended against the introduction of an unforgeable national identification card, which is undeniably critical to coping with illegal immigration. Without this national identification system, control of illegal immigration becomes a mere charade. This recommendation gutted the commission's attempt to resolve this problem.

Despite this priest's evident concern for his country, his Church's agenda prevailed. In my own view, his appointment to head this commission was the equivalent of leaving a fox to guard the chicken house door.

No consideration is given by the Church to even the short-term implications of the problem. Already Californians and Floridians are arming themselves as they bear witness to intensified criminal activity. The wave of violent crime is attributed to unemployment, both that of illegal aliens and of Americans displaced from their jobs by illegal aliens. Labor unions stand silent under intimidation by the Church. As tens of millions of illegal aliens migrate into these states, the resulting social disorder will subsequently make them uninhabitable.

Following the Church's alternative, in a few decades we can expect the United States to become either ungoverned under the crunch of hundreds of millions of illegal aliens or one of the iron-clad authoritarian governments described by Heilbroner in *The Human Prospect*. In either case, the security of the United States' citizens will be lost. Their civil rights will be trampled by these hundreds of millions (Latin America's population is projected by the U.S Census Bureau to increase from 360 million to 676 million in just twenty years and to add 100 million every several years thereafter). A few decades hence the deprivation, misery, hunger, and insecurity that characterizes Latin

America will also characterize the country to the north. The United States will no longer be attractive to immigrants, since these conditions will have equalized throughout the Americas and the Caribbean. The U.S capability for contributing to world peace and prosperity will be destroyed. If America becomes chaotic, all hope for a humane world at peace will be lost for many generations to come. Then what alternative will the Roman Catholic Church offer?

The United States has a system of government, personal freedoms, prosperity, and security unparalleled by any nation in history. Although population will take its toll around the world in the coming decades (projected by the U.S. government's heavily documented *Global 2000 Report*), it is imperative that people of all nations retain the hope that these freedoms, prosperity, and security will be enjoyed by their heirs, at least. It is clearly in the best interest of all peoples that the United States remain socially organized, free, and secure. A socially organized America is not only a paradigm but will serve as a launching site for efforts to solve the problems engendered by overpopulation. If there is no source from which organized efforts to deal with these problems can emanate, then the Four Horsemen of the Apocalypse will ravage the peoples of the Earth. The Catholic Church's alternative to effective family planning and abortion is unworkable; the Church should show some humane concern for the hundreds of millions of destitute who will not be able to make the voyage to America.

Given that illegal immigration and its underlying cause of overpopulation are most serious threats to our security (forcefully documented in the National Security Council's Fourth Annual Report of its Ad Hoc Group on Population Policy), it would seem that our elected public officials and other civil servants who cannot bring themselves to deal with these imminent threats on religious grounds owe it to their fellow Americans to step down. Only through the concerted efforts of all public officials can we confront the significant issues involved in the control of illegal immigration and overpopulation. Maintenance of U.S security and global peace is at stake. Whatever the original humane intent of the Roman Catholic Church, through its hierarchy's activities concerning illegal immigration, it seriously threatens the security of the United States.

The Administration's Plan

On July 30, 1981, the Reagan Administration's plan for dealing with illegal immigration was announced. According to the administration, the plan would cut the flow of illegal immigrants by half, as if this would be adequate! This proposed program is doomed to failure.

The single act of failing to include the tamper-proof Social Security card in the package dooms the program. With a couple of phony documents in hand, millions of employable aliens will continue to swarm across our borders for decades to come. No serious student of this problem, including former Secretary of Labor Ray Marshall, believes that the flow can be slowed without both the card and the administration's proposed employer sanctions.

The amnesty program and the enforcement component border on the ridiculous. The package calls for a 50 percent increase in spending for enforcement. Yet, even today the INS estimates that, for each alien apprehended, two escape detection. A 200 percent increase would have been more consistent with reality, but even then we would have to assume that the flow will not increase. And it most certainly will.

Jorge Bustamante, a sociologist at El Colegio de Mexico and a frequent advisor to the Lopez Portillo government, said on August 4, 1981: "All parts of the program are conducive to an increase in the flow."

Some 5 million (many believe the number exceeds 10 million) who state they were present before January 1, 1980, and can produce some flimsy, phony documentation to "prove" it, will be granted amnesty. According to MIT illegal immigration expert Michael Piore, the program will cost in excess of a billion dollars, far more than the $235 million allocated by the government. The largest cost will be in certifying each alien for amnesty. This means that the certification process will take years. In the meantime, many millions more will flow through our borders, false documents in hand. The government certification system would never catch up, and the number would swell to many times the 5 million.

The plan says that dependents of aliens granted amnesty could not migrate to the States. How could they be stopped? It's not possible. If each alien worker has an average of five dependents (the average Mexican completed family size is seven children), then the population of the United States could grow by 30 million in a few years. Many service systems would collapse. All Americans would be receiving fewer services.

One must question whether the administration's plan, endorsed in the August 11, 1981, issue of *Executive Intelligence Review*, a conservative Roman Catholic publication that called the plan a "viable, though minimum, program for immigration," was designed to ensure failure, as desired by the Church. One must also question the Reagan Administration's commitment to the security of the United States.

Notes

1. R. S. Johnson, "Our Undocumented Aliens, Part VI," *Empire Magazine, The Denver Post* (July 30, 1978), p. 23.

2. West Germany, Italy, and the United Kingdom are the three largest countries and also the most food deficient in Europe. According to E. P. Kraly ("Limits in the Land of the Free," *American Demographics*, March 1980, 2:3:18,

> Over one-half of the foreign-born population in 1970 came from Europe. Italians comprised 10 percent, Germans and Canadians each 9 percent. . . . Over 40 percent of all naturalized citizens are immigrants from the United Kingdom, Germany, Italy, and Canada, which are the historical sources of immigration to the United States.

3. D. R. Vining, Jr., "Airborne Migrant Study Urged," *INTERCOM* (November–December 1979), 7:11,12:3.

4. E. P. Kraly, "Limits in the Land of the Free," *American Demographics* (March 1980), 2:3:17.

3.

Abortion:
A National Security Issue

In public discussion of abortion, proponents frequently point to its positive aspects, particularly regarding the individual. Only rarely are the social benefits of legal abortion cited, and then in terms of the savings in billions of dollars of welfare funds and tens of billions in federal, state, and local tax-supported social expenditures (for example, education and health). However, the national security implications of abortion have not been addressed in a public forum but could come to be the single most important facet of the abortion debate.

Abortion has been and will remain an essential variable in fertility control. Any serious attempt at population growth control in the next few decades will have to recognize the role abortion plays in birth rate decline. Currently, an estimated 40 to 50 million abortions are performed worldwide each year, one-half of them illegal.[1] Since world population grows at a rate of about 80 million persons per year,[2] in the absence of abortion, annual growth would approach approximately 120 million. Growth of this magnitude would probably place intolerable strains on the economics and environments of some countries. Given the inadequacies of current contraceptive technologies and the poor prospects for improved technologies in the near future, the universal availability of abortion becomes critical in control of population growth in the decades ahead.

To recognize the role of abortion in fertility control is not to promote abortion simply to avert births but to emphasize the inescapable need for abortion as one element in any comprehensive family service.[3,4] Contraceptive advice must be available after abortion (but is not normally given when abortion is illegal), while the availability of abortion for contraceptive failure makes reversible methods of family planning more acceptable. Recent experience in Tunisia documents that legal abortion can accelerate the adoption of family planning,[5] perhaps with less total fetal destruction in the long run.

World population growth as a threat to national and global security has been previously described in chapter one.[6] Two National Security Council reports[7,8] agree with this characterization. More recently, Camp and Green of the Population Crisis Committee pointed out the strategic importance of many developing countries whose internal stability is threatened by excessive population growth. This excessive growth leads to chronic unemployment and the frustration of the goals of hundreds of millions of people, perhaps particularly those who migrate to the overcrowded cities of the developing world looking for a better life.

While this new threat to the security of individual nations and ultimately to global security has not been widely acknowledged, it is beginning to capture the attention of people of different professions and distinctive political persuasions.

An extensive search of the literature reveals that one of the earliest to express his concern was the founder of the World Population Society, Dr. Charles Cargill. At the First Annual Meeting of the World Population Society in February 1974, Cargill emphasized the relationship between national security and population. He brought the message to many groups, including the House Select Committee on Population in 1978.

In 1976, former Assistant Secretary of State George W. Ball referred to demographic pressures in his book, *Diplomacy for a Crowded World.*[9] Former World Bank President Robert McNamara underscored the importance of the problem as he addressed an audience at the Massachusetts Institute of Technology in April 1977 when he declared:

> Short of thermonuclear war itself, it is the gravest issue the world faces over the decades immediately ahead. . . .
>
> Indeed, in many ways rampant population growth is an even more dangerous and subtle threat to the world than thermonuclear war, for it is intrinsically less subject to rational safeguards and less amenable to organized control.[10]

At about the same time, the former director of the Central Intelligence Agency, William Colby, made a similar observation during a television interview and has since reiterated his belief that world population growth is the most serious threat to United States security (as noted in an article, entitled "Population," in the *Cincinnati Enquirer*, August 13, 1978, referring to a statement made by Mr. Colby in testimony before a congressional committee a few days earlier). Lester Brown, ecologist and president of the Worldwatch Institute, has emphasized the salience of population growth factors in his treatise, "Redefining National Security."[11] In February 1978, Ambassador Marshall Green, then coordinator of population affairs, United States Department of State, outlined its significance in testimony before the House Select Committee on Population.[12] Retired Army General Maxwell Taylor acknowledged the threat before the same committee in April 1978.[13] Ambassador Richard Benedick, coordinator of population affairs at the State Department, made a forceful plea for greater efforts for security reasons in testimony presented before the Senate Foreign Relations Committee in April 1980.[14] Former Secretary of State Alexander Haig, during his Senate confirmation hearings, asserted:

> I think perhaps the greatest, the most pervasive problem by which mankind will be increasingly wrenched is our declining ability to meet human needs in the areas of food, raw materials, and resources, counterpoised against what are clearly rising expectations of growing populations. I think this is the grist from which many of the controversies in the period ahead will evolve.

It is becoming increasingly apparent to family planning professionals that the vociferous debate on abortion in this country is having a serious negative effect on the struggle to provide legal abortion services throughout the developing world where population growth rates are the highest. It is also becoming apparent that, as the abortion struggle in the United States goes, so goes the struggle in the developing world.

The following facts are indisputable:

- World population growth is a threat to the security of all nations, including the United States.
- Abortion is essential to any effective population growth control effort.
- Abortion is a national security issue.
- As the availability of legal abortion in the United States goes, so goes the availability of abortion in the developing world.

The American College of Obstetrics and Gynecology is to be congratulated for its unyielding commitment to making legal abortion an available choice for all American women.

Notes

1. T. M. King, "Abortion and Abortifacients," *The Draper Fund Report* (Summer 1978), 6:27.

2. 1980 World Population Estimates Sheet, Washington, D.C., 1980, The Environmental Fund.

3. I. Nazer, "The Tunisian Experience in Legal Abortion," *International Journal of Gynaecology and Obstetrics* (1980), 17:488.

4. M. Potts, P. Diggory, and J. Peel, *Abortion* (Cambridge University Press, 1977).

5. J. van der Tak, *Abortion, Fertility, and Changing Legislation: An International Review* (Lexington, MA: Lexington Books, 1974).

6. This report was prepared in collaboration with the Georgetown University Center for Strategic and International Studies and was later published as "Population Growth and Global Security: Toward an American Strategic Commitment" in *The Humanist* (January/February 1981), 41:1:6–18.

7. U.S. International Population Policy, Third Annual Report of the National Security Council Ad Hoc Group on Population Policy (Department of State, January 1979).

8. U.S. International Population Policy, Fourth Annual Report of the National Security Council Ad Hoc Group on Population Policy (Department of State, April 1980).

9. G. W. Ball, *Diplomacy for a Crowded World* (Boston: Little, Brown & Compa y, 1976), p. 233.

10. R. McNamara, "Address to the Massachusetts Institute of Technology" (Washington, DC: World Bank, April 28, 1977).

11. L. Brown, *Redefining National Security*, Worldwatch Paper No. 14 (Washington, DC: Population Reference Bureau, 1977).

12. M. Green, "Rapid Population Growth Politically Explosive," *INTERCOM* (Population Reference Bureau, April 1979), 7:4:13.

13. M. Taylor, *Precarious Security* (New York: W. W. Norton & Company, 1976), p. 12.

14. R. E. Benedick, U.S. International Population Policy and National Security, testimony presented before the Senate Foreign Relations Committee (April 29, 1980).

4.

The Catholic Church and Social Justice Issues

Numerous books have been written by both Catholic clergy and lay-persons charging that the Vatican and Catholic hierarchy in general concern themselves too much with dominance and too little with social justice, that struggle for and retention of power enjoys the highest priority, and that positive stands on social justice are taken only when they are expedient and do not threaten the equilibrium of the Church. Among these Catholic critics are writers such as Malachi Martin,[1] Andrew Greeley,[2] and Jean-Guy Vaillancourt.[3] This preoccupation with power has serious implications for non-Catholics as well, regarding some of the most sensitive and important social issues of our day. They include the Equal Rights Amendment, the environmental movement, legalized abortion, family planning and population growth control, and illegal immigration control. This chapter discusses the sources and current threats to the power of the Church and some of the bold actions the Vatican has taken to counter these threats.

The past few years have been very active for the Roman Catholic Church in America, and, as time passes, its activities have become less thinly veiled and its intentions more evident. Particularly since the Pastoral Plan of Action of November 1975, the Catholic Church has placed in gear its formidable political machinery. Although American bishops said that this plan for political mobilization was designed in response to the legalization of abortion, astute observers now recognize that abortion was simply an excuse for the American Church to mobilize politically.

At the 1975 annual meeting of the National Conference of

Catholic Bishops at which the Bishops' Pastoral Plan for Pro-Life Activities (often referred to as the Pastoral Plan of Action) was announced, then Archbishop Joseph Bernardine of Cincinnati told the nation's Roman Catholic bishops that "the will of God and the law of reason" demand an unrelenting fight against abortion. This "will of God and law of reason" justified, in the Church's eyes, the implementation of the Pastoral Plan of Action and what the influential *National Catholic Reporter*, a lay-edited weekly, referred to as the creation of a new political party, an American Catholic Party.[4]

Sources of Power

The Roman Catholic Church is an organization whose influence exceeds that of most governments of the world. How did the Church arrive at this position? What are its principal sources of power?

First, the Church establishment is an absolute monarchy. In this highly autocratic situation, the chain of command is well defined, and all in positions of authority are absolutely responsive to their superiors. When the pope speaks, his subordinates listen—at least through the rank of priest. Anyone who steps out of line is quickly dealt with, usually very quietly. Father Drinan and Hans Kung are examples. Unquestioning loyalty to the monarch who sits on St. Peter's throne is demanded and received.

Second is the claim of infallibility, a rather recent invention, first proposed in the early 1880s. For centuries, the Church had maintained considerable temporal power. About this time it became apparent to the Vatican that it was about to lose all of its temporal power, so it struck upon this idea of infallibility—its new source of power.

Third is the ever-present threat of excommunication: a person may be excluded from entering heaven by declaration of the pope. Bishops and priests also possess this power as they can recommend excommunication to the pope. This is probably the most powerful social engineering weapon ever devised by humankind. For the true believer, there is absolutely nothing worse than excommunication, not even death. Such a ruthless weapon says much about the nature of the relationship of the hierarchy to the communicant.

The fourth is indoctrination, which is fundamental to control over the laity. It is this source of power that the Church sees seriously threatened by numerous efforts to improve the quality of life, such as:

1. democracy in general
2. the Equal Rights Amendment (ERA)
3. legalized abortion

4. the family-planning movement
5. the control of illegal immigration
6. the protection of the environment
7. the *Global 2000 Report*[5]

Each of these thrusts threaten the power of the Church by undermining its carefully indoctrinated authority. Certain tenets have been persistently inculcated during the process. If these tenets are undermined by civil law instituted by temporal authorities, then the authority of the Church itself is undermined and, in the eyes of its followers, the power of the Church diminished.

The Social Justice Issues

True democracy is very threatening to the Church. As long as it can control the lawmakers, as it did when the Christian Democrats held sway in Italy for several decades, the Church has no problem with democracy. However, when a democratic government implements advances that tend to diminish influence of the hierarchy and thus weaken its hold on the populace—such as legalized abortion and equal rights for women—these actions can become very irritating. Furthermore, a democratic political system encourages clergy and laypersons to demand a more democratic Church such as existed in the earliest years of the Church. These demands can be exasperating to a Church leadership that rules absolutely. Why should the Church share its power? Its success lies in the fact that it is the most monolithic organization on earth.

The Church has found itself most effective in alliances with right-wing dictatorships. Being very conservative itself, it feels most at home with conservatives. Right-wing dictatorships and the Church coexist in a symbiotic relationship. The Church can deliver the control of the masses, and the right-wing governments permit the Church to conduct its business and its wishes, including ensuring the passage of laws which enhance its power.

Three popular modern movements—ERA, family planning, and legal abortion—all undermine Church authority and power by having as their ends the legalization and promotion of acts that completely counter the tenets with which the Church leadership has indoctrinated its congregants.

The Equal Rights Amendment would, in effect, encourage women to seek out interests outside a role devoted to a lifetime of reproducing and rearing faithful Catholics. Most important, the adoption of the Equal Rights Amendment by the secular will soon lead to demands by women belonging to Catholic religious orders to be recognized as first-class citizens. No longer would the Church have at its disposal a force of millions of docile and obedient nuns. Actions such as the recent suit filed against a bishop in New England would become commonplace. There would be unending challenges to the authority of the all-male leadership of the Church by these women. This prospect has undoubtedly generated many nightmares for the occupants of the Vatican. Furthermore, calls for democracy within the Church would be strengthened. The ERA, therefore, seriously threatens the power of the leadership of the Catholic Church.

The Church has staked much of its authority on the issues of family planning and abortion. Initially, the Church took up these issues because it has always been highly pronatalist, believing that through numbers comes strength, and the greater the number of Catholics the better.

The Church's claim that abortion and contraception are immoral continues to be eroded. What is moral is pretty much determined when a consensus is reached. Murder is immoral. There is a consensus. However, on the issues of abortion and contraception, America continues to slowly move away from the Church's position. A majority of Americans belong to religious groups that do not believe that abortion and family planning are immoral, including nearly all of the major Protestant groups. An intimate knowledge of the sex lives of individuals gained through confessionals gives priests considerable power over individuals, and ultimately this power is exercised by the Vatican. The celibate males of the Church have always given considerable attention to the sexual lives of their followers, and concern with family planning and abortion became natural concerns.

On these issues of abortion and family planning the Church went out on a limb, staking much of its authority on these two issues. It cannot lose on these two issues without seriously damaging its authority with subsequent substantial loss in power. Both the Vatican and its critics agree here. The Church cannot lose these two battles nor can it reverse its positions. The course is irrevocably set. The Catholic leadership persists on these two issues because its power and authority are at stake. Therefore, abortion and family planning are issues of power—principally Catholic power issues—not moral issues.

Environmental protection and the *Global 2000 Report* threaten the Church indirectly but nevertheless quite seriously. The basic thesis of the environmental movement, with its inherent premise of population stabilization based on the limitations of the land, is that, if one exceeds the carrying capacity of our ecosystem, an irreversible process is set in motion. Environmental degradation caused by excessive stress on the ecosystem continues to reduce the carrying capacity of the ecosystem until it approaches zero. Desertification is one ultimate result. If this premise is accepted, then it becomes obvious that population growth cannot continue as it has for long. Once this is recognized, changes in social mores and previously pronatalist attitudes will soon bring acceptance of family planning and abortion by the Catholic laity. Thus, the environmental movement threatens the authority of the Church and therefore its power.

The *Global 2000 Report* was prepared by the most distinguished scientists in our government and is by far the best study of the earth as an ecosystem ever undertaken. I believe that it is unquestionably among the most important reports ever prepared by our government. It examines projections in twelve areas including world food supply, water supply, energy, minerals, and population growth. Although the findings are conservative and far too optimistic, it makes a powerful case by providing an enormous amount of evidence that the world is in deep trouble, that the ecosystem cannot hope to provide for the world's rapidly expanding population. One of the firm conclusions is that population growth must be sharply curbed if we are to avoid a world in chaos. This means wide availability and use of family planning and abortion. Thus, if the *Global 2000 Report* is recognized as truth, then family planning and abortion will be accepted as necessary for survival. Thus the Global 2000 movement threatens the Church.

Another threat to the Church is the illegal immigration control movement. If this movement succeeds, and what is perceived by Latin Americans and other governments as an escape valve is shut off, these governments would logically say, "Our demographic course cannot continue." These governments would have little choice but to confront the Church and say, "If we are to survive as governments, then we must get serious about population growth control. Otherwise, we in Latin America are destined to become a sea of chaos. We, as Latin Americans, must make family planning and abortion services fully available and enourage their use." Turning off the valve to illegal immigration is therefore a serious threat to the power of the Church.

This movement threatens the Church in another way. The charge is that the Vatican strongly desires to see a Catholic majority in America so that the Vatican can exercise much greater, if not complete, control over the American democratic process, in the same way that the Vatican controlled the government of Italy for decades through the Christian Democratic Party. Many authors have advanced this idea. I have read this charge time and again over the past decade or so, and, until recently, I thought the idea ridiculous. But after observing the Church's bold and thinly veiled actions in the Reagan Administration, I now believe these authors are probably describing reality. If 150 million Latin Americans legally and illegally migrate to the United States in the next twenty to thirty years, this apparent goal can be achieved. And, as I discussed at length in chapter two,[6] these numbers are demonstrably not farfetched.

The Reagan Administration is clearly being manipulated by the Catholic Church, apparently with the president's blessing. In an April 1982 speech before the National Catholic Education Association, Reagan made the incredible statement, "I am grateful for your help in shaping American policy to reflect God's will. . . . And I will look forward to further guidance from His Holiness Pope John Paul II during an audience I will have with him in June."[7] Mr. Reagan is obviously leaning on the Vatican for a lot of help, and he's getting it—much of it not in the best interest of the United States.

If the United States government shows no more willingness to deal with illegal immigration than has been shown by the Reagan Administration, then a migration from Latin America of the magnitude described above is certainly imminent. A Catholic majority in the United States and Vatican control of our government would greatly enhance the power of the Church not only in this country but worldwide.

The Abortion Movement

In 1980, Federal Judge John Dooling, United States District Court, Eastern District of New York, declared that the Hyde Amendment, which prevented Medicaid payment for abortion, was unconstitutional. (Copies of Judge Dooling's 328-page decision in *McRae* vs. *HEW* are rare. During a recent conversation with the Brooklyn United States District Court, I was told that their copy had disappeared and, for this reason, they were not in a position to reproduce it.) Judge Dooling had spent a year gathering evidence and studying the anti-abortion movement, and his findings showed that the anti-abortion movement was essentially a Roman Catholic movement with a little non-Catholic window dressing.[8] The amendment, says Dooling bluntly, was a ploy by anti-abortion congressmen frustrated in their attempt to pass a constitutional amendment that would override the Supreme Court's 1973 pro-abortion decision; its purpose was quite simply to circumvent the Court's ruling and prevent as many abortions as possible. Dooling, a practicing Catholic, makes short shrift of the anti-abortionists' pretensions to be a spontaneous grass-roots movement that owes its political victories to sheer moral appeal. He confirms that the right-to-life's main source of energy, organization, and direction has been the Catholic Church, and he describes in detail how the movement uses one-issue voting to put pressure on legislators, candidates, and the party organizations that nominate them—a tactic that gains influence far out of proportion to its numbers. Please see appendix one for excerpts from Judge Dooling's decision in *McRae* vs. *HEW*.

What is most significant in this extract is Judge Dooling's finding that *the anti-abortion movement's main source of energy, organization, and direction has been the Catholic Church.* The bishops' Pastoral Plan prompted the creation of the Moral Majority. Richard A. Viguerie, a Catholic, is the man most responsible for the development and success of the New Right, and he will be the first to claim that honor. He was also involved in the original discussions that led to the creation of the Moral Majority and, as its fundraiser, can be credited with its financial success. Paul Weyrich, a Catholic, claims credit for originating the idea for the group and the name itself. In their search for an attractive front man for the organization, they chose Jerry Falwell, who, according to intimates, has an insatiable lust for power—and, thus, Moral Majority, Inc., was born.[9]

It is inconceivable that these Catholic laymen were not responding to the bishops' Pastoral Plan. Much went into avoiding public disclosure of the role of the Catholic Church in the creation of the Moral Majority. Maxine Negri, in "A Well-Planned Conspiracy," exposed involvement of the Catholic hierarchy in the Moral Majority.[10] Then, the June 21, 1982, issue of *U.S. News and World Report* noted:

> At the heart of Moral Majority is a direct-mail operation. . . .
> Membership claims . . . put the number of Moral Majority's active supporters at roughly 4 million Roman Catholics, Protestant fundamentalists, and orthodox Jews. The organization says its "hardcore contributors," numbered at more than 400,000, include a cadre of 80,000 priests, ministers, and rabbis organized into fifty autonomous chapters.

This claim of autonomy should not be taken seriously. What is described here is exactly the organization described in the Pastoral Plan of Action down to the details.

None of us who has ever worked extensively with fundamentalist churches or lived among fundamentalists ever took the claim that the Moral Majority was a fundamentalist organization seriously. One characteristic common among fundamentalists is a keen sense of individualism, and individualists are often fundamentalists because of this trait. There is self-selection. They strongly resist the "herding" that characterizes other major denominations such as the Catholic Church. It is very difficult to organize two or three local fundamentalist churches to carry out even a local short-term civic activity. Organizing much beyond this is inconceivable. In contrast, the Catholic Church, with its keen sense of organization acquired over a two-thousand-year history, found the "organization" of the fundamentalists a relatively simple task by providing with few exceptions the entire organization infrastructure, including the organization of the fifty autonomous state chapters and the organizations in the 435 congressional districts.

The far more experienced and autocratic Catholic Church found the fundamentalists easy prey. They created "leader" Jerry Falwell and they sought out for other visible positions others who also had an insatiable lust for power. These fundamentalists tow the line of the Catholic Church to maintain their newly acquired visibility and their sense of power. And, of course, the purse strings of the Moral Majority are controlled by those who collect the money—represented by Richard Viguerie. As the old adage goes, "he who controls the purse strings, controls the organization."

The Family-Planning Movement

There is little doubt that virtually all opposition to the family-planning movement is Roman Catholic. The anti-family-planning movement's main source of energy, organization, and direction clearly has been the Roman Catholic Church. Most people outside the family-planning field are not aware that this anti-family-planning movement continues to score major victories, such as preventing the U.S. sale of Depo-Provera, the birth-control injectable given every three months, a method which all available data indicate is safer than birth control pills. Depo-Provera is used by tens of millions of women around the world and is now approved by over one hundred countries, including most European countries, WHO, and other prestigious groups. Other victories include successfully laying roadblocks that prevent tens of thousands of women from receiving sterilization operations when they want them, roadblocks which result in thousands of unwanted births yearly. Far more important are the successes of the Church in minimizing U.S. assistance to family-planning efforts in developing countries.

Many of these victories for the Church come under the heading "Administrative Areas" in the bishops' Pastoral Plan of Action. Two recent examples of Catholic Church activity are the mandatory notification of parents of teens who seek contraceptives at federally funded clinics and the banning of federal funds for family-planning clinics which provide abortion.

The ERA Movement

The Equal Rights Amendment died June 30, 1982. I am certain that its failure was the result of the success of the Catholic hierarchy's bold efforts to defeat it. As with the anti-abortion movement, the main source of energy, organization, and direction of the anti-ERA movement is the Roman Catholic Church.

In June 1978, I received a Planned Parenthood Washington Memo which contained an article entitled "U.S. Bishops Block Pro-ERA Statement." In part, it read:

> The Roman Catholic hierarchy, in early May, refused to permit issuance of a subcommittee's statement supporting the Equal Rights Amendment, indicating that the fight against legal abortion takes precedence as its preeminent concern.
>
> The pro-ERA statement was supported by the bishops' six-member Ad Hoc Committee on Women in the Church and Society, which took pains to separate support for ERA from any connotation of accepting abortion. Furthermore, they sought only to issue the statement in their own behalf and had reportedly consulted with the Family Life section of the bishops' Department of Education, which apparently approved their conclusions "that the ERA will not threaten the stability of marriage in family life."
>
> According to a report of the National Catholic News Service, acceptance of the statement had been urged by ninety-four employees of the National Conference of Catholic Bishops and the U.S. Catholic Conference, but advance disclosures about the issue also generated heavy mail from the "right to life" groups opposing the ERA. The NCCB's forty-eight-member administrative board, which sets policy for the 345 U.S. Roman Catholic bishops, rejected the pro-ERA document during an early May meeting in Chicago, contending that it could hurt anti-abortion efforts.

It is now apparent that this move by the bishops was a brilliant ploy. The Church not only evaded taking a positive stand on an important social justice issue which threatens its power but it has worked diligently to defeat the ERA by using the very same political action organization used to combat abortion!

In my home state of North Carolina, one of the last hopes of the ERA movement, we saw statewide polls in May 1982 show that two-thirds of our citizens favored the amendment, and, in June 1982, we saw two-thirds of our lawmakers vote to defeat it. Clearly, a vast superior organization killed the ERA in North Carolina, a finely honed and skillful operation, one two thousand years in the making—the same one continuing to fight legalized abortions in our fair state.

Actions Taken by the Church

What actions has the hierarchy taken to counter the abortion, family-planning, and ERA movements?

In 1980, Jean-Guy Vaillancourt, a Canadian Roman Catholic professor of sociology at the University of Montreal, published a book entitled *Papal Power: A Study of Vatican Control Over Lay Catholic Elites.*[11] This is a study of the techniques intensively used by the Vatican in many countries to control Catholic laypersons in Italy over the past one hundred years. In 1875, the Vatican created a system of local parish committees of at least five members each, called Catholic Actions. These committees were created to organize laypersons to assist the Vatican in seizing control of local, state, and national political machinery. Over the years, the Church gained considerable experience in organizing these committees and in ensuring obedience and a very high degree of responsiveness to the chain of command by the committees. These committees and their more recent counterpart, civic committees, are highly effective in mobilizing Vatican efforts. Vaillancourt places the role of the committees in proper perspective by discussing

> a famous open letter presented to the Pope in 1968 by dissatisfied Catholics from France and elsewhere. The letter severely criticized the Vatican's excessive attachment to wealth and power, stressing the idea that Church authorities are too repressive and manipulative:
>
> "The whole Church apparatus is organized for control: the Roman Curia controls the bishops, the bishops the clergy, the clergy controls the laity . . . and the lay Christians control (what an illusion!) mankind. Hence a multiplication of secretaries, commissions, structures, etc., with their programs and rules. . . . Underhand influences have suffocated the openness which had manifested itself at the lay conference in Rome, a congress which had very little communication with the bishops who were then meeting in a synod."
>
> After this attack on the abuses of social and legal power by church authorities, the letter goes on to describe three of the favorite techniques of control used by the Vatican: secrecy (there

are secret files even against bishops), spying and informing, and repression (used even against some of the most respected theologians).

Secrecy can be classified as either a legal or a social method of control, depending on whether it is used as an administrative-legal procedure or as a simple social defense mechanism. Spying and informing would clearly be instances of social power, since they entail the use of social processes. Finally, repression, as discussed in the open letter, refers to a mixture of legal, coercive, and even remunerative power. Concretely, it includes the habitual recourse by Church officials to excommunications, censures, condemnations, demotions, and the removal or firing of offenders from their ecclesiastical jobs.

In researching *Papal Power*, Vaillancourt studied Vatican control over lay Catholic elites for years, spending a large part of his time at the Vatican. To effect this control, Vaillancourt has found that the Vatican exercises eight kinds of power—all of which have been used and have proved effective in opposing social issues in the United States.

ECOLOGICAL POWER, based on the physical control of material environmental conditions. An example of this is the use of territory, buildings, or real estate to control people through the domination of their environment.

REMUNERATIVE POWER, based on material or nonmaterial rewards or compensations. An example of this is the way the Pius XII Foundation uses its funds to support some lay activities and not others.

COERCIVE POWER, based on physical or psychic violence. Examples of this are burning at the stake, torture, imprisonment, banishment, blackmail, removal from office, denouncement.

SOCIAL POWER, based on the use of structural-organizational or psycho-sociological mechanims such as Catholic Action congresses, peer-group pressures, rumors, co-optation, social ostracism, socialization, use of mass media, nepotism, and selective recruitment. An example of social power is "conditioning." . . .

LEGAL POWER, juridically founded, or simply based on bureaucratic and administrative norms, procedures, and maneuvers. An example of this is the rule of secrecy which affects, under the pain of "grievous sin," the affairs of the Secretariate of the Pope and the Council for the Public Affairs of the Church in their relations with Vatican diplomats and other high-ranking prelates. Another example is censorship, through the *nihil obstat* and *imprimatur.*

TRADITIONAL POWER, based on the use of traditional symbols, rituals, ideas, and sentiments. The cementing of loyalty through a mass of torch-lit procession during a congress would be an example of this kind of power. Appeals to practices (for example, speaking Latin) and documents popular or prevalent in previous times are also instances of the use of traditional power.

EXPERT POWER, based on professional, technical, or scientific or purely rational arguments. An example of this is the recourse to commissions of experts in theology or the social sciences to bolster one's position. Pius XII's speeches to numerous groups on a multitude of topics was also an effort to control through expert power.

CHARISMATIC POWER, based on exemplary or ethical prophecy. Examples of this are calls for social justice and equality (used extensively in recent years) or the giving away of some of the Church's possessions for certain causes (for example, a ring in a Brazilian slum). In a less prophetic vein, the replacement of personal charisma of office and the routinization of charisma are other examples of the use of this kind of power.

The Vatican with one hundred years of experience in controlling nations through these lay Catholic organizations, has chosen to export this highly developed mechanism for control of lay Catholics and democratic processes to the United States. In 1975, the Church launched its Pastoral Plan of Action. The "committees" discussed in this plan are the same "committees" discussed by Vaillancourt that are used to control lay Catholics and to serve as political machinery. These "committees" which make up anti-abortion organizations are openly being used by the Vatican to manipulate the American democratic process. This includes the Moral Majority organization, as unsuspecting Protestants lend their support. For those who have figured out that they are being used, the lust for power or attention given them is enough to keep them in the fold.

The Pastoral Plan of Action was supposedly initiated by the Vatican because "the will of God and the law of reason" demanded an unrelenting fight against abortion. However, by 1978, it became apparent that the Vatican had simply seized upon a golden opportunity to mobilize Catholic America into a political party using its "right-to-life committees"—including the Moral Majority. Some observers began to recognize that these very same "committees" were being used to fight the other "enemies" of the Catholic Church: the ERA, family planning, the environmental movement, illegal immigration control, and support for the *Global 2000 Report*. I am now convinced that *abortion* was simply an excuse to politically mobilize the American Catholic Church and create, *de facto*, an American Catholic Political Party. The same techniques and tactics developed and used by the Church one hundred years ago to manipulate local, state, and national governments on other continents are exactly the same techniques and tactics seen in America today!

In 1977, victory for the ERA movement seemed almost certain. Few Americans realize the fantastic amount of organization and mobilization of human resources, funds, and commitment it took on the part of the Vatican to turn apparent victory for the ERA into defeat. Phyllis Schlafly, a Catholic, and the "organization" she headed, got more help from the Vatican and the American bishops than most Americans can possibly imagine. Judge Dooling found the anti-abortionists' claim that they were a grass-roots movement to be spurious; the belief that the anti-ERA forces are also a grass-roots movement is ridiculous.

As serious observers study the opposition to the family-planning movement, the environmental movement, illegal immigration control, and the *Global 2000 Report*, they recognize just how sophisticated the opposition is—the amount of energy, organization, and direction each has—and that the opposition is all the same people, *the same committees.*

Conclusion

This is not an abstract theory. Such organization has been effective in Italy and other countries and was described by Vaillancourt before it got underway in earnest in the United States. Until those of us who are concerned about these social justice issues are willing to confront the Catholic hierarchy, there will be no significant advances in these areas of social justice. So long as the Church can act "undercover," it will continue to be effective in thwarting significant advances. Our willingness to permit the Church to act in secrecy in America vastly enhances its power. It is absolutely essential that our silence be shattered. If not, then no matter which of these causes is "our cause" it's a lost cause. Just as important, the strength of a threatening Vatican-controlled political party in America will continue to grow. American

Catholics who are seriously concerned about social justice must take the pope and the Vatican at their word when they say that they do not intend to change their course. Catholics must be aware that the pope and the Vatican are choosing their social justice issues very selectively. In the 1970s, Cardinal Leo Suenens proposed that the position of pope and the Vatican, as we know it, be eliminated and that four "mini-pope" positions be created; this is consistent with Catholic teachings. He insisted that this is feasible. Perhaps it is time for socially responsible American Catholics to break the American Church away from the control of the Vatican. Otherwise, they as individuals stand to be accused of the same hypocrisy practiced by their Church hierarchy.

Notes

1. Malachi Martin, *The Final Conclave* (Briarcliff Manor, NY: Stein and Day, 1978).

2. Andrew M. Greeley, *The Making of the Popes, 1978: The Politics of Intrigue in the Vatican* (Kansas City: Andrews and McNeil, Inc., 1979).

3. Jean-Guy Vaillancourt, *Papal Power: A Study of Vatican Control Over Lay Catholic Elites* (Berkeley: University of California Press, 1980).

4. "U.S. Bishops Spark New Abortion Debate," *INTERCOM* (1976), 4:1:13.

5. *Global 2000 Report to the President: Entering the Twenty-First Century*, Vol. 1 (Washington, DC: U.S. Government Printing Office, 1980). 0-256-752.

6. "Illegal Immigration, National Security, and the Church" first appeared 1 *The Humanist* (November/December 1981).

7. A. Menendez, "Of Presidents and Popes," *Church and State* (1982), 35:6:1.

8. D. J. Dooling, decision in *McRae vs. HEW*, New York: U.S. District Court. See, Appendix I for a more complete extract from Judge Dooling's decision.

9. P. D. Young, "Richard A. Viguerie: The New Right's Secret Power Broker," *Penthouse* (December 1982), p. 146.

10. Maxine Negri, "A Well-Planned Conspiracy," *The Humanist* (May/June 1982), 42:3:40.

11. Vaillancourt, *Papal Power*.

Christopher Dawson, *Religion and the Modern State*.

5.

The Vatican and Population Growth Control: Why an American Confrontation

The rationale for the Church's posture on population growth control as well as other social issues has been discussed in the preceding chapters. My purpose in this chapter is to document why an American confrontation with the Vatican over its anti-family-planning efforts is prerequisite to removal of this obstruction to the common good.

There has been little success in bringing the growth rate of the human race down at all, much less to a level that is sustainable in the long term. The most optimistic assessment is that this growth rate has fallen from 1.9 percent (1960–1965) to 1.8 percent (1975–1979), if we exclude China.[1] Except for China, organized efforts to date have given us, through total births prevented, less than one additional year to deal with overpopulation. Population scientists have puzzled over the "determinants of fertility" to explain this irrational response. It has been demonstrated that, when all methods of fertility control are made readily available and political will exists to control rapid population growth, growth rates decline rapidly. A missing factor in their analysis to date is the role of the Roman Catholic hierarchy in thwarting organized family-planning efforts.

For decades, there have been claims from within the population establishment (often made by Catholics) that the only way to get the Vatican to change its position on this issue is through "communication." It is now understood that the reason the Church has not "communicated" is that it recognizes that it cannot change its position and still retain its power. A change in position would result in a tremendous loss of authority, precipitating a loss of power. Communication with the leadership of the Church will not occur for reasons that are discussed in this report.

A "Catholic" Administration

If the stakes are high for the Church as an institution, they are critical for all nations and people, including Americans. That world population growth poses a serious security threat has been well established.[2] Under the Carter Administration, the National Security Council first acknowledged this threat,[3] which was subsequently reaffirmed.[4] The election of President Reagan has introduced an administration that is the most Catholic in American history. His first National Security Advisor, Richard Allen, a Catholic, halted within the Council further discussion of population growth as a national security threat. His second National Security Advisor, William Clark, a Catholic, announced that the Carter council had "erred" in this determination and that this "error" must be corrected. Reagan's CIA director, William Casey, a Catholic, ignores any intelligence that would indicate that overpopulation is a security threat. Alexander Haig, a Catholic who was Reagan's first secretary of state, supported the Carter council's position on this issue but, according to Haig, was drummed out of office by his Catholic colleagues. His replacement, George Shultz, a Catholic, remains silent in this regard.

Margaret Heckler, a Catholic, as secretary of Housing and Human Services, is responsible for the U.S. government's support of domestic family-planning services. She is both anti-abortion and supportive of the administration's restrictions on family-planning services. Attorney-General William French Smith, a Catholic, is responsible for the Immigration and Naturalization Service and for the execution of U.S. immigration laws. The attorney-general has chosen to give little attention to this responsibility and to ignore the fact that our bishops and thousands of clergy commit a felony every time they aid or abet an illegal alien (90 percent of our illegal aliens are Catholic). The mathematical odds of this arrangement happening by chance are fantastically low in this nation which is only 20 percent Catholic. The Church has managed to cover all key highest level positions that would be concerned with the population growth and security issue.

Population Growth Control Losing Ground

There is a growing consensus among population workers that, for the past few years, wherever attempts were made to control population growth, losses have outweighed gains. For example, from a November 26, 1982, *International Herald Tribune* article:

> The family planning programme in the Philippines, once highly regarded, is in danger of being dismantled. The head of the nation's population agency has been dismissed because of his opposition to funding cutbacks, and the new five-year plan barely mentions family planning and, unlike previous plans, sets no specific demographic targets. Aid from Western agencies is held up by Filipino officials, and UNFPA is cutting back its funding because previous allocations have been underspent. The problem is . . . the influence of a senior governmental official, Placido Mapa, highly regarded by President Marcos, and a member of Opus Dei.

Opus Dei, of which Placido Mapa is a member, is a Vatican-controlled lay Catholic organization.[5]

Losses have also outweighed gains with respect to assistance given through bilateral and international donor agencies. The U.S. agency responsible for all international population assistance, the U.S. Agency for International Development, has seen its real purchasing power cut by 34 percent over the past ten years.[6] Among the international agencies, the United Nations Fund for Population Activities (UNFPA), the World Health Organization (WHO), the International Planned Parenthood Federation (IPPF), and the World Bank, despite the good intentions of most of their staffs, have all been manipulated and compromised from within and without by the Catholic Church. The result? Most of their "population moneys" are being spent for "general development" and not on family planning. Astute observers have recognized for years that the Vatican's strategy was to siphon off family-planning and population funds into "development" activities. The "development will take care of population growth" school of thought was an illogical concoction of the Vatican that has been propagated and promulgated primarily by dutiful Catholic laypersons. This strategy has successfully devastated family-planning activities of some international donor agencies and certain countries.

The successes of the Church have occurred despite a large unsatisfied demand for family planning. Among countries studied by the World Fertility Survey, typically one-half of the fertile married women who want no more children are not using any method of contraception. On the Indian subcontinent these levels exceed 90 percent. As a rule, one-third to one-half of those interviewed reported that their last child was unwanted.[7] Worldwide, more than two in three women at risk of pregnancy (about 450 million out of 670 million women) lack access to modern contraceptive methods.[8]

The decline of the world population growth control effort of the past couple of years has coincided with the activities of Pope John Paul II and his Vatican. Virtually every American is familiar with his position on family planning and population growth control: "The will of God and the law of reason demand an unrelenting fight against immoral contraception." His position has been well covered by the American press. It is indeed unfortunate that the actions of the Vatican to intervene in our national affairs have not been equally publicized. This silence of the American press has given the Vatican enormous power to undermine family planning worldwide. The Church is completely candid about its implorable opposition to birth control and professes that it will do everything possible to accomplish its purposes.

The Vatican has called on its bishops, all of whom are completely loyal (though they may appear at certain moments to be otherwise) to thwart efforts for population growth control. The Church, through its two thousand years of experience, has learned that responsiveness to the chain of command in this truly monolithic organization can best be guaranteed by selecting persons for leadership positions who have an intense lust for power. In this monolithic organization, anyone who steps out of line faces an immediate and permanent loss of power. If they, as persons, have an intense need for power, they will not step out of line and face losing it. In this way, obedience can be maximized. The highly successful television mini-series, "The Thorn Birds," based on the bestselling novel, was about just such a person. Father Ralph denied everything that made him human in order to satisfy his intense lust for power, only to become aware in the last few moments of his life of what had driven him to make this denial. Pastoral men remain as priests and are not driven by power. They never obtain leadership positions, but they serve a very useful purpose by creating the image that the Vatican wishes to project—that all priests are nice men and pastoral in orientation.

The Vatican has also called upon a tiny fraction of its laity who are also completely loyal for the same reason as the bishops—an intense lust for power. These men, who are more ruthless than religious, find that, if they are absolutely loyal to the Vatican, they can attain positions of power that they would never be able to obtain without Vatican support. These positions may be elected government positions, appointed positions, in government bureaucracies, in public and private corporations, and in private nonprofit organizations. They are found within the population establishment or are peripheral to it. Under the protection of the power of the Church, they operate in complete secrecy, undermining the efforts of population organizations.

Since the election of President Reagan, they have acted with increasing impunity.

Vatican Power Over Governments

It is also true that the Vatican controls governments whenever possible—either completely or partially. Until this strong hold on Catholic countries or those with substantial Catholic leadership is greatly reduced, we can expect very little improvement in world efforts to control population growth. The Vatican's strong influence on international donor agencies must be eliminated as well.

Jean-Guy Vaillancourt, professor of sociology at the University of Montreal, a Catholic, and author of *Papal Power: A Study of Vatican Control Over Lay Catholic Elites*,[9] has studied extensively Vatican efforts to achieve this dominance:

> [The] Vatican is, above all, an organizational weapon in the hands of the papacy and other top ecclesiastical officials. Religious ideology has increasingly become subordinated to organizational imperatives. Among these internal and external organizational imperatives, organizational control of lay elites seems to have become a major preoccupation and necessity for Church authorities.[10]

> No matter who the pope is, there are structural and institutional influences that operate because the Vatican is not only a religious institution and a center of political power but also an economic institution with vast financial and real estate holdings, a "fiscal paradise" which ranks alongside Monaco and Hong Kong as a haven for tax evasion.[11]

> In spite of the purely religious image that it endeavors to put forward, the Vatican is deeply involved in Italian and international politics and finance, promoting conservatism and capitalism while professing a Christian approach to democratic reforms. The Vatican is constantly intervening in Italian politics to protect its interests, including its economic interests. The Vatican is not only a political and a religious entity, it is also an important financial enterprise. . . . Church authorities have let themselves be used by political and economic elites as ideological legitimators of capitalism and conservatism, in return for economic advantage and political favors.[12]

It is a fact that the Vatican exercises enormous control over governments in predominantly Catholic countries:

> From its inception, the Catholic Church has moved gradually from grass-roots democracy and collegial authority to a vast concentration of power and authority in the hands of the hierarchy, and especially in the hands of the pope and his curia. This development has been accompanied by the alliance of these ecclesiastical leaders with the dominant classes and elites in civil and political society.[13]

"Shogun," another recent highly successful television mini-series based on a novel, dramatized the development of just such an alliance in an Asian country three centuries ago.

This alliance is truest in developing Catholic countries and developing countries that have substantial Catholic leadership and is less true now than it once was in countries in which the population is well educated, such as France, Italy, Belgium, and The Netherlands:

> On the basis of its office charisma, the Church obtains certain privileges from the state, like tax exemptions, special subsidies, and protection from disrespect and even from secular jurisdiction.
>
> In particular, the Church establishes a distinctive way of life for its officials. This requires a specific course of training and hence a regular hierocratic education. Once it has created the latter, it also gains control over lay education and, through it, provides the political authorities with officials and subjects who have been properly brought up in the hierocratic spirit.
>
> From parochial schools to Catholic colleges, from minor seminaries to the pontifical universities in Rome, the Catholic educational system, with few exceptions, was organized under the central control of the Catholic hierarchy and the Vatican. . . . Building on all these educational institutions, with the help of a private taxation system and important investments, the Church developed a far-reaching system of socialization and controls which ultimately functioned to block threats to the established secular system. This ecclesiastical system of controls included, besides the various educational facilities, a whole network of mass media and meeting places for retreats, meetings, and various other kinds of sessions and congresses of groups and organizations, the most important of which have been examined in some of the preceding chapters.

The relative independence of the Catholic Church bureaucracy vis-a-vis political and socioeconomic forces permit it to fulfill better the role of agent of ideological control which the ruling class assigns to it, and which it willingly assumes because of its links with that ruling class. Conservative Church officials do not have to receive direct orders from businessmen and from politicians to act in accordance with interests, since their own interests coincide with those of the ruling class.[14]

The Church functions optimally when it teams up with a right-wing dictatorship or single-party government such as commonly seen in Latin America, certain African countries, and the Philippines. The government offers an environment in which the Church can prosper and the Church reciprocates by controlling the masses—the laity—and ensures the status quo for the government. Referring to Italy as an example, Vaillancourt says:

> The papacy gives religious legitimation to the socioeconomic and political status quo in Italy in exchange for political and economic advantages. It is itself controlled partly by the remunerative power of the ruling class, and in return it uses various kinds of normative and social control mechanisms to keep the laity loyal to itself and to the socioeconomic and political system that supports it. It helps reproduce the monopoly capitalist system and is in part determined in its own internal control activities by economic and political imperatives.[15]

The Church controls the masses using techniques that took centuries to develop. These have been classified by Vaillancourt as: (1) ecological power; (2) remunerative power; (3) coercive power; (4) social power; (5) legal power; (6) traditional power; (7) expert power; and (8) charismatic power. (*See*, chapter four, p. 48).

Through its control of large segments of the population, the Church can and does perpetually intimidate governments. Persevering and monolithic (two well-recognized characteristics), the Church is eminently qualified to overcome the resistance of any government on any issue, given sufficient time.

The Church is accurately described as a totalitarian international government:

> After the financial power which is practically uncontrolled, the ecclesiastical hierarchy exercises an authoritarian power. The accession to the episcopacy comes through a system of artistocratic co-optation. The people of God, the faithful, have no controlling power. The bishop's power, once acquired, is nearly absolute, as long as one respects the supreme norms of orthodoxy

that the ruling stratum itself has established. Without elections, without parties, without unions, ecclesiastical power rules according to the model of absolute monarchy. . . . In its relationship with political power, ecclesiastical power is in perfect symbiosis, as long as there is no mutual disagreement. . . . The financial basis and the power of the Church condition its doctrine and its ideology.[16]

Its preoccupation with power also affects the way in which it defines morality. Because the Vatican answers to no one, it can define morality in any way it chooses—and it does. Anything that threatens its power is automatically deemed immoral. For example, legalized abortion seriously threatens its authority and thus its power. It is thus immoral and great attention is given to this immorality. Illegal abortion, on the other hand, does not threaten the authority of the Church, because the goverment has passed no law confronting the Church's authority. Its authority over the people is upheld, and the government does not try by legalizing abortion to assume greater authority over the people than held by the Church. For example, Portugal, Argentina, and Uruguay all have illegal abortion rates greater than five hundred abortions per one thousand live births— even higher than the rate seen in the United States.[17] However, the Church pays only lip service to illegal abortion since it does not directly threaten Church authority and thus Church power. "Illegal" abortion is apparently much less "immoral" than "legal" abortion, and little attention is given it by the Church leadership. Abortion thus becomes an issue of power—not morality!

A Colonial Power

Vaillancourt also points out that the world is really faced with Vatican imperialism to some extent. The modern Church is little changed from the days when its Holy Inquisition burned heretics at the stake.

In certain aspects, the Church also resembled the mode of production known as oriental despotism, since an absolute ruler (the pope) governed with the help of a bureaucracy (the Roman Curia) centered in the imperial city (the Vatican) but having local ramifications (bishops and pastors). That despot was not served by a hereditary nobility but by educated eunuchs (the clergy) co-opted by a complex system of socialization and favoritism legitimated by canon law and tradition.[18]

Catholic countries with right-wing dictatorships are, de facto, colonies of the Vatican, making it the world's last great colonial power. It is true that the clergy is rarely an officer of a government. The Vatican fears such an arrangement, because the clergy represents a greater immediate threat to its authority than the laity. For this reason, the hierarchy prefers to manipulate lay office holders instead. Priests are normally more dependent upon Church authorities than laymen; but, once that dependence is broken, they are potentially much more dangerous, because they influence their constituents, even when they disagree with their superiors, and because they are insiders who cannot easily be dismissed as heretics.

The Church, in effect, controls most governments in Latin America and many in Africa and the Philippines. Authorities in these countries live under constant intimidation by the Church, which can threaten to bring about the downfall of a regime by arousing its citizens through pastoral letters and other means should the government refuse to conform to the Church's agenda. This ultimate step is ordinarily avoided through manipulation—by weeding out "troublemakers" before they rise to power. On the other hand, those who are loyal are well rewarded in their search for positions of power; they are assisted by the Church in their ascension to high positions in government. Government leaders who owe their first loyalty to the Vatican represent different proportions of office holders in different governments.

For the reasons presented here, many senior decision makers are responsive to the Church and its perceived needs on such matters as family planning and population growth control. The most democratic Catholic countries, such as France and Italy, are no longer completely dominated by the Vatican. At the same time, they have excellent family-planning programs (which include the wide availability of government-funded abortion) and a very positive attitude toward population growth control.

Why an American Confrontation?

Unfortunately, none of the Catholic countries with right-wing dictatorships can confront the Vatican on family planning and population growth control issues and survive. This is the censensus of our own intelligence agencies. The only government in modern times to successfully eliminate Vatican influence in domestic affairs is China. Mao Tse-tung recognized the Church's attempts to dominate the government of China for more than half a century. In 1949, he terminated all contact between the Chinese Catholic Church and the Vatican. Mao made no attempt to eliminate the Chinese Church, which continues today as the Chinese Catholic Church and is completely independent of the Vatican. The Chinese government has rebuffed all attempts by the Vatican to regain control over the Church in China.

Such an arrangement is quite consistent with Catholic teachings. The late Cardinal Leo Suenens urged the elimination of the current "super pope" position and the creation of four "mini popes," pointing out that Catholicism did not require churches to report to a central authority.[19]

It is nothing short of ridiculous to expect right-wing Catholic countries to seriously approach family planning. They cannot do so and survive the blandishments from the Vatican. In Latin America, for example, resistance to the Vatican on this issue would undoubtedly destabilize any regime in a matter of months, to be replaced by one sympathetic to the needs of the Church.

A case in point is Mexico. Despite the lengths to which the Mexican government has gone to check Vatican influence, it is powerless to fully implement the rigorous family-planning program (which necessarily must include wide availability of *legal* abortion) the country desperately needs. Throughout the 1970s, their program grew at a phenomenal pace. Then with the election of John Paul II, the reactionary Vatican began to bear down on Mexican officials. Now losses appear to exceed gains and, certainly, the momentum of the mid-seventies has been lost. Mexico's failure to keep its population size in balance with its resources by bringing into the world millions for whom it is utterly incapable of providing has tremendous implications for Mexican and U.S national security. All Americans will find their lives directly affected and less secure as a result; of course, Mexicans will be in even greater jeopardy. Attempted illegal immigration of tens of millions of Mexicans into the United States can be expected in the coming decades.

This holds true throughout Latin America, a region of the world with substantial overpopulation. The Church is evidently strongly promoting illegal immigration to the United States, and for two salient reasons (*see,* chapter two): first, to achieve a Catholic majority in America, the most powerful nation on earth. Second, the overpopulation of Latin America is driving its followers to communism, which, through its similar indoctrination techniques, strongly competes with the Church for the "claim to a rightful empire over the minds of men."[20]

Catholic theologian Father Arthur McCormack recently pointed out that the Vatican, because of its position on population growth control, threatens the security of all nations.[21] Latin governments cannot proceed with the efforts necessary to achieve population growth control as long as Vatican resistance continues. There is only one nation equipped to challenge the Vatican on population issues and survive: the United States. It has the power, stability, and leadership for this absolutely critical undertaking.

Until the United States confronts the Vatican on this issue, nothing significant is likely to happen in the population growth control effort. And if we do not do so, as Americans, we are faced with a tremendous loss of security as projected in the *Global 2000 Report*.

There are many in the population field who demand that the Church be given "ample time" to change within and that confrontation from without be avoided at all costs. This position is often taken by those Catholics in this field who consciously or unconsciously coopt others and by coopted non-Catholics in this field. It is inevitable that American Catholic laypersons will be held ultimately accountable for the Vatican's actions. The Vatican is not going to change its position. As Vaillancourt has pointed out:

> Papal control over the laity is not an end in itself but rather a means to attain certain goals, some of which are political and economic rather than purely and uniquely religious. Since it is unlikely that the Vatican will abandon in the near future its preoccupation with economic and political power to revert to its original religious goals, it seems rather inevitable that manipulative means of control will continue to be part of the standard operating policies of the Roman Catholic Church.[22]

Separation of the American Catholic Church from the Vatican is therefore a prudent objective of concerned American Catholics.

For over thirty years, the attempts of thoughtful members of the Church, both laypersons and clergy, to impress the hierarchy with the terrible consequences of overpopulation have met with failure. Since the Church thereby seriously threatens the security of all Americans, it would seem that the time for the Church to change from within has run out. American non-Catholics, consciously or unconsciously, are certain to hold Catholic laypersons responsible for the actions of their Vatican. American lay Catholics must break the American Church away from Vatican control.

The Vatican's carefully orchestrated, well-synchronized resistance to population growth control must be firmly dealt with so that humankind may live in harmony with the resources of the planet. Weak governments would not survive such an effort; only the United States is strong enough to undertake this essential confrontation, survive, and succeed.

Notes

1. U.S. Bureau of Census, International Population Dynamics 1950–1979, ISP-WP-79(A). (Washington, DC: U.S. Government Printing Office, 1980), p. 9.

2. R. E. Benedick, "U.S. International Population Policy and National Security," testimony presented before the Senate Foreign Relations Committee (April 29, 1980).

3. U.S. International Population Policy, Third Annual Report of the National Security Council Ad Hoc Group on Population Policy (Department of State, January 1979).

4. U.S. International Population Policy, Fourth Annual Report of the National Security Council Ad Hoc Group on Population Policy (Department of State, April 1980).

5. "Threat to Philippines Family Planning Programme," *IPPF Open File* (December 3, 1982), p. 18.

6. *IPPF Open File* (March 11, 1983), p. 18.

7. "World Fertility Survey Answers Some Questions That Have Long Puzzled Population Policy-makers," *International Family Planning Perspectives* (1980), 6:3:114.

8. "Population Crisis Committee: World Abortion Trends," *Population* (1982), 9:4.

9. Jean-Guy Vaillancourt, *Papal Power: A Study of Vatican Control Over Lay Catholic Elites* (Berkeley: University of California Press, 1980).

10. Ibid, p. 15.

11. Ibid, p. 245.

12. Ibid, p. 283.

13. Ibid, p. 11.

14. Ibid, p. 261.

15. Ibid, p. 284.

16. Ibid, p. 265.

17. Stephen D. Mumford and Elton Kessel, "Is Wide Availability of Abortion Essential to National Population Growth Control Programs? Experiences of 116 Countries," *American Journal of Obstetrics and Gynecology* (July 15, 1984), 149:6:639–645.

18. Vaillancourt, *Papal Power*, p. 270.

19. A. Greeley, *The Making of the Popes, 1978: The Politics and Intrigue in the Vatican* (Kansas City: Andrews and McMeel, Inc., 1979).

20. Vaillancourt, *Papal Power*, p. 272.

21. A. McCormack, "Countdown to Disaster," *The Tablet* (London, November 6, 1982), p. 1109.

22. Vaillancourt, *Papal Power*, p. 175.

6.

What Are Catholics Saying?

The previous chapters were written over a period of four years. Throughout that time, I felt that any change in the attitude of the Catholic Church on population affairs would inevitably come from within. I was convinced that, once American Catholic clergy and laypersons realized how seriously their church was threatening the security of their country by opposing population growth control activities, there would be an outcry among them for change. I was very much interested in learning the opinions of both clergy and laypersons. Responses have been mixed.

Father Arthur McCormack, the leading Vatican expert on population growth, was a special advisor to the 1974 World Conference on Population and a consultant to the United Nations on population. On November 6, 1982, his article, "Countdown to Disaster," appeared in the London publication, *The Tablet*. He was unequivocal in his statement that population growth is a serious security threat: "The population explosion . . . poses a more immediate threat to human lives and *to human life* than the possibility of nuclear war and nuclear explosion." He gave two examples reflecting the refusal of the Roman Catholic Church leadership to deal in a straightforward fashion with the enormous problem of overpopulation. Father McCormack went on to cite recent statements by Norman Borlaug, a Nobel laureate in agriculture, and others who have been responsible with him for the Green Revolution.

And these scientists are not suspect when they make prophecies of doom, unlike some professional population experts.

But Norman Borlaug does not fool himself, he does not blind himself to facts or pretend that theories, however plausible and well thought out, will cope with immediate pressing and complex situations.

Above all, he does not rely on the lessons of history to fit us to deal with situations without precedent, unlike Julian Simon or Herman Kahn or members of the renowned Hudson Institute in the United States, whose optimism gets good notices, even in papers like the *New York Times*.

The facts behind the scientists' alarm are genuine facts, not myths. These should be so well known as to be boring to repeat, but it still seems to me that they are either not absorbed, especial-ly . . . in the Church, or are deliberately overlooked or ignored.

This deeply concerned priest condemns the Church for its flagrant irresponsibility in failing to sound the alarm on the population explosion while protesting the proliferation of nuclear arms:

We hear increasingly in the Church, bishops, priests, and others protesting, sometimes stridently, against even the possession of nuclear arms or the threat to use them. How many official voices are raised in the Catholic Church to warn about the other explo-sion—population? Even in the slums of the Third World, while there have been plenty of warnings against "immoral" methods of birth control, there has been no suggestion of a population problem of the magnitude I have indicated, or of realistic efforts to deal with it.

There was hardly any mention of population in the 1980 Synod of Bishops on the Family, where not one recognized popu-lation expert was included among the advisers. Yet surely Catho-lics should be warned about the consequences of excessive population increase and told of the part that the Church could play in contributing to the solution of a problem which will have to be faced squarely some time: possibly when it is too late.

Father McCormack demanded:

Is it not time the responsibility [of the Vatican] was considered more seriously and factually? High birth rates and low death rates, causing a rapid rate of population increase, cannot long continue. Either birth rates must be reduced or death rates will rise, due to lack of food and other resources. That is the stark choice. One may differ about the timing but in the end everyone will have to be antipopulationist.

The Vatican has to take one side or the other. It must put its influence behind lowering the birth rates or, if it feels this is doctrinally not feasible, boldly state that death rates must regrettably be allowed to rise rather than break what it claims is the law of God.

The article contained a stern warning: if it continues to treat the "population explosion" as heresy, the Church will be doing little more than following the example of the Chinese and find later that its earlier position was untenable.

Even with a limit of one child per couple, the present population of 1 billion will reach 1.3 billion by the year 2000. Running as fast as they can, the Chinese will barely be able to feed that number. How could they manage more?

Father McCormack further observed:

Although I have given a good deal of study (including the writing of a booklet) to the speeches of Pope John Paul II in all his fourteen journeys I cannot remember any reference to those subjects [the danger of overpopulation] and they are not a very prominent subject in Catholic literature, except in more extreme works by Catholics to prove that there is no serious problem. Could we in the Church learn something from China before it is too late?

"Otherwise," he asserts, "if the chaos responsibly foreseen by extremely reputable men materializes, the Church will bear a heavy burden of responsibility."

It took great courage for Father McCormack to publish this article. Only one other Catholic clergyman has offered significant leadership in the control of population growth. The work of this man, Father Francis Murphy, will be discussed later.

Four weeks after Father McCormack's article was published, a response written on behalf of the Vatican by American Catholic Monsignor James McHugh, special adviser on population issues to the Holy See's Permanent Observer Mission to the United Nations, appeared in *The Tablet* (December 11, 1982). Monsignor McHugh presents the usual Vatican arguments against the existence of a population problem and offers not a single substantive criticism. Monsignor McHugh refers to the observations of Rafael Salas, director of the United Nations Fund for Population Activities, "The experience drawn from over a decade of population activities augurs well for the future."

For the record, Monsignor McHugh considers *population explosion* an inept and excessively limited term to describe the world population situation, because it does not address the variety of population problems we presently face on a worldwide scale. To illustrate, he quotes estimates and projections by the United Nations of "declining trends in fertility . . . and . . . the prospect of world population stabilizing at 10.5 billion in the year 2110."

The European Population Conference, sponsored by the Council of Europe (Strasbourg, 1982), is given as another example:

> Except in a few countries where the birthrate remains high, the outstanding feature of the present demographic situation is the sharp decline in the number of births since about 1965. Although the decline has since come to a halt in most countries, the present level of fertility is no longer sufficient in many countries to ensure the replacement of the population in the *long run.*
>
> And, even in the high fertility nations of the Third World, population explosion is not an accurate term because "for the world as a whole, the new estimates and projections indicate a slow but steady decline of the crude birth rate from 36.3 per 1,000 in 1950–1955 . . . to 17.9 in 2020–2025" (*World Population Prospects*).

Monsignor McHugh attempts to refute Father McCormack's argument that there is insufficient food for the unnumbered millions. He offers an encapsulated analysis of worldwide economic and agricultural production and distribution, including the reasons for failed policies under various political regimes. He expects us to accept uncritically his analysis. He criticizes Father McCormack for belittling those who are presently caught up in the debate about nuclear war. He does "not accept Father McCormack's analysis of the world population situation nor his implied solution to it, that is, a radical and immediate decrease in population growth."

Ironically, Monsignor McHugh never mentions that the U.N. population projections he cites assume widespread use of abortion and contraception, which he and his Church are currently successfully thwarting.

Positive lay responses have been nearly as scarce. A practicing Catholic in Lexington, Kentucky, shared a copy of a letter, dated September 21, 1981, that he had sent to about seventy Catholic friends. Excerpts follow:

> Dear Friend:
> . . . I am haunted by a vision of millions of starving children. Last

year, according to UNICEF estimates, 30 million children under age five died from starvation. The World Food Council estimates that 450 million adults are severely undernourished. Under the current teaching on birth control of the Roman Catholic Church, we are supporting a system that insists it is God's will to bring hundreds of million of children into the world in the next few decades only to have them suffer briefly and then perish. If we externally support this church, even while making reservations in our conscience for ourselves, we are contributing to an incredible injustice.

I have become convinced that we Catholics are as blind today as were Christian slaveowners of 1840. Aside from the facts above, we are on a collision course with world hunger which greatly affects world peace and security. The main support throughout the world for unlimited births is the Roman Catholic Church. This may be a greater danger than the proliferation of nuclear weapons or the spread of terrorism.

We are hypnotized by papal teaching that places authority and power in Rome. The direct political consequence is to increase the dependency, leading to passivity, of laity, priests, and bishops. Dialogue on many of these issues is not even permitted. Why shouldn't it be? Few of us have any sense of the history of change in the Roman Catholic Church, i.e., how wrong or how recent some teachings have been.

Catholics would be shocked to learn how much of the teaching of the church is of recent origin. The more regal the rule, the more accepted his monarchy, the more blind the populace is to other ways to view both the emperor and their own cultural predicaments. The greater the aura, the more entranced are beholders.

Few Catholics know the story of how the Pope was defined as Infallible. This act stressed that authority and power reside in Rome rather than in the bishops or the body of faithful. The definition at that time, 1870, was as much an exercise to elevate the papacy and compensate for the impending loss of temporal power in Italy as it was the needed culmination of the development of Christian doctrine. It proclaimed a religious monarchy and created a centralized and authoritative Roman Curia with immense bureaucratic power.

Now the Church is in a Catch-22 situation. To revise its proclamation on birth control would seriously undermine its claim of infallibility (even though only the Assumption has been so defined) and weaken the power of the Vatican. Such changes would be an admission of guilt for untold human suffering, death, and misery inflicted upon millions of men, women, and children since the days of Margaret Sanger.

Because the laity have no concept of the development of teaching, they have no way of accepting change and admission of error. The Vatican fears to undermine central power and to scandalize the laity.

The Church rightly supports the sanctity of human life. It is concerned about the right to life from its very beginning. It does not yet seem to be able to separate the right and responsibility not to conceive from the rights and responsibility of what is conceived. So it permits no interference with human fertility other than abstinence because of its obsession with biological determinism. How can celibates understand human sexuality and the useful and necessary bonding that occurs from mutuality in genuine affection?

As the Church fails to modify its teaching, the coming years will find an increasing awareness of the relationship between overpopulation, premature death and human suffering, and the Roman Catholic Church among more and more of the earth's populace. This is a no-win situation the Vatican finds itself in.

Numbering about 2 billion just fifty years ago, global population is now over 4 billion, and growing by some 74 million a year, or 1 million every five days! (Population Reference Bureau, Washington, D.C.; other reports are higher). By the year 2000, only two decades hence, the total is expected to be 6 billion, despite a further slight drop in the growth rate to about 1.5 percent. In other words, as several population reports state, we are on an international suicide course, with world hunger, starvation, and malnutrition. The Vatican together with the passivity of Catholic laity and bishops are leading the world in this direction of massive poverty.

Because its refusal to recognize the need for effective contraception is crushing human dignity under massive grinding poverty, illiteracy, disease, malnutrition, and unemployment, the most destructive force in Latin America with respect to human rights is the *Roman Catholic Church!* Government-oriented oppression is irrelevant by comparison.

This Catholic layman was responding to the material in chapter one, which, in the form of a monograph, had been sent to all U.S. bishops, hundreds of Catholic publications, and more than 200 bishops in developing countries—950 copies in all. There was not a single response from a Catholic bishop.

However, the official Church did respond through Virgil Blum, president of the Catholic League for Religious and Civil Rights. Because Werner Fornos, director of the Population Action Council, distributed the monograph, Mr. Blum addressed him:

December 8, 1980

Dear Mr. Fornos:

Far from being the serious work of scholarship that it purports to be, Dr. Stephen Mumford's monograph, "Population Control and Global Security: Toward an American Commitment," is an undisguised anti-Catholic polemic which casts discredit not only upon its author but also upon its primary distributor, the Population Action Council.

Typical of Mumford's absurdly false assertions is his claim that the Catholic Church wields enormous worldwide political power, determining by sinister means the policies of nearly every nation on earth, including the United States. He even makes the blatantly anti-civil-libertarian claim that American prelates are actually the agents of a foreign government and should not therefore be permitted to exercise their civil rights in influencing American public policy. In the last century, such a statement would have brought cheering throngs of Know Nothings to their feet in admiration.

Your disclaimer that you "do not necessarily agree with all of the assumptions and conclusions contained in Dr. Mumford's paper" does little to mitigate your responsibility for disseminating what is in essence an appeal to religious bigotry.

Surely you must realize how irrational Mumford is when he compares the Church's opposition to birth control (for its own voluntary members!) with "the threat of Hitler." Surely you detect a certain fanaticism in his exhortation to "confront the Church on this issue now!" A person in your position must surely realize that the Church could reverse its stand on birth control tomorrow without appreciably affecting the size or growth rate of world population. Few of the world's 760 million Catholics are reproducing indiscriminately.

It is true that Catholics oppose Mumford's distorted vision of Utopia in which he and his cohorts would license parenthood. But then, so would every other self-respecting citizen of the United States who is committed to our constitutional rights and liberties.

Sincerely,
Virgil C. Blum, S.J.

A response from Elmer von Feldt, editor of *Columbia*, the magazine of the Knights of Columbus with a circulation of 1.3 million, came in the form of an editorial (April 1981), entitled "Sowing the Seeds of Bigotry":

> There is a prejudicial virus among certain intellectuals that is as persistent as the common cold. No amount of good will, reasoning, explanation, or dialog seems to cure it.
>
> The openness of the Catholic Church during the Second Vatican Council and the periodic world Synod of Bishops has not dispelled fear and distrust of the Church among some.
>
> A new example is a vicious article featured in the January/February issue of *The Humanist*, published in Buffalo, New York, an official organ of the American Humanist Association. Though it has a circulation of only 25,000, it has considerable influence because it goes to a large number of college professors and other professionals.
>
> The article deals with the "population crisis," holding that the world's present population growth inevitably will lead to starvation, global unrest, and terrible violence. It adds that the situation could be remedied, if only it were not for the obtuse attitude of the Roman Catholic Church.
>
> The author is Stephen Mumford, described as a scientist at the International Fertility Research Program and author of the 1977 book, *Population Growth Control: The Next Move is America's.*
>
> He sets forth the thesis that current population control is ineffective. He adds, "If we are to reverse this trend, the United States must overcome the formidable obstacle that the Roman Catholic Church presents."
>
> The author proposes this population-control program: universal sex education, availability and promotion of contraceptives for teenagers, availability and promotion of abortion, and infringement on total reproductive freedom.
>
> "The Church's teachings and the hierarchy's insistence that they be followed is resulting in unintentional suppression of a vast knowledge of the consequences of overpopulation: ultimately, that either man or nature will sharply limit population and that abortion, contraception, and sterilization must be used by every at-risk fertile couple on earth if global peace and security is to be maintained," Mumford states. "While the Catholic Church is no longer influential with its followers in the United States in matters of reproduction, it is nevertheless a powerful political force. Ironically, it is upon the policymakers that the Church's influence is greatest. . . . The Church maintains its political power

through the forewarning of our nation's elected officials by either using or threatening to use its vast resources (funds, communication network, and so forth), and its organization against them."

At this point, the author resurrects the old bugaboo of a Vatican tunnel to the White House. "What has made this tolerance for Catholic influence in U.S. public policy particularly perplexing is that the leadership of the Catholic Church in America owes its allegiance to the leadership in Vatican City. . . . Thus, the leaders of the Church in Vatican City are orchestrating this interference in American political affairs. In effect a foreign power is interfering with U.S. governmental affairs."

Mumford undercuts the Church further by insisting that its concern is not moral but political. "The power struggle within the Catholic Church over the past twenty years has made it apparent, even to the casual observer, that abortion, contraception, and population growth control are political issues within the Catholic Church leadership, not moral issues."

Mumford's fear of an impending disaster from overpopulation is not shared by all other experts. Among those who disagree with Mumford's thesis is Dr. Colin Clark, a fellow of the Faculty of Economics at Monash University in Melbourne, Australia, a fellow of the Royal Statistical Society and a member of the Academy of Agriculture in France.

He insists that a large part of the world's potential agricultural land is still unused and much of what is used is producing far below capacity. To produce an abundant diet such as now consumed in the United States, he declares, only a quarter of a hectare of land—less than an acre—is needed. He notes the world has 3.2 billion hectares of arable land and 3.6 billion hectares of grazing land. With multiple cropping, this builds up to 9 billion hectares, Clark states, and is capable of feeding 36 billion people or nine times the world's present population. If people settle for the current Japanese diet, the world, with present technology, could support almost three times more people or about 100 billion, Clark says.

Mumford's accusation of "absolute insistence on overpopulation" by the Church reveals either gross ignorance of the Church's teachings or deliberate distortion of them. The idea of responsible parenthood is put forward in the encyclicals, *Populorum Progressio* and *Humanae Vitae*. Responsible parenthood means that a couple should plan its family so it would have no more children than it can support and educate, keeping also in mind world conditions regarding population growth. However, the Church insists that family planning be carried out by moral methods. The basic one is natural family planning, which means foregoing intercouuse during the wife's fertile cycle. If followed carefully this is as effective as any artificial means, with no harmful side effects.

Mumford brushes aside any moral objective in Church policy. Nevertheless the Church's opposition to abortion is based on the commandment, "Thou shalt not kill." The Church considers the destruction of human life wrong at any stage of development, whether in the womb or old age.

Logically Mumford would have a novel program to remedy the overpopulation in prisons. If killing the pre-born is the solution to a crowded world then perhaps killing new prisoners is the solution to crowded prisons. One form of killing should be no worse than the other, except the pre-born are totally innocent. They have committed no crime.

Mumford's recommendation of universal sex education and promoting contraceptives for teenagers is a bankrupt policy. It has been tried for the past decade with disastrous consequences. There is more extensive sex education and a greater availability of contraceptives among teenagers than ever before. But it has led only to increased precocious sexual activity, increased sexual irresponsibility and disease, and more teenage pregnancies than ever before.

However murky Mumford's arguments are, one thing is clear. He detests the Church. Perhaps it is because the Church is a great world force that it has to live in the shadow of suspicion, prejudice, and even hate. But Christ warned His followers, "If you find that the world hates you, know that it has hated me before you." And He identified the source of that hatred as Satan.

Elmer von Feldt

Recently, I wrote to the layman from Lexington, Kentucky, and asked him to share the responses he received from the seventy letters he had sent to friends. He responded with the following letter, dated February 14, 1984:

I am a graduate of [the University] of Notre Dame, a former Benedictine monk and Roman Catholic priest. The basic reason I resigned from the Roman Church was the population issue. As I got some training in psychology and marital therapy, and did more counseling, I began to see what a burden the teaching of the Roman Catholic Church was on the marital peace of many couples. I slowly began to realize that in this matter the Vatican had deserted the gospel. With much pain, agonizing self-analysis, and prayer, I resigned in 1968. I wrote a long letter to all family, friends, and acquaintances at that time explaining my action.

The September 21, 1981, letter was sent to about seventy selected persons: graduates of Notre Dame, Catholic friends and professionals, family, etc. Most ignored it. I had about seven responses: two from expriests expressed some sympathy; several from Catholics who felt the same way and were on the point of either leaving the Church or staying with their reservation of conscience; and only one a history professor from the University, who attempted a dialogue. One lawyer waited until the Notre Dame annual picnic [the] next year to gripe to my wife about "secret letters," a reference apparently to the fact that I had not sent it to all of the Notre Dame alumni club here.

The response of the history prof was as he said "personal": that my letter was prophetic, righteous, and unself-critical. He said my statement was "also a bit passe: mostly the hierarchy are now asking, not demanding, and most [Roman Catholics] are simply following their own conscience. The population problem is more cultural than doctrinal, a Third World thing rather generally." He also suggested that my letter "bespeaks some guilt."

I have continued a letter correspondence with him for several years, attempting to get him to consider the *sitz im leuben* historical contingency aspects of all doctrines, but his faith commitment is such that he does not apply his historical discipline to the [Roman Catholic] Church in any way. I doubt if he is even aware of the critical-historical approach to the Bible.

That's it, believe it or not! Only one person was interested in any dialogue. I became convinced that the security needs of Roman Catholics, even educated professionals, are such that they cannot or will not criticize current practice of the Church wherever it does not press on them personally! I am as convinced as ever of what I said in the September 1981 letter, but I really have no forum to say it. I am not willing to be quoted by name, unless I could edit how I would be quoted. I hope this response is useful.

Recently, I did another mailing to essentially these same people— some 950 persons in all—that included the material contained in chapters four and five. The following appeal accompanied that material:

To the leaders of the Roman Catholic Church in America:
There are occasions when the best interests of the Vatican and the best interests of the United States are not the same. I

recently wrote the two articles enclosed, "The Catholic Church and Social Justice Issues" and "The Vatican and Population Growth Control: Why an American Confrontation?" These two articles appeared in *The Humanist* magazine and they discuss some of these occasions. I believe that you will find both to be of interest.

These issues are particularly important to American Catholic leadership. It is inevitable that the 20 percent of Americans who are Catholics will pay an even greater price than the other 80 percent of Americans if these issues are not squarely dealt with.

In the next short twenty years about 350 million people will be added to the population of Latin America, which now has a population of 385 million. Since the land and economies of not a single Latin American country can adequately provide for their current population, it is all but certain that well over 100 million Latin Americans will attempt to illegally immigrate to the United States; most of them will seek work. This would require more than a doubling of the number of jobs in the United States in just twenty years. This simply will not happen. The tens of millions who cannot find work will turn to violence and crime in unprecedented proportions. Our streets and homes will no longer be safe, [but more] like those in Bogota, Lima, and Rio de Janeiro, where I was recently robbed at knife point by two of the 40 million street children in Latin America.

Some Americans are aware of the Church's highly successful efforts to undermine government support for family planning, abortion, and population growth control in most countries of the world. Americans are aware that during his October 1979 visit to New York, Pope John Paul II declared in a major address that all aliens have the right to freely immigrate to the United States. Americans are aware that the Catholic Church is the only significant promoter of illegal immigration in America and the only significant opposition to illegal immigration control. They are also aware that 90 percent of all illegal immigrants are Roman Catholic, making them suspicious of the Church's motives.

As tens of millions of Americans lose their jobs to illegal aliens, as security in our neighborhoods and homes slips away, anger like that following Martin Luther King's [Jr.] death will surface. As a young second lieutenant assigned to an airborne brigade airlifted to Baltimore during the worst of the rioting, I witnessed a mass of human beings temporarily lose the qualities we think of as human. I never want to witness such a complete loss of security again, nor do I want my children to be such witnesses. But I fear that I will. I have said, Americans recognize the Catholic Church's essential role in the overpopulation of this hemisphere. As the anger surfaces, it is likely that it is going to be directed at the Catholic Church and unfortunately at the Catholic laity who are themselves victims.

Realities in our hemisphere cannot be ignored any longer. Any excuses that might be offered by the American Church leadership will most surely be ignored. Americans are already too well informed. Please allow yourself to consider the issues set forth in these two articles. I urge you, the leadership of the American Church, to act and act now to do whatever is necessary to bring an end to the Church's unrealistic and illogical opposition to population growth control.

Sincerely yours,
Stephen D. Mumford, Dr.P.H., M.P.H.

From the bishop of the diocese of La Crosse, Wisconsin, dated September 21, 1983:

Dear Dr. Mumford:

I have received your letter with copies of your articles in *The Humanist*.

After reading your letter and glancing through the articles, I was disgusted with myself for having taken the time to read such "garbage." However, on second reflection, I suppose I was overcome with compassion for you because of your complete ignorance, total misunderstanding, or deliberate misrepresentation of the attitudes of the Roman Catholic Church in America and in other parts of the world. I shall certainly pray for you that you will come to recognize these facts.

May I simply tell you that the Roman Catholic Church stands for the defense of human life above all other forms of creation. I believe its record in most parts of the world, especially in our time, will bear that out in spite of the distortions that some writers have tried to develop, e.g., with the Jewish people in Germany. A great many Catholic people, priests and laity, were also involved in that holocaust. I can personally testify to that because I spent several years in Germany just before the war.

In your letter you state, "I witnessed a mass of human beings temporarily lose all the qualities we think of as human." May I simply ask you the question, do you consider the slaughter of more than one million unborn children through abortion each year as a human quality? I share your fears that the judgment of God will soon come upon us if we continue to demand for ourselves the major percentage of all the material conditions of this world. All of the great revolutions of modern times have resulted from that type of greed by a few ruling class in many countries of the world. The same will come to us soon if we do not change our attitudes.

Finally I predict for you that the Roman Catholic Church, including the American Catholic Church, will more and more be recognized as the defender of human life and of human rights.

Sincerely yours in Christ,
F. W. Freking
Apostolic Administrator
Diocese of La Crosse

Father Aedan Manning, S.T., Catholic Diocese of Jackson, responded with the following, dated October 3, 1983:

Dear Dr. Mumford:

I have just finished reading the two articles that you authored for *The Humanist* (July/August 1983 and September/October 1983). They proved once again that a string of degrees does little to blot out the prejudice that an author possesses. Unfortunately, prejudice does not give way to reason since it is rooted in emotion. Only a true, interior conversion of the heart eradicates prejudice.

Not since the days of Paul Blanshard and some of the backwoods, fundamentalist preachers have I read such blatant and virulent anti-Catholicism. About the only old saw that you missed was the charge that priests and nuns having children together and then eating them in their loaves of bread at the Eucharist.

You have managed to trivialize history and present-day reality, distort truth, offend scholarship, and draw conclusions that if taken seriously could re-introduce the dark moments of our American history where such bigotry whipped up hatred and vigilante persecution against Catholics, Jews, blacks, Mormons, etc. Fortunately, your argumentation is so paper thin that most men and women of learning and goodwill will be embarrassed.

Dr. Mumford, if you wish to continue to write about or against Catholics and Catholicism, at least have the intellectual honesty to find out factually who we are and what we teach.

Sincerely,
Father Aedan Manning, S.T.

Father Claude R. Daly, Colombo, Sri Lanka, responded with the following dated October 7, 1984:

Doctor Mumford,

Your circular letter addressed "To the Leaders of the Roman Catholic Church in America," along with two articles of yours, arrived in Colombo on February 6, 1984. The envelope was post-marked September 22, 1983.

It will come as no surprise to you that I do not agree with your position. You seem not to appreciate the fact that members of the Roman Catholic Church in the United States of America, like those in other countries, believe that Jesus Christ died and rose from the dead, and that he will come again to judge all men according to what they have done. They believe also that the Pope is the visible representative of Jesus Christ on earth. People who hold such beliefs—even if they are lay persons—will not voluntarily take part in any effort to "break the American Church away from Vatican control." The Roman Catholics of Communist China, if they were allowed to practice their religion free of government pressure, would welcome the guidance of the bishop of Rome in matters of faith and morals.

As for your advocacy of the killing of unborn human beings as a means of "population control," even without reference to religion there are reasons to judge that that is not a good method. There are good reasons for asserting that an unborn child is a human being, and that killing a human being before it is born is just as unacceptable as the killing of a human being after one is born or even after one has reached adulthood.

There are other and better ways of "population control," several of which are completely in accordance with the teaching and practice of the Roman Catholic Church. It is a misrepresentation to write as if the Roman Catholic Church were totally opposed to all forms of "population control."

In expressing my disagreement with your opinions I by no means question your sincerity and good faith, and I trust you will admit my own.

Yours truly,
Claude R. Daly

This collection of letters, articles, and editorials account for the most intellectual of the responses I have seen to the information offered in the previous chapters. The leadership of the Church and the devout laity are not listening to Father McCormack or the layman from Lexington, Kentucky.

This is a horrifying set of circumstances! The leadership of the Church is out of touch with reality, and, because of the immense political power they exercise over our national, state, and local governments, they are seriously threatening the security of the United States (and all other nations). Since the political power of this institution ultimately comes from the American Catholic laity, indirectly and unconsciously they too threaten the security of the United States.

Consider the following: if an American allows himself to be identified as a Catholic, he necessarily becomes an instrument of power exercised by Church leadership *by their design.* Therefore, each Catholic American has no choice but to take responsibility for the actions of the leadership since he is a source of the political power being exercised by his Church which threatens U.S. security.

Remember, American Catholics get abortions at the same rate as non-Catholics, and they use modern methods of contraception at essentially the same rate as non-Catholics. It is obvious that American Catholics *have taken* responsibility for the control of their own individual fertility, over the strongest objection of the Church leadership.

There is an evident contradiction here. Why? What is there about this institution that makes for this contradiction? American Catholic laity have made the strongest possible statement that can be made on fertility control: they *live* fertility control every day by using contraception and abortion at the same rates as non-Catholics! How can the leadership of the Church maintain and exercise its enormous power in these matters under these circumstances?

Born and reared in a devout Methodist home, in a neighborhood that was mostly Catholic and fundamentalist, I never developed an interest in learning the difference between Catholicism and Methodism. I never really cared. Deeds revealed no differences. About a decade ago, after years of research and study, I realized that the greatest single obstacle to world population growth control was the Roman Catholic Church and that the other obstacles could not be seriously addressed until the Church obstacle was addressed. I began studying the *effects* of the Church, and these findings appear in earlier chapters.

However, as I received and studied the stunning responses like the ones offered in this chapter, as well as the paucity of responses, I came to realize that I must study the foundation and inner workings of the Church in order to at least partially understand the *causes* of this obstacle. How could 50 million American Catholics (or 25 million practicing Catholics, as noted on page forty of *USA Today*, November 28, 1983) make such a strong statement on fertility control through their actions, while their leadership takes the opposite position *and* exercises nearly complete control over U.S. domestic and foreign policy on fertility control issues? The remaining chapters are a product of this study.

7.

The Origins of Vatican Power in America: A Guide for Population and National Security Specialists

To understand the population problem and the inertia currently seen in dealing with this problem, one *must* understand the origins of Vatican power. The Catholic hierarchy, unchallenged, has used American freedom as a cloak to undermine the population movement and, thus, U.S. security. Their methods deserve close scrutiny.

The pope and his hierarchy claim that papal or Vatican power originates from God. However, there are more earthly explanations for the origins of their power. Very few Americans have ever been exposed to the more earthly explanations. If the intentions of the founding fathers in their drafting of the United States Constitution had prevailed until today, those freedoms of thought, expression, speech, and the press, which we cherish, would not be jeopardized by the Vatican, a sovereign foreign power, influencing the American democratic process and domestic and foreign policy.

American Protestants are taught as children that you simply never criticize another person's religion, that you should not think about the negative aspects of another person's religion, that freedom of religion means that other people have the freedom to do whatever they want to do in their religion, that criticism of religion is always inappropriate, that we should be tolerant.

Roman Catholicism was a relative latecomer to the United States. At the time of the American Revolution, Catholics accounted for less than one percent of the population. Catholics had virtually no influence on the creation or form of the American government. It was not until the great migrations of the late 1800s and early 1900s that the proportion of Catholics became significant. Until then, the United States was a nation of Protestants. A complete taboo on criticizing another person's religion had become a strong national ethic before the arrival of a significant Catholic presence.

Surrendering the freedom to think that another person's religion might have certain negative implications in a Protestant America seemed to have produced no ill effects. (Only the Mormon Church was organized for the specific purpose of attaining political power, but this came later!)[1]

However, with the arrival of a significant presence of the Catholic Church, this national ethic was soon to be exploited by a church with a long history of lust for political power. It had already become dominant in a province in Canada, as well as in Mexico, Central and South America, most of Europe, much of Africa, and the Philippines, and had tamed many Asian countries including India, Sri Lanka, Thailand, Indonesia, and, until recently, Vietnam.

In order to enhance our cherished freedom, the freedom of religion, we denied the possibility that another person's religion might do a wrong. The problem is, when one no longer talks about something, one ceases to think about that thing. By the time of my birth in 1942, the freedom to think about another person's religion was extinguished.

This was fatal to two other cherished freedoms. When some people in this country became aware, at last, of the negative influence of the Catholic Church hierarchy on American democracy, the freedoms of speech and the press were diminishing. The Vatican had succeeded in exploiting an innocent America. How? What characteristics of the Catholic Church led to this exploitation?

The Church as a Totalitarian Institution

This characteristic of the Church is essential to our discussion. It is a fact that the best interests of the Vatican and the best interests of the United States are not always the same. This is the source of the conflict. If the American Catholic Church were a democratic institution, like most other mainstream American religions, I believe that I can say with some certainty that it would have been unnecessary to write this book. Current American Catholic fertility behavior is proof that the overwhelming majority of American Catholics have the best interests of the United States foremost at heart.

Totalitarian as defined in *Webster's Third New International Dictionary Unabridged* (1970) means:

1a. of or relating to centralized control by an autocratic leader or

hierarchy regarded as infallible. Authoritarian. Dictatorial. b. of or related to a political regime based on subordination of the individual to the state and strict control of all aspects of the life and productive capacity of the nation [especially] by coercive measures, such as censorship and terrorism.
2a. advocating the concept that the end justifies the means.

The totalitarian character of the Roman Catholic Church has been noted for some time. In 1948, Karl Barth, a leading European Protestant theologian wrote of the kinship between Catholic and communist political policy in a comment he made to a Jesuit journalist:

> To be honest, I see some connection between them [Roman Catholicism and communism]. Both are totalitarian; both claim man as a whole. Communism uses about the same methods of organization (learned from the Jesuits). Both lay great stress on all that is visible. But Roman Catholicism is the more dangerous of the two for Protestants. Communism will pass; Roman Catholicism is lasting.[2]

Pope Leo XIII, in his encyclical, *Chief Duties of Christian Citizens*, stated that Catholics owe "complete submission and obedience of will to the Church and to the Roman Pontiff, *as to God Himself.*" The pope sits on the throne of St. Peter and, as television has shown Americans, is worshipped as a king. The infallible spokesman of God, he is also worshipped "as God Himself." This is by intention.

In chapter four, I cited a passage from a famous open letter presented to the pope in 1968 by dissatisfied Catholics from France: "The whole Church apparatus is organized for control: the Roman Curia controls the bishops, the bishops the clergy, the clergy controls the laity . . . and the lay Christians control (what an illusion!) mankind." The pope is an absolute ruler who governs an empire reaching to the grass-roots with the help of a bureaucracy (the Roman Curia) located centrally (the Vatican), with the assistance of bishops and pastors.

Obedience is an essential qualification for securing and holding Church office. The mechanism for the screening of potential bishops is so thorough that there is virtually little possibility of the appointment of any bishop who is not subservient to his own bishop and to the hierarchy.[3] Inside the closed cultural system, the priest is supplied at second hand with all the arguments against Catholicism and learns stereotypical answers. He takes his religion from others above him as a matter of duty because he has always been taught that *submission to Church authority is the essence of "freedom."* Likewise, the members of the parish church are taught to be guided in turn by the priest, with what has been described by one Catholic writer as "the apron-string mentality which leaves the clergy to do all thinking for the faithful."[4]

This institutional arrangement of unquestioning obedience makes it nearly impossible for some faithful Catholics to participate in American democracy.

Noted British Catholic Christopher Dawson, who was named as one of the "forty contemporary immortals" among the Gallery of Living Catholic Authors, said:

> . . . There seems to be no doubt that the Catholic social ideas set forth in the encyclicals of Leo XIII and Pius XI have far more affinity with those of fascism than with those of either liberalism or socialism. In the same way, it is clear that Catholicism is by no means hostile to the authoritarian ideal of the state. Against the liberal doctrines of the divine rights of majorities and the unrestricted freedom of opinion, the Church has always maintained the principles of authority and hierarchy and high conception of the prerogatives of the state. The ruler is not simply the representative of the people, he has an independent authority and a direct responsibility to God. His primary duty is not to fulfill the wishes of the people but to govern justly and well, and so long as he fulfills this duty any resistance on the part of the people is a *grave sin*.[5] *Religion and the Modern State*

Thus, to resist a government that is fulfilling its duty to govern "justly and well," as judged by the Vatican, is a *"grave sin."* This control of the people is often offered by the Church to right-wing dictatorships in return for special privileges.

This concept of grave sin is but one of many controls exercised by the Vatican.

Words and Deeds

Americans tend to be far too uncritical of information they receive about the Catholic Church, most of it ultimately originated by the hierarchy, though rarely identified as such. We seldom measure the consistency of the rhetoric and the actions. We often see the Church or churchmen described in high-sounding terms, and we do not subject the institution to any serious examination when it enters any arena other than its appropriate one. Unfortunately, no one else is doing this for us. Upon close scrutiny, one finds that deception abounds. Standard meanings of words are often revised or modified to fit a prefabricated conclusion. It will be of interest to review some deliberate attempts to deceive and thus to understand this manipulation.

1. "The Vatican is principally concerned that the basic right of the couple to choose the size of their family should be respected."[6] This is the reason offered for Vatical opposition to government family planning programs and Vatican pursuit to block government family planning programs. However, if this statement were true, the Church would be promoting the best methods of contraception and abortion and ensuring that couples have no more children than they want. However, more than two of three women capable of becoming pregnant (about 450 million out of 670 million women worldwide) lack access to modern contraceptive methods. Access to good abortion services is even worse.[7]

2. "The Vatican is principally concerned that international population programs and policies should protect the rights of national sovereignty and individual conscience."[8] This is the reason offered by the Vatican for their "right" to meddle in all international population agencies and in the domestic affairs of all governments that are donors or recipients of population monies.

3. The pope wants one thing for every nation: the freedom for each to "live its own life." But, according to columnist Robert Blair Kaiser, this is just one more broken promise by the pope.[9] Freedom for each to live his or her own life does not include the use of contraception or anything else that in any way threatens the Church.

4. According to the Vatican, education is the function of the parent, not the state. However, nowhere does the Church leave the decisions regarding education to the parent (as is done in U.S. public education). The Church expects to exercise absolute authority in all matters related to the education of Catholic children.

5. "He [the pope] also called on Christians to examine the teachings of the Church in their search for social justice."[10] However, the Church vastly undermines its own calls for social justice by actively working to halt population growth control. The Church's teachings work against social justice. As Father Arthur McCormack has frequently pointed out, social justice is not possible in the absence of population growth control.

> The present pope has also gone further than Paul VI in stressing human rights. "Human rights" is a noble goal to work toward, but the attainment of human rights in the fullest sense can never be achieved as long as hundreds of millions of poverty-stricken people lack basic necessities. They do not mean much to a person with an empty stomach, a shirtless back, a roofless dwelling, the frustration and fear of unemployment and poverty, the lack of education and opportunity, and pain, misery, and loneliness of sickness without medical care.[11]

Agreement with this observation requires but a modicum of common sense.

6. Pope John Paul II called for world leaders "to free themselves from the 'slavery' of power worship."[12] Nearly always, books written about the Vatican by Catholic writers, including clergymen, describe the leadership of the Church as being far more concerned with power politics than social justice. But in this statement the pope is implying that "slavery of power worship" is not a problem to the Vatican. This is an act of deception.

7. The Raleigh, North Carolina, *News and Observer* referred in its December 26, 1983, paper to Pope John Paul II's "forceful championing of political freedom" (4A). This statement implies that the pope is always a forceful champion of political freedom. However, when the exercise of political freedom threatens the power of the Church, suddenly he is a forceful opponent. For example, in March 1983, while visiting Nicaragua, the pope sharply condemned the "popular church," a grass-roots movement in that country committed to revolution. This church, in effect, is the formation of another Protestant church. Any political freedom that permits the formation of another Protestant church is going to be opposed by the Vatican.

8. "The pope does not confuse politics with religion."[13] The pope says that priests should not be active in politics and demanded that Congressman Drinan (who is pro-abortion) resign, yet, according to columnist Robert Blair Kaiser, the pope "has been in politics up to his eyeballs since before he became John Paul II."[14] Of all of the deceptive pronouncements of the Church, this claim that the Church is not active in politics and is not mixing religion and politics is the most dangerous to American democracy and population growth control.

9. The Committee on American Citizenship from Catholic University exists to serve as the censor of Catholic school syllabuses and textbooks.[15] Frequent use is made of such euphemistic names for organizations that are quite different in function from that which is implied in the name. The sole function of this organization is censorship of school material that might be threatening to Church dogma. This censorship is not consistent with American citizenship.

10. ". . . the high skill and untiring work of Pope John Paul II for peace and a just solution of the grave problems that threaten humanity."[16] This is but one of hundreds of examples that I have collected over the past few years from reporters who have gone to great lengths to give the pope and the Church the best possible public image. The statement above is in the words of the reporter—not a quotation of a Church official. It is offered as truth—but on faith alone—since no empirical evidence is found on the pages of nearly all newspapers and news magazines. Usually, these reporters are Catholic or they have

Catholic editors. However, they are rarely identified as Catholics. You find these statements scattered among what is otherwise reasonably objective news reporting. But such placement of these value judgments based upon faith make them dangerous. They are dangerous because most of us let these statements register as objectively derived facts even though they are not. We gradually find ourselves questioning the "goodness" of the Catholic Church less and less. Many have almost stopped questioning the actions of the Church hierarchy.

Most Americans look for goodness. We want to believe in goodness. The Catholic Church is constantly telling us of their good works. For example, Michael Novak, columnist and Catholic theologian writing for *USA Today* (10A, April 5, 1983):

"Today the world watches Pope John Paul II's daily struggle to become another exemplar. . . .

"He wants to be wholly faithful to God. . . .

"Three principles guide him.

"1. He must condemn every abuse of human dignity." (Of course, denying family planning is not.) "There must be one single standard for all humanity.

"2. That standard can only be met in regimes which permit liberties of conscience, freedom of association, and institutions of consent. Totalitarianism, coercion, the absence of institutional structures protecting human dignity—such structures threaten both soul and body." (This is a standard that cannot be met in the Vatican empire.)

"3. Third, the clergy by their vocation have a special symbolic role, above and beyond partisan politics, nonviolent, transcending human and earthly structures."

We seldom seem to notice the frequency with which the hierarchy says one thing and does the opposite. Few question. The mass media avoid such findings.

The Elevation of Priests to a Higher Class of Citizens: How and Why?

Michael Novak is not identified as a Catholic theologian. His article gives the impression that he is speaking of facts when he is speaking of faith. We get a wonderful impression of the goodness of the pope, the Church, and the priest, never recognizing the special interests of the source.

Novak, in his third principle, elevates the priest and disarms the reader, frankly stating that the priest is "above and beyond partisan politics." He tells the reader (non-Catholic) not to look for the priest's political activities, that what may be seen as political activities really are not. Since the priest "transcends human structures," he should be looked upon as the natural leader. So says Novak, the unidentified Church spokesperson.

The Church, besides having its Novaks for almost two thousand years, has developed a sophisticated system in order to elevate men who have been most responsive to the Church's indoctrination process and who are most loyal and obedient to the hierarchy.

It is a "superman" quality that makes the priest so effective as the hierarchy's front line political operative. Since every priest is perceived as always speaking on behalf of all the Church, the priest with his "superman" qualities excessively intimidates democratically elected politicians and bureaucrats to the point of undermining democracy itself. This intimidation has, in recent years, been practical in population growth control and sexual matters more than in any other area.

The Catholic Church and Sex

The Church's preoccupation with sex stems chiefly from three very different concerns of power or control: (1) control of priests and nuns; (2) control of lay persons; and (3) control of nations.

The control of nations is seen by the Church, as by many other institutions throughout history, as being a function of numbers. The Church, from the beginning, was concerned with "out-reproducing" other groups. Sex, to some extent, became a concern on those grounds.

For the Church's first four hundred years, it was a democratic institution.[17] Then it evolved into an absolute monarchy as its lust for power grew, resulting in the need for absolute control of priests and laity. This control derived in no small part from the exploitation of their human sexuality, though this exploitation was different for priests than for the laity. For each group, an elaborate system of controls related to human sexuality was developed, and these controls were classified as "morals" (as defined by God, of course).

Earlier religions and primitive groups exalted virginity as a status of perfection. The Catholic Church adopted this concept as a step toward producing clerical leadership for the masses. The self-control required for celibacy was looked upon as evidence of an inner strength not possessed by ordinary men and women. These celibates of the Church were promoted as men and women worthy of leadership positions in the community or people who should be respected, admired, and unquestionably followed. Then the Church bestowed a number of characteristics upon the priest to literally "create" leadership that was at the same time devoted, subservient, loyal, and obedient to the hierarchy. The priest is obliged to relinquish certain personal prerogatives that we all would agree are essential for responsible and responsive participation in American democratic life.

> No one has stated this systematic subjection of the Catholic mind to clerical guidance more frankly than the noted British Catholic writer, Hilaire Belloc:
> "The religion of the Catholic is not a mood induced by isolated personal introspection coupled with an isolated personal attempt to discover all things and the maker of all things. it is essentially *an acceptance of the religion of others;* which others are the Apostolic College, the Conciliar decisions, and all the proceeds from the authoritative voice of the Church. For the Catholic, it is not he himself, it is the Church which can alone discover, decide, and affirm."
> With such an attitude toward his own personal doubts and toward any independent thinking in his own congregation, the parish priest becomes primarily the Voice of Authority. He is not a man among men. He is a member of a special caste. He follows a routine which is almost military in its severity, and he must obey his superiors with military precision. He wears special uniforms and does not marry. He is called "Father" to emphasize his paternal supervision over his people. He has certain special powers that distinguish him from his fellows, and by using those powers he becomes a purveyor of certain supernatural benefits to all believers.
> The Catholic priest is also armed with several special and effective devices of concern over his people. The people are told that under certain circumstances he is able to forgive sin and grant absolution and he performs these operations with impressive dignity.[18]

Thus, much, if not all, of the priest's behavior is directed by the need to control his large flock to provide the control demanded by the hierarchy. Democracy or the needs of people that are different from the needs of the hierarchy cannot be given serious consideration.

Control of the laity through exploitation of their sexuality was probably initially related to desire of the hierarchy to out-reproduce non-Christians. Thus, controls were placed on all human sex-related activities imaginable. Since maximum reproductive output was the goal, anything and everything that inhibited maximum output was made "immoral."

1. Masturbation was forbidden. Making intercourse the only sexual outlet maximized reproduction.

2. Sex among the unmarried was made immoral since, on the average, women will have more exposure to intercourse and, in turn, be more likely to conceive and produce more children if all sex were limited to marriage.

3. Homosexuality was made immoral because it obviously reduces reproduction.

4. Contraception, which had already been practiced for centuries, was made immoral because this practice reduces reproduction.

5. Abortion was made immoral because it obviously reduces reproduction.

6. Divorce was made immoral because it, too, often meant the termination of reproduction by women before they reached menopause.

7. Sex education has traditionally been immoral because it inevitably results in fertility control actions on the part of the couple. In a reluctant compromise, the Vatican now allows limited sex education which does not include information on any of the effective methods of fertility control, such as the modern methods of contraception and abortion. Education that includes effective fertility control measures continues to be immoral.

8. Prostitution was made immoral because it reduced the number of marriages and thus family formations and lessened sexual activity among married couples.

Nearly all sex-related acts that are considered immoral by the Church can be traced to the reduction of reproduction. Others not mentioned here are related to the Church's absolutism, but nearly all can be traced to the "immoralities" listed above.

I used the past tense in the list because it is unlikely that the Church, if it were making its list of "immoralities" in 1984, would include these immoralities given the problem of overpopulation. However, because it cannot change its "infallible" teachings, it is locked into this set of "immoralities."

Now that these "immoralities' are accepted by the laity, priests can use them for purposes of control, as well as fundraising. Since virtually everyone is guilty of at least some of these "sins," and since foregiveness of sins has to be sought and only the priest can give such foregiveness, he retains a considerable amount of control over his flock. The power that the priest derives from this control is ultimately transferred to the Vatican.

The great tragedy in all of this is the tremendous social injustice caused by the Church because of these "immoralities" which seem to have at their root a lust for power. The untold mental anguish caused by production of guilt feelings, as well as physical harm brought about by these "immoralities" is unconscionable.

The importance of the control of education of youth in control of the laity becomes all the more apparent in the face of these "immoralities."

Catholic Education: The Rock on Which the Whole Church Structure Rests

I was raised in a Catholic neighborhood. I walked past a Catholic elementary school in order to reach my own public elementary school. Some of my closest friends were Catholics who attended Sts. Simon and Jude Elementary School in Louisville, Kentucky. Yet, I never realized that there were any significant differences between our schools. It has been only in the past few years that I have discovered that there are *major* differences. This discovery was prompted by my observation that some (but certainly not all) Catholics in the population and environmental fields simply to not complete their thought processes in instances in which the Catholic Church might be threatened. They will start, taking one logical step at a time, until they reach a point where it is evident that the outcome will probably point to the Catholic Church as culprit and then quickly abort the entire thought, frequently citing some kind of dogma. I found their behavior most perplexing. Then, with more experience, I began to recognize a pattern. These people included only those who were instructed solely or for the most part in Catholic schools and universities. Exceptions to the pattern were few.

Recognizing this pattern over the past few years, I decided that I must examine the Catholic education system in an attempt to understand these differences in behavior. In most public schools, children are encouraged to think for themselves; they are given empirical knowledge and taught the meaning and value of the U.S. Constitution. In Catholic schools, children are taught that they owe "complete submission and obedience of will to the Church and to the Roman Pontiff, as to God Himself."[19] They learn that the pope "should rule America in moral, educational, and religious matters,"[20] without having it made clear that all matters can be interpreted as moral matters. They are impressed with the Catholic Church as a sovereign power. Indeed, "it has the three requisites of a sovereign power, legislative, executive, and judicial, including the power of coercion. The ruler of the Church, the pope, claims sovereignty by divine right."[21] It is a power that extends "everywhere where there are Catholics. It claims that it is a supernatural institution with complete territorial jurisdiction."[22] "If there is a dispute between the Catholic Church and the state over the right to rule any specific area, the Church and the

Church alone has the right to decide who wins. And 'the Church' means Rome. . . ."[23] In effect, it is claimed that it is the supreme ruler of the United States:

> In particular areas the authority of the Church is superior to that of the United States government and of all governments, and no government is conceded the moral right to deny this. The pope is a kind of special world monarch who rules a synethetic moral empire that overlaps and penetrates the sovereignty of all earthly governments. His special territory is religion, education, and family life, but he also has supreme power over a vaguely defined areas known as "morals." Also he has special and exclusive jurisdiction over any matter which may affect the life of the Church either directly or indirectly. . . .
>
> In practice, "immoral and irreligious laws" are sometimes laws that non-Catholics consider supremely moral. Under the theory of two powers, divine and civil, democracy is simply one of a number of acceptable types of civil government which may exist side by side with the divine kingdom of the Church. As far as the hierarchy is concerned, the acceptability of a form of government depends upon its attitude toward the Church. As Leo XIII said in his encyclical on *Human Liberty*, "It is not of itself wrong to prefer a democratic form of government, if only the Catholic doctrine be maintained as to the origin and exercise of power." If a democracy favors the Church, then the hierarchy tolerates it; if it opposes the Church, then that proves that the government is godless and lacks the necessary divine authority. If a democracy in Spain expels the Jesuits and seizes Church property, then it is a murderous outlaw. If a democracy in The Netherlands supports all the Catholic schools with taxpayers' money and pays the salaries of the priests, its divine right to govern is recognized as authentic. . . .
>
> There is a certain understandable shrewdness in this attitude toward the democratic welfare state. If the hierarchy once conceded that ultimate sovereignty lies wholly in the people, anything might follow. The state might then rightfully expand its jurisdiction over many fields of authority now claimed by the Church. Because of this danger, the American Catholic bishops who praise democracy always utter their praises with an important mental reservation, that the real source of the authority of the American government and of all governments is God and not the people. And when the bishops use the name of God in this connection, they do not mean a genial or undenominational deity of all the people; they mean the particular Catholic Deity who

established Roman primacy through St. Peter, whose vicar on earth is the pope.[24]

Catholic school children are taught that the concept of the separation of church and state is an error[25] and that no Catholic may positively and unconstitutionally approve the policy of separation of church and state.[26] Also they are taught that the government has no primary right to educate at all and that that right has been given by God, the source of all governmental power, to the Roman Catholic Church.[27] They are taught that submission to Church authority is the essence of freedom and that true freedom comes to men only through the Roman Catholic hierarchy:

> Freedom of thought in the official Catholic system means freedom to accept Catholic truth, not to reject it. The *Catholic Almanac* defines freedom of thought as follows: "liberty to think the truth. In our day the expression has come to mean liberty to think as one pleases; this is an error. Our rational nature demands that we think only the truth, whatever the impact of outside forces or our own appetites." And, of course, supreme religious and moral truth comes to men only through the Church. Such truth is an ecclesiastical entity, unchanging and unchallengeable, over which the Church has a permanent monopoly.[28]

To accept these teachings requires a great deal of faith and, as the old saying goes, "Great is the power of steady misrepresentation." Catholic children are conditioned and indoctrinated systematically in the educational system from the kindergarten through the university or seminary. In other words, the school system is designed to form Catholic minds, to prepare children for the Catholic way of life as opposed to the American way, the democratic way, of life. The system serves to condition children to accept and endure priestly control. Few Americans appreciate how completely the Catholic school system is an instrument of the Catholic hierarchy.

What does this priestly control of education mean in terms of intellectual freedom? The question can be answered by listing samples of Catholic popular beliefs that no teachers in the Catholic school system dare to challenge publicly without danger of penalties:

1. The pope is the infallible leader of mankind, and, when he speaks for the Church in matters of faith and morals, he cannot make a mistake.
2. The Virgin Mary returned to the earth six times in 1917 and told three peasant children of Fatima, Portugal, what the

Western world should do to avoid destruction by Soviet Russia.

3. It is a grave sin for an American Catholic deliberately to join the Masons or Odd Fellows.

4. No good Catholic may positively and unconditionally approve of the principle of separation of church and state.

5. Thomas Aquinas is the greatest philosopher of all time.

6. It is a sin to teach the evolution of man as a whole from animal life.

7. In general, no Catholic has a moral right to secure a divorce and remarry even if married to a syphilitic, insane, or adulterous murderer; and any Catholic who does remarry after such a divorce is guilty of adultery.

8. The Reformation was a backward step in human history, and many of the worst evils of fascism and communism flow from it.

9. It is a grave sin for a Catholic under ordinary circumstance knowingly to own or use a Protestant Bible.

10. The pope is the head of a sovereign temporal state which has coequal rights with that of the government of the United States.

11. The rights of the Church as educator are prior to and superior to the rights of the state as educator, and no government has the legal right to infringe upon this divine prerogative.[29]

Bishop John F. Noll of Fort Wayne, founding editor of America's most noted Catholic family paper, *Our Sunday Visitor*, summed up the priestly apprehensions about the American public school by writing a pamphlet called *Our National Enemy No. 1—Education Without Religion*. Its public enemy No. 1 was the American public school without Catholic religion. The Jesuit magazine, *America*, declared in an editorial: "That the Catholic and non-Catholic school systems are absolutely irreconcilable is an indisputable fact."[30]

Catholic schools really are different from public schools and these differences account for the different behavior of many trained scientists in population and related fields. In the next chapter, we will elaborate further on these differences in training and behavior. We will examine how they are accounting for the rejection of the relationship of overpopulation and national security and why some Catholics feel justified in their efforts to undermine population growth control efforts.

Catholic Hospitals: The Roles They Serve and Don't Serve

For years after I had completed a doctorate in public health and had worked for some time in hospitals and clinics, I was still under the impression that the Catholic Church substantially supported and administered hospitals solely because of its concern for the social value of health. I assumed that the Church was in the hospital business because of the value of the enterprise. More recently, I have become aware that Catholic hospitals receive billions of dollars in federal monies, although they sharply restrict the delivery of family-planning services. All couples (Catholic and non-Catholic) who use these facilities for fertility related services are provided less than adequate medical care and those who do not have easy access to non-Catholic hospital services find certain choices restricted altogether.

I have learned that bishops regard the building of Catholic hospitals next in importance to the building of churches and schools, not only because of the general social value of hospitals but also because they serve a useful purpose in winning and holding Church members.[31] During times of illness or death, whether one's own or that of a family member, people are most vulnerable to exploitation. Examples of this exploitation abound. Catholic hospitals are used as partisan and sectarian agencies in spite of public claims by the clergy that they are "community enterprises." Similarly, priests attempt to impose as much of their moral code as possible on non-Catholics using Catholic hospital services, particularly in such areas as contraceptive sterilization.[32]

Absolutism and Controls (or Morals) and Their Implications for Family Planning

With the recent advances of medicine that have allowed embryo transfers, test-tube babies, and artificial insemination, many Americans have been perplexed by the Catholic Church's strong negative responses to these advances, given the Church's so-called pro-life position. However, Americans should not be perplexed.

The Church claims that such conceptions are against "natural" law, and great pains are taken to defend this doctrine with elaborate theological reasoning, all of it sheer nonsense. There is a different reason for its opposition. The very existence of the Church is threatened by these advances. How?

The Catholic Church is an absolute monarchy under absolute and infallible leadership. The Church claims and actually exercises sovereignty over nearly 800 million Catholics. It has a system of law called "canon law," and, in the "domain" in which the claim of sovereignty is made, canon law is applied. Yet, the Catholic hierarchy exercises this sovereignty without the direct use of force, armies, police, or weapons. How is this possible?

Instead of using physical weapons, the Church uses psychic weapons. The most extreme case was discussed in chapter four: the threat of excommunication. Over the centuries, the Church devised an elaborate system of controls that rely nearly completely upon "psychic terrorism." The concepts of morals and sins which can only be forgiven by certain members of the hierarchy are examples of controls. Of course, it is purported that both have as their ends "goodness," and adherents believe this. Yet, some thoughtful people recognize other "ends," including the maintenance of the power of the Catholic hierarchy and the enhancement and advancement of this power.

All tyrannies in human history that relied upon force have disappeared. Reliance upon force made them conspicuously evil, and people inevitably rose up and destroyed them. What distinguishes the tyranny of the Catholic Church is its explanation of its actions in terms of "virtue." With the help of great numbers of priests and nuns (today numbering more than one million), the Church has sold the concept of these morals and other controls. Through the Vatican's constant presentation of the Church's actions as "virtuous," recognition of the Church as a tyrant has been thwarted. Characterizing all actions in terms of "goodness" has allowed this tyranny to survive for nearly two thousand years while all others have failed. The effectiveness of the Vatican in convincing the world of the "virtue" of these morals and other controls is best exhibited by American acceptance of the incredible new claim of papal infallibility in the 1870s, despite the fact that it was obviously a move to maintain vast power in the Vatican. It is almost inconceivable that Americans would have accepted this obvious grab for power. (Currently only 50 percent of Catholic Americans believe in the papal claim of infallibility.) The Catholic hierarchy has been appropriately described as a cabal of power that moves under the guise of benevolence. How could this be possible in America?

The pope and the Vatican promote only the most obedient and loyal priests to positions of authority in the hierarchy. It is an extensive review process for promotion of only the most conditioned and indoctrinated. Those who are not are culled as quickly as possible. Hans Kung and Father Drinan are examples. This process assures maintenance of the tyranny but at the same time "changes or adjustments from within" are made most difficult or impossible. In general, this highly obedient hierarchy tells its American priests in great detail what to believe. Usually, the parish priest has no strong inclination toward heretical belief inasmuch as he is the product of the Catholic educational system. A glance at any biographical list of prominent Catholic clergy shows how few of them ever stray from the Catholic educational system.

Since the Vatican has no military apparatus or personnel to physically impose its laws (canons) and maintain and expand its power, it must control its communicants through their minds and through social action. To accomplish this, they use their control over their priests, including American priests.

The Vatican has drawn up a set of rules (morals) by which all must abide. Since the hierarchy had to rely upon more than one million subordinates to ensure that the laity abided by these rules, they had to make these rules simple. The "end" desired by the Church was to out-reproduce non-Catholics everywhere, and many of the rules or laws (morals) of the Church are devoted to this purpose.

To ensure that these rules are enforceable, they made them both simple and *absolute*. They related to sterilization, abortion, divorce, homosexuality, prostitution, masturbation, and so forth. *No* exceptions were allowed or ever entertained. Absolutism. With this modality, the Church cannot afford the luxury of exceptions. With interpretations, rules break down.

This, combined with the absolutism imposed by the claim of "infallibility," is the real source of the opposition of the Catholic Church to family planning and population growth control. So much of the Church is built on the absolutes related to population growth that it cannot even permit "embryonic transfer" without taking a significant risk that the whole system of morals might collapse around them. As soon as the Church begins making exceptions, the whole system of controls would be in jeopardy. Ultimately, there would be so many exceptions and so many special cases that moral judgment would have to shift to the local priests and then to local people. The power of the Vatican would be considerably weakened.

If one examines all of the sex-related prohibitions of the Church, the common denominator is the promotion of the quantity of Catholics produced! *This is not a coincidence.* There are few exceptions. The needs of the Church with regard to a cadre of celibate priests were discussed earlier, as was the fact that Catholic education represents the rock upon which the whole Church rests and that celibate nuns who work for low wages are the backbone of that system.[33] These two exceptions represent "higher order" needs of the Church than reproduction. Imposed celibacy certainly represents the highest form of perversion of the "natural order," yet celibacy of nuns and priests is an additional absolute.

It is interesting to examine some of the population-growth-control-related *absolutes*. For most Americans the "theological reasoning" will be as shocking as the outcomes themselves. The following are all published teachings for priests.

1. Regarding sterilization:

Question: A woman has had two children, both of whom were brought into the world by a Caesarian operation. On the second occasion the attending obstetrician declared that the woman would never be able to give birth to a child normally and that another pregnancy would very probably prove fatal. Accordingly he recommended that the fallopian tubes be tied up as protection against such an occurrence. Would such a procedure be permissible? In other words, would ligature of the tubes in such circumstances be regarded as a lawful therapeutic sterilization?

Answer: The tying up of the fallopian tubes in the circumstances described would be a grave sin against the law of God, an unlawful act of sterilization. The fact that another pregnancy would probably (or even certainly) cause the woman's death does not justify the procedure by rendering it a lawful therapeutic sterilization. A lawful therapeutic sterilization takes place only when an operation or treatment is given which, though it produces sterility, also *by its very nature* confers a physical benefit sufficiently great to compensate for the evil effect, sterility. Thus the excision of the reproductive organs when they are seriously diseased is permissible, since such an operation *by its very nature* has a notable beneficial effect on the health of the patient, in addition to its sterilizing effect.

In such a case we legitimately apply the principle of the double effect, so frequently used in moral theology. But in the case presented the ligature of the tubes in itself contributes nothing toward the well-being of the woman; it merely produces sterility. It is true, this is directed to a good effect inasmuch as it prevents the physical harm which would (probably or certainly) be consequent on another pregnancy. But this good effect is produced *by means of* the bad effect, hence, one who would hold that such an operation is lawful would have to admit that a good end can justify a bad means. If the woman in question wishes to avoid the dangers of another pregnancy, the only lawful method is abstinence from sexual relations, either completely or periodically.[34]

2. Regarding abortion:

If it is morally certain that a pregnant mother and her unborn child will both die if the pregnancy is allowed to take its course, but at the same time, the attending physician is morally certain that he can save the mother's life by removing the inviable fetus, is it lawful for him to do so?

Answer: No, it is not. Such a removal of the fetus would be direct abortion.[35]

Human life is not subject to comparison of values. A living human fetus, even though a monster, may not be sacrificed to save all the human lives in the world. . . . If you say: Why should a mother suffer the hazard and the ills of the Caesarian section to save a monster whose hours are numbered and who never could be a useful member of society? I answer because the monster is a human individual with the inalienable right of life. A beggar idiot may not be directly sacrificed to save the life of the most useful member of society; nay not to save the lives of all the members of society.[36]

The assertion that an undeveloped fetus in the womb is not as valuable as the mother of a family is beside the question, and in certain vital distinctions it is untrue. Any human life as such, whether in a fetus or an adult, is as valuable as another, inasmuch as no one but God has any authority to destroy it, except when it has lost its right to exist through culpable action. Secondly, the quality of motherhood is an accidental addition to a mother's life, not substantial as is the life itself. This quality of motherhood does not create any juridic imbalance of values which justifies the destruction of the rights inherent in the fetus. That the fetus may not be able to enjoy these rights if the mother dies is, again, an irrelevant consideration. . . . An innocent fetus an hour old may not be directly killed to save the lives of all the mothers in the world.[37]

3. In regard to contraception: only total abstinence and the rhythm method are approved by the hierarchy under any circumstances whatsoever.

If space permitted, an entire chapter could be devoted to Church "absolutes" regarding reproduction. The hierarchy claims to control the entire ethical code surrounding propagation. "Behind the Catholic formula in regard to all of these 'quality' problems in human beings is the philosophy that creating Catholics is a good thing in itself, and that, even if they are diseased, feebleminded, and a menace to normal community life, no *medical* act should be permitted to prevent their conception, their survival, or their freedom to produce other human beings."[38]

How can this "absolutism" of the Church in matters of reproduction and population growth and this pattern of "morals" go undiscussed in the scientific literature and in the lay press? "Professor Earnest A. Hooton, head of the department of anthropology at Harvard, expressed the conviction of most experts in this field when he said over forty years ago:

> The hypocrisy of certain organized religions and governments in endorsing deliberate killing in warfare, for whatever motives, and at the same time opposing the restricting of that fatal overproduction of low-grade human life which leads to warfare, should not be tolerated by the leaders of human biological science.

"American Catholic scholars cannot admit the truth of such statements. They are under Papal orders to stress quantity rather than quality in population and to resist every medical and political reform that might sacrifice one for the other."[39]

For decades there has been extensive censorship of both Catholic and non-Catholic Americans. Few Americans realize how pervasive it is, and I would have been similarly unaware had it not been for my fifteen years of experience in population research, an area that has received particular attention by the Church's censorship efforts. No other Church activity has thwarted population growth control as much as this censorship activity.

> Because good Catholics are accustomed to the imposition of general boycotts and taboos by their priests, the censorship of literature and art is accepted as part of the Church routine. Catholics are taught that the Roman Catholic Church is the supreme guardian and purveyor of truth, that the Pope has infallible judgment in moral matters, and that "union of minds requires not only a perfect accord in the one Faith, *but complete submission and obedience of will to the Church and to the Roman Pontiff, as to God Himself.*[40] [emphasis added]

> The general rule is: "All men are forbidden to read books that are contrary to faith in God, good moral conduct, and Christian virtue"—a rule so sweeping that it can be interpreted as banning a large proportion of all modern works on science, medicine, and morals. *In practice this rule means that no Catholic is allowed to read knowingly and without special permission any book attacking any fundamental doctrine of the Catholic Church.* [emphasis added] "The Church is not afraid of truth," says Father John C. Heenan in his *Priest and Penitent*, "but She is very much afraid that a

clever presentation of falsehood will deceive even the elect." *The Church teaches that literature is "immoral" if it is opposed to Catholic standards, and that "no one has a 'right' to publish such literature any more than one has a right to poison wells or sell tainted food."*[41] [emphasis added]

The justification for censorship: just as we are not free to take as food for our bodies matter that will disease, deprave, and destroy them, so too for our minds—far more precious—we may not take ideas that similarly vitiate the very functions for which the mind was made.[42]

When a book has been denounced by official authorities it is a grave sin for a Catholic knowingly to buy, sell, borrow, own, read, or lend it to any other person. The penalties apply to booksellers, publishers, readers, and reviewers unless they secure special permission to handle contraband goods.[43]

Catholic cardinals are not isolated and they are rarely spontaneous. The censorship system of the Roman Catholic Church in the United States is neither a spasmodic nor an intermittent phenomenon. It is a highly organized system of cultural and moral controls that applies not only to books, plays, magazines, and motion pictures, but to persons and places.[44]

We believe that the rulers of a Catholic country have the right to restrict the activities of those who would lead their people away from their allegiance to the Catholic Church . . . they possess the right to prevent propaganda against the Church. This is merely a logical conclusion from the basic Catholic tenet that the Son of God established one religion and commanded all men to accept it under pain of eternal damnation.[45]

The justification given by the hierarchy for their acts of censorship is that the information, interpretation, finding, and so forth is "offensive" to the Catholic people. However, upon close examination, it becomes apparent that, in virtually every instance, that which is being censored actually threatens *the power of the hierarchy*. The hierarchy has vigorous concern for stamping out threats to its power that arise in the mass media. Labeling something "offensive" is simply an excuse. Its control of our media to thwart discussion of the implications of world overpopulation is seriously threatening the security of the United States.

This censorship system of the Church was purported to be primarily a Catholic affair directed at Catholics and acceptable under the guise of religious freedom. But is it primarily a Catholic affair? The strictures of the Catholic hierarchy upon its own people could never be isolated from the rest of the community. We have witnessed the way in which Senator Joseph McCarthy, a Roman Catholic, communicated closely with the Vatican, and we are witnessing the way in which the issue of abortion is being used by the Vatican to build a powerful political force in contemporary America. It becomes more evident that this system of censorship has been directed at the American political system. In fact, it was always directed at non-Catholics under the guise of being directed at Catholics. Its affairs have invariably resulted in the acquisition of political power. The use of "McCarthyism" and the "red menace" and now the "abortion issue" for this purpose is not mentioned. How did this come to pass?

Every city editor in the United States knows of the unofficial Catholic censorship of American news, but almost all publishers avoid discussion of the phenomenon out of fear of reprisals. The Church frequently succeeds in intimidating the most powerful newspapers by using organized protest and boycott, even though in many cases the facts suppressed have great social significance. Through the use of organized protest and boycott, the Vatican in effect holds the power of economic life and death over many authors, editors, publishers, and producers who must rely upon American Catholics for patronage and support.[46] The techniques are highly developed and widely used:

> American priests habitually use their pulpits to condemn any newspaper that publishes material critical of the Church, and they are particularly vehement in condemning any editor who publishes facts unfavorable to priests and nuns. Whenever a newspaper prints a news story reflecting upon the character of a priest, local Catholic organizations, directed by priests, write, telephone, and telegraph vigorous protests to the editor and frequently approach the business office of the newspaper with threats to boycott the paper's advertisers. As a result of this policy of siege and boycott, very few publishers in the United States are courageous enough or wealthy enough to deal frankly with Catholic social policy or stories of priestly crime.[47]

A Jesuit priest, Charles J. Mullaly, has published in the Jesuit magazine, *America*, a point-by-point description of Catholic techniques in boycotting an American newspaper and a censorship program for priests and laymen. Father Mullaly tells with perfect candor how a priest and four or five Catholic laymen, with the help of an impressive letterhead bearing the names of prominent citizens, can terrorize any editor with the specter of a great wave of Catholic indignation.[48]

Father Mullaly concluded this revealing document with a platform of action for punishing critical American newspapers:

1. Do not attack a magazine or newspaper through its editorial department but act through its business office.

2. When a magazine or newspaper is attacking your religion, write to the business manager and inform him that you will not buy the offending periodical again, and mean it.

3. Call the attention of the merchants with whom you deal to the insults and tell them that as long as they advertize in any offending paper you will not buy their goods, and mean it.

4. Tell your news-dealer that as long as you see the magazine or newspaper on his stand as an open insult to you, you will not buy from him, and mean it.[49]

In chapter nine, I will offer in some detail specific examples in which I have been a recent victim of this censorship.

All Catholic publishers must submit before publication all books of a religious nature to a censor appointed by his bishop. "A Catholic publisher who issues a book on religion or morals without this Imprimatur risks immediate excommunication and nationwide boycott under Canon 2318. Also, says the *Catholic Encyclopedia*, Catholic laymen must not write for newspapers or periodicals hostile to Catholicism or morality, unless for a just and reasonable cause approved by the local ordinary."[50] Non-Catholic publishers who print criticisms of Catholic policy are threatened with boycotts and flooded with letters of protest. As a result of this type of pressure, scarcely any publishers in the United States will even consider any manuscript that might expose them to a Catholic boycott.

As described by Father Henry Davis, in the most authoritative Catholic work on doctrine, *Moral and Pastoral Theology*, all Catholic bishops must enforce a boycott against the following classes of books:

1. Books by any writers which defend heresy or schism or attempt in any way to undermine the very foundations of religion;

2. All books . . . which affect to prove that true divorce is permissible in the case of adultery;

3. Books which attack or hold up to ridicule any Catholic dogma, such as the creation of man, original sin, the infallibility of the Pope;

4. Books which professedly treat of, narrate, or teach matters

that are obscene, such as the defense of methods of birth control.[51]

I personally know four authors who have been victims of this type of censorship through intimidation of publishers. All four books spoke directly to the Church's actions in successfully thwarting population growth control, and one of them dealt candidly with the Vatican's obvious intention of "Catholicizing" the United States by encouraging tens of millions of Catholics to illegally immigrate to this country.

Two of these authors were able to finance the publication of their own books through vanity presses. Robert Rienow, distinguished service professor of political science, State University of New York at Albany, and his wife, Leona Train Rienow, are the authors of twenty-five books, both trade and text, including their best-selling *Moment in the Sun.* When they attempted to publish their book, *The Great Unwanteds Want Us: Illegal Aliens—Too Late to Close the Gate?*[52] none of their previous publishers would touch this fact-filled book, and neither would any others.

Waldo Zimmermann spent thirty-five years preparing his exceedingly well-written fact-filled book, *Condemned to Live: The Plight of the Unwanted Child,*[53] which thoroughly examines the actions of the Catholic Church to thwart legal access to abortion services. A few of the publishers who rejected the book made it clear that they were responding to Catholic pressure.

Not only are individual writings blocked through censorship but this censorship biases national perceptions of the past, governmental policy, and the national images of the Church in order to present the Church in the best possible light.

How is it possible to think that the Vatican can be capable of any wrongdoing or in any way harm America? All we see is *goodness!* There is virtually no negative press whatsoever. The dangers that lie in the continuation of this arrangement are stunning. The very security of the United States is threatened by this arrangement whereby the Church ultimately hopes to gain control of our democracy through sheer numbers.

Numbers and Power

It is unquestionable that the pronatalist position of the Catholic hierarchy throughout the history of the Church has always had as its goal achievement of power through numbers. This position has been common to most institutions in history, especially those that have survived for any length of time. As has been pointed out, much of the system of "morals" maintained by the Church is devoted to this end.

However, in the United States, the hierarchy has almost completely lost its control over communicants with regard to matters of reproduction. American Catholics are ignoring the wishes of the hierarchy and have adopted desired family sizes identical to non-Catholic Americans. They are using the same contraceptive methods with the same frequency and are resorting to abortion at the same rate. The result is that American Catholics are not outbreeding American non-Catholics.

Traditionally, there had been a "Catholic differential" in fertility and even as late as the early 1960s Catholics had, on the average, one more child than non-Catholics. However, during the 1960s, this differential all but disappeared even though the clergy took every prudent measure to stop the loss of this differential without causing an even greater exodus from the Church than had occurred.

In the late 1960s and early 1970s, the hierarchy recognized that, under existing American democratic conditions, little could be done to reverse this trend. Another course was decided upon to achieve the same goal. This course included the Church-assisted influx of tens of millions of illegal aliens, nearly all of whom are Catholic. This plan is well underway as literally millions are now coming each year to the United States, mostly from Latin countries. If illegal immigration is not firmly dealt with, and current trends continue, the United States will have a Catholic majority before I retire.

In chapter ten, I will discuss the considerable national security implications of the Catholic Church's vast promotion of illegal immigration.

National Divisiveness and the Vatican

Few non-Catholic Americans understand the relationship between American Catholics and their Vatican, yet this relationship has enormous implications for loyal Catholics working in the population or national security fields or any other area in which the best interests of the Vatican do not invariably parallel those of the United States. This relationship is one that generates divisiveness:

> Unfortunately, the Catholic people of the United States are not citizens but subjects in their own religious commonwealth. The secular as well as the religious policies of their Church are made in Rome by an organization that is alien in spirit and control. The American Catholic people themselves have no representatives of their own choosing either in their own local hierarchy or in the

Roman high command; and they are compelled by the very nature of their Church's authoritarian structure to accept non-religious as well as religious policies that have been imposed upon them from abroad.[54]

From the *Catholic Almanac:*

The Catholic citizen is in conscience bound to respect and obey the duly constituted authority provided faith and morals are thereby not endangered. Under no circumstances may the Church be subjugated by the State. Whatever their form may be, states are not conceded the right to force the observance of immoral or irreligious laws upon a people.[55]

Since "morals" can define any human activity, the Vatican, accordingly, is the supreme ruler of the United States. As Pope Leo XIII said in his encyclical on the "Chief Duties of Christian Citizens," setting the stage for anarchy at the pope's command:

If the laws of the state are manifestly at variance with the divine law, containing enactments hurtful to the Church or conveying injunctions adverse to the duty imposed by religion, or if they violate in the person of the Supreme Pontiff the authority of Jesus Christ, then truly, to resist becomes a positive duty, to obey, a crime.[56]

The Vatican has even been divisive within the American Catholic Church:

Rome has always been careful not to elevate any bishopric in the United States to a position of primacy. For a time the bishops of Baltimore enjoyed a kind of primacy of honor, but even this has now disappeared. Leo XIII, instead of creating an American primate whose viewpoint and background might be fundamentally American, created an Apostolic Delegacy at Washington, and each succeeding Pope has sent his own representative to occupy the spacious building in Washington which, in effect, is the general Roman headquarters of American Catholicism. Since the Pope's appointee is always an Italian, whose line of promotion runs toward Rome instead of the United States, there is little danger that he will become infected with the "heresy" of Americanism.[57]

There is no doubt that the parochial school, whatever may be its

> virtues, is the most important divisive instrument in the life of American children. It keeps Catholic children separated from the main body of American childhood during the most impressionable years of life and develops in them a denominational narrowmindedness.[58]

> Even when both schools emphasize patriotism and community spirit, the fact that they exist as separate establishments tends to divide the community emotionally and culturally.[59]

Catholic parents must send their children to Catholic schools when they are available *under moral law*.[60] In other words, it is "immoral" to send Catholic children to public schools if Catholic schools are available.

Catholic schools teach intolerance and oppose national solidarity when the Vatican is threatened. Abortion is an example. We need only to look to the north to observe the logical conclusion of this arrangement:

> The major lesson for the United States in the Canadian experience is quite clear. A nation that compromises with the Catholic hierarchy on the control and support of common schools is doomed to be either a clerical state or a house divided. In Canada the Roman Church has built a state within a state because the British government permitted public revenue to be used for a school system that conditioned Catholic children to be Catholics first and Canadians second. Many Canadians believe that it is too late now to rescue the province of Quebec.[61]

The general rule against marriage with Protestants, Jews, and those of schismatic persuasion has served to be most divisive, since loyal Catholics tend to shun Catholics who have married outside the Church. If this rule could be strictly enforced, and the Vatican wishes it could be, it would split the American community clearly down the middle by religious bigotry.

The intolerance toward other American religions taught from childhood will ensure a continuation of divisiveness:

> The *Homiletic and Pastoral Review* of February 1947, in answering a question for priests as to whether it is right to use the word "faith" to describe other religious groups, said: "For, if there is anything in Catholic teaching, it is the doctrine that the Son of God established only one religion and imposed on all men the obligation of embracing it; consequently no other religion has a

real objective right to exist and to function, and no individual has an objective right to embrace any non-Catholic religion."[62]

The hierarchy's use of ethnic power bloc politics has been a major source of power in the United States for a century. Traditionally the Church used the Irish, Polish, German, and Italian Americans for this purpose. More recently, the Church has used Mexican Americans, Puerto Ricans, Cubans, Vietnamese, and Haitians. In the near future, since one-ninth of the population of El Salvador has illegally immigrated to the United States, many of them will similarly serve the Vatican.

The Catholic Church draws upon these power blocs to manipulate both domestic and foreign policy in ways that are discussed in chapter ten. Millions of voters, wishing to maintain some cultural identity, find that their bishops "feel compelled" to speak out "on behalf of" their ethnic minority group. This is especially true where a large proportion of the group does not speak English. The Church then uses these power blocks to achieve its own political ambitions.

Conflict and disunity are bred by cultural and linguistic differences. Bilingual education fosters these in the extreme. It is no accident that the Church has been the only significant proponent of bilingual education in the United States. Almost all recipients of bilingual education are Roman Catholic. Having created this separate cultural group, it would be the "duty" of the bishops to speak "for them."

There is a persistent pattern of acts that create divisiveness at the international level (in the United Nations and its agencies), at national, state, and local government levels, and in voluntary organizations. Through the use of the abortion issue, more than any other, the Catholic hierarchy has divided the country and has made enormous political gains, including helping to elect a president who represents the Church on *all* issues the hierarchy considers important (*see,* chapter ten).

In no other area of human activity is the Church's use of the "divide and conquer" technique more apparent than in the population growth control field. In the remaining chapters, specific examples of their use of this technique will be provided.

Anti-American Positions of the Vatican

There is nothing distinctive about the "American" Catholic Church. It is, first and foremost and always, Catholic. American democracy has not made it democratic, any more than, for example, the Polish national church. It does not stand for the causes of freedom of the press, speech, or worship (for Protestants) any more than do the Catholic Churches in Latin countries. Regarding freedom of speech, from *The New Scholasticism,* published by Catholic University of America, "Free speech is not free to injure faith, hope, charity, prudence, justice, temperance, truth, or any other virtue protecting the welfare of the individual or society."[63] Of course, only the Church can judge what "injures" and what "protects" the welfare of the individual or society. Regarding freedom of the press:

> Father Mullaly's platform is entirely consistent with Papal pretensions. The Vatican does not stand for freedom of the press as the term is commonly used in the United States. The Church tolerates freedom of the press only up to a certain point, and with restrictions. In 1946 Pius XII told a group of American editors that freedom of the press "does not allow a man to print what is wrong, what is known to be false, or what is calculated to undermine or destroy the moral and religious fiber of individuals and the peace and harmony of nations." The Church, of course, is the supreme judge of all requisites of worthy public expression. Most Americans will agree with *The Christian Century* that this is "a totalitarian conception of the freedom of the press."[64]

Regarding freedom of assembly, Cardinal Hayes once ordered the break-up of one of Margaret Sanger's birth control meetings by New York Catholic police.[65]

Regarding freedom of worship, two great Catholic writers, Monsignor John A. Ryan and Father Moorhouse F. X. Millar, in their standard work, *The State and the Church,* answer the question: "Should such persons [non-Catholics] be permitted to practice their own form of worship?"

> If these [practices] are carried on within the family, or in such inconspicuous manner as to be an occasion neither of scandal nor of perversion to the faithful, they may properly be tolerated by the State. . . . Quite distinct from the performance of false religious worship and preaching to the members of the erring sect, is the propagation of the false doctrine among Catholics. This could become a source of injury, a positive menace, to the religious welfare of true believers. Against such an evil they have a right of protection by the Catholic State. . . . If there is only one true religion, and if its possession is the most important good in life for States as well as individuals, then the public profession, protection, and promotion of this religion and the legal prohibition of

all direct assaults upon it, becomes one of the most obvious and fundamental duties of the State.[66]

And from the official world organ of the Jesuits, *Civilta Cattolica:*

> The Roman Catholic Church, convinced, through its divine prerogatives, of being the only true church, must demand the right of freedom for herself alone, because such a right can only be possessed by truth, never by error. As to other religions, the Church will certainly never draw the sword, but she will require that by legitimate means they shall not be allowed to propagate false doctrines. Consequently, in a state where the majority of the people are Catholic, the Church will require that legal existence be denied to error, and that if religious minorities actually exist, they shall have only a *de facto* existence without opportunity to spread their beliefs. . . . In some countries, Catholics will be obliged to ask full religious freedom for all, resigned at being forced to cohabitate where they alone should rightfully be allowed to live. But in doing this the Church does not renounce her thesis, which remains the most imperative of her laws, but merely adapts herself to *de facto* conditions, which must be taken into account in practical affairs. . . . The Church cannot blush for her own want of tolerance, as she asserts it in principle and applies it in practice.[67]

Regarding the principle of separation of church and state, Pius IX, in his *Syllabus,* condemned the principle of separation of church and state as one of the "principal errors of our time."[68] In no nation does the Church honor this principle; the hierarchy feels that no nation has the right to impose this principle since it has a "divine right" to direct nations in matters of faith and morals (and "morals" in some way touches on all human activities).

Regarding public education, the Church recognizes that its schools are the rock upon which the Church is built. Likewise, public schools are viewed by most Americans as the rock upon which democracy is built. Father William McManus, representing the hierarchy, said before a Senate hearing in 1947:

> The school, particularly the private school, is the battleground between the forces of totalitarianism and those of freedom and democracy. In the totalitarian nation, the government is the teacher; the government controls all the schools which it uses for the mental enslavement of the people. In the free nation, the government refrains from direct educational activities.

As Blanshard notes, "The special meaning of the word *free* should be noted. A *free* nation in priestly parlance appears to be a nation that permits priests to control education. The nation that operates its own schools through school boards elected by the people is, by inference, totalitarian."[69]

Regarding Defiance of American Law

American Catholic priests and bishops defy American law daily. Thousands commit a felony each day by aiding and abetting illegal aliens, for example. This is openly Church policy:

> In some cases the alien-controlled hierarchy demands defiance of existing American law; in other cases it notifies the government that it *would* defy certain laws if they were passed; in still other cases it urges temporary submission without conceding the state's moral right to enforce a law; and in almost all cases in which the Church and the American people disagree the hierarchy uses ecclesiastical penalties to punish its members for making their own choice in good conscience between Church policy and public policy.[70]

In population growth control matters, American Catholics are openly encouraged to defy and circumvent laws and public policy. Pope Pius XI, in his *Casti Connubii*, not only condemned sterilization of the insane and feebleminded but said that the government, by doing so, is arrogating to itself "power over a faculty which it never had and can never legitimately possess." This defiance of modern government was justified by Pius XI, who said that "the family [meaning the Church] is more sacred than the State and that men are begotten not for the earth and for time but for Heaven and eternity." A recent example of this defiance regarding sterilization appears in chapter ten.

It is undeniable that the Vatican maintains many un-American doctrines. These doctrines clearly threaten American democracy and American security. The needs of the Vatican are placed above the needs of the United States. They also suggest a certain discomfort with American democracy.

The Pope as "Ruler" of America?

Now that 150 million Latin American Catholics are poised for illegal immigration to the United States, a Catholic majority in the United

States is clearly achievable in the next fifteen years. The Church merely needs to continue successfully thwarting illegal immigration control efforts for fifteen more years. With a Catholic majority, the Church will no longer tolerate a feeling of discomfort with American democracy. "The Catholic hierarchy is perfectly willing to compromise with democratic forms of government so long as its own special areas of power are respected. In a Catholic America the principal institutions of American democracy might be permitted to continue if they were operated for Catholic objectives."[71]

As mentioned earlier in this chapter, the Vatican claims sovereignty everywhere there are Catholics in the areas of faith and morals, including the United States, and their claim is based upon "divine right." Who determines what subjects come within the broad sweep of "faith and morals"? The pope, of course! The power to define jurisdiction makes authority almost limitless. The word *morals* is so broad that it invites indefinite expansion; similarly the word *faith*. "If faith deals with ideas and morals deals with behavior, is not the whole range of human experience encompassed within the papal claim?"[72]

Three-and-one-half decades ago, the editor of the leading diocesan paper in the United States, Monsignor Matthew Smith, made the position of the Catholic bishops quite clear. They favor a *partial* union in which the Church will have a privileged position as the recognized sovereign of the nation's moral and religious life. "Where the Catholics are in overwhelming majority, it is theoretically better to have an official union of Church and State, with the state participating from time to time in public worship and using the machinery of government, when needed, to help the Church."[73]

There must be concern that American democracy will find itself less and less tolerated by the Vatican as it achieves more and more power in America. "The Vatican's affinity with fascism is neither accidental nor incidental. Catholicism conditions its people to accept censorship, thought-control, and, ultimately, dictatorship. Says Count Coudenhove-Kalergi, who was reared as a Catholic:

> Catholicism is the fascist form of Christianity of which Calvinism represents its democratic wing. The Catholic hierarchy rests fully and securely on the leadership principle with the infallible Pope in supreme command for a lifetime. . . . Like the Fascist party, its priesthood becomes a medium for an undemocratic minority rule by a hierarchy. . . . Catholic nations follow fascist doctrines more willingly than Protestant nations, which are the main strongholds of democracy. . . . Democracy lays its stress on personal conscience; fascism on authority and obedience."[74]

With increasing power of the Catholic hierarchy, we are seeing more and more defiance of American law. Specific examples will be discussed in later chapters. Under existing circumstances, we can expect this trend to continue.

The Catholic hierarchy constantly uses American Catholics by identifying its clerical ambitions, including its design to acquire more power, with the supposed wishes of its people. We have reviewed the major methods the hierarchy uses to fulfill these aspirations. Many of the hierarchy's social and political policies are clearly incompatible with Western democracy and American culture and *no American should ever apologize because he or she objects to these policies.*

A good understanding of the hierarchy's methods and policies are essential to understanding the population problem. Many of the population field's most distinguished scientists and field workers have personally been victims of the hierarchy's methods and policies and have been driven from the field. Among the survivors are many advocates of a policy of appeasement and limited cooperation with the Church. That they have survived is no doubt by Catholic hierarchy design, as will be shown in the next chapter. A few may be idealists of unquestioned integrity, though I am not sure I have ever met such a person. Most are cowards. They refuse to accept the facts about the Catholic Church discussed in this book and attempt to pass off their lack of courage for "tolerance and broadmindedness."

These "idealists" fall back on the cliche, "You should never criticize another man's religion." That innocent-sounding doctrine, born in a Protestant America before the arrival of a significant Vatican presence, is full of danger to U.S. security. It ignores the duty of every good citizen to stand for the truth in every field of thought, most importantly, in matters of national security, including population growth control. It fails to recognize that a large part of what the Vatican calls religion is also politics and economics. The facts suggest that silence about "another man's religion" means acquiescence to a complete loss of national security.

The remaing chapters will deal with specific cases of the Vatican's application of these techniques and policies. Offered here are the disastrous results of the policies of the population field's advocates of appeasement and "cooperation."

Notes

1. Joseph Smith became a candidate for president of the United States in 1844, only fourteen years after founding his church.

2. Paul Blanshard, *American Freedom and Catholic Power* (Boston: The Beacon Press, 1950), p. 259. [Quoted from the Catholic weekly, *De Linie.*]

3. Blanshard, *American Freedom and Catholic Power*, p. 19.

4. Ibid., p. 35.

5. Ibid., p. 245. [Quoted from *Religion and the Modern State*.]

6. Monsignor James McHugh, *The Tablet* (London, June 11, 1983).

7. *World Abortion Trends*, Population Briefing Paper No. 9, Population Crisis Committee, Washington, D.C. (1982), p. 4.

8. McHugh, *The Tablet*.

9. Robert Blair Kaiser in *U.S.A. Today* (April 5, 1983), 10A.

10. J. Kohan, "To Share the Pain," *Time* (March 14, 1983), p. 38.

11. Father Arthur McCormack, "A Catholic Views Word Overpopulation," *Popline* (August 1983), 5:7:1.

12. *News and Observer*, Raleigh, North Carolina (December 24, 1983), 3A.

13. Michael Novak in *U.S.A. Today* (April 5, 1983), 10A.

14. Kaiser, *U.S.A. Today*, 10A.

15. Blanshard, *American Freedom and Catholic Power*, p. 78.

16. *Chapel Hill Newspaper*, Chapel Hill, North Carolina (December 31, 1982), 3A.

17. Jean-Guy Vaillancourt, *Papal Power: A Study of Vatican Control Over Lay Catholic Elites* (Berkeley: California Press, 1980), p. 24.

18. Blanshard, *American Freedom and Catholic Power*, p. 35.

19. Ibid, p. 338. [Quoted from Pope Leo XIII's encyclical, *Chief Duties of Christian Citizens*.]

20. Ibid., p. 339.

21. Ibid., p. 40.

22. Ibid., p. 41.

23. Ibid., p. 45.

24. Ibid., pp. 45–47.

25. Ibid., p. 22.

26. Ibid., p. 340.

27. Ibid., p. 65.

28. Ibid., p. 294.

29. Ibid., p. 76.

30. Ibid., p. 82. [Quoted from the Jesuit magazine, *America*.]

31. Ibid., p. 117.

32. Ibid., p. 123.

33. Ibid., p. 155.

34. Ibid., p. 152. [Quoted from the *American Ecclesiastical Review*.]

35. Ibid., p. 112. [Quoted from Father Patrick A. Finney, *Moral Problems in Hospital Practice*.]

36. Ibid., p. 114. [Quoted from Medicus, *Medical Essays*, used in Catholic seminaries.]

37. Ibid., p. 113. [Quoted from Dr. Austin O'Malley, *The Ethics of Medical Homicide and Mutilation*.]

38. Ibid., p. 147.

39. Ibid., p. 149.

40. Ibid., p. 181. [Quoted from Pope Leo XIII's encyclical, *Chief Duties of Christian Citizens*.]

41. Ibid., p. 183. [Quoted from Father John C. Heenan, *Priest and Penitent*.]

42. Ibid., p. 194. [Quoted from the Boston *Pilot*.]

43. Ibid., p. 184.

44. Ibid., p. 180.

45. Ibid., p. 186. [Quoted from the *American Ecclesiastical Review* on "Preserving

the Faith Inviolate."]

46. Blanshard, *American Freedom and Catholic Power*, p. 195.

47. Ibid., p. 195.

48. Ibid., p. 196.

49. Ibid., p. 198. [Quoted from Father Charles J. Mullaly in the Jesuit magazine, *America*.]

50. Ibid., p. 188.

51. Ibid., p. 184. [Quoted from Father Henry Davis, *Moral and Pastoral Theology*.]

52. Robert Rienow and Leona Train Rienow, *The Great Unwanteds Want Us: Illegal Aliens—Too Late to Close the Gate?* (Monterey: Viewpoint Books, 1980).

53. Waldo Zimmermann, *Condemned to Live: The Plight of the Unwanted Child* (Vita Press, 2143 Poplar Avenue, Memphis, TN 38104; 1981).

54. Blanshard, *American Freedom and Catholic Power*, p. 5.

55. Ibid., p. 46. [Quoted from the *Catholic Almanac*.]

56. Ibid., p. 50. [Quoted from Leo XIII's enclyclical, *Chief Duties of Christian Citizens*.]

57. Ibid., p. 27.

58. Ibid., p. 302.

59. Ibid., p. 60.

60. Ibid., p. 65.

61. Ibid., p. 278.

62. Ibid., p. 32.

63. Ibid., p. 295. [Quoted from *The New Scholasticism*, published by Catholic University of America.]

64. Ibid., p. 198.

65. Ibid., p. 146.

66. Ibid., p. 53. [Quoted from Monsignor John A. Ryan and Father Moorhouse F. X. Millar, *The State and the Church*.]

67. Ibid., p. 295. [Quoted from *Civilta Cattolica*.]

68. Ibid., p. 237. [Quoted from Pius IX in his *Syllabus*.]

69. Ibid., p. 81.

70. Ibid., p. 52.

71. Ibid., p. 267.

72. Ibid., p. 25.

73. Ibid., p. 50. [Quoted from the Denver *Catholic Register*.]

74. Ibid., p. 257. [Quoted from *Crusade for Pan-Europe*.]

8.

The Catholic Hierarchy's Cooptation of the American Population Establishment

Since the days of Margaret Sanger, the Church has ordered members to infiltrate population organizations to collect intelligence and undermine them from within. Documented cases of this in Planned Parenthood organizations across the country probably number in the hundreds. For example, while I was working at Planned Parenthood of Houston, a recently hired Catholic woman was caught photocopying the clinic's foundation contributor list which she had no reason to have in her possession. She admitted that she had been asked to get the list by local leadership of the Catholic hierarchy.

However, by far the most significant example of infiltration and cooptation occurred during the 1970s. The target was the U.S. Agency for International Development's Office of Population, which provides international population assistance. Dr. Reimert T. Ravenholt, that office's first and only director until 1980, is unquestionably the most important leader in the international population field, a man of great courage and intelligence. From the very creation of this office in 1966, Ravenholt was the subject of intensive personal and professional attacks, some of them prompted by the Church, which often used unsuspecting non-Catholics to criticize his tactics and judgment. A few non-Catholics sought personal gain in return for their attacks. Despite the intense Catholic hostility directed at the program, successes of the program were considerable, a reflection largely of Ravenholt's considerable courage and inner strength but also because the people of recipient nations greatly desired what this program offered.

Ultimately, the Vatican succeeded in forcing Ravenholt from

office. Just prior to his departure, he sent to selected colleagues the following memorandum, which documents some of the techniques used by the Church to force him out. (Notes in brackets are my own.)

MEMORANDUM   June 2, 1980

TO: Population Colleagues
FROM: R. T. Ravenholt
SUBJECT: The Population Jungle

The crocodile battles along the Potomac have flared repeatedly during the last year as a virulent coalition of those opposed to A.I.D.'s population program on ideological grounds and political appointees seeking to grasp the program more closely for their own political purposes usurped direct control of the program.

Whether they have introduced a comma or a period into my own long sentence as director of this program will depend upon the outcome of my Appeal to the Merit System Protection Board, now moving toward a formal Hearing.

At this time I wish to briefly communicate the accomplishments of A.I.D.'s population program, the evolution of adversary activities, and reflect upon recent events. . . . [Author's note: The first section, "Nature and Accomplishments of A.I.D.'s Population Program," an eight-page overview of significant accomplishments, is deleted for the sake of brevity.]

Adverse Action

With the above record of accomplishment, one would expect strong support for the further implementation of A.I.D.'s population programs. But alas, political appointees have during the current administration incessantly attempted to decapitate the program, culminating in a letter from then acting administrator Robert Nooter [to the effect that he was demoted and could appeal].

Adversary Activities

A brief account of events and activities leading to this adverse action may be of interest:

Reproduction and its control, a controversial issue for centuries, became even more of a public issue in the 1950s and 1960s with the growing movement to launch population and family planning population programs to solve many fundamental social problems, both in the United States and in the developing world.

A thorough study of the events, activities, and controversies in the population field during the 1950s and the 1960s which led to fundamental change in U.S. foreign policy and initiation of population program assistance in 1965 has been published (P. T. Piotrow, *World Population Crisis: The United States Response*, New York: Praeger Publishers, 1973).

Controversey both within and without A.I.D. attended virtually every action toward creation of the population program. In particular, controversy swirled about those actions aimed at making the most effective means of fertility control—oral contraceptives, condoms, intrauterine devices, surgical sterilization, and abortion—readily available to entire populations in developing countries.

While authority for this action was dispersed in A.I.D. during the first half dozen years of the population program, reaction to diverse initiatives was diffused. But with the reorganization of 1972 which created a unified Office of Population in the Bureau for Population and Humanitarian Assistance, with me as director, and therewith the accelerated implementation of a central strategy, adversary activities became progressively more intensely polarized.

As the Office of Population moved with increasing strength to take the many concerted actions needed to achieve meaningful contraceptive availability in developing countries, diverse elements coalesced in opposition thereto and often did their utmost to obfuscate such actions.

Many program actions now taken for granted, such as the annual purchase and delivery of huge quantities of contraceptives, household distribution of contraceptives, and extensive support for voluntary sterilization, were initially intensely resisted by adversary groups, though now generally accepted by the Agency and many countries.

Repeatedly, "Right to Life" adversaries invoked the assistance of Congressman Clement Zablocki [a Catholic] of the House International Relations Committee and his assistant, John H. Sullivan [a Catholic], when attacking me and A.I.D.'s population program; and Congressman Zablocki insistently demanded of A.I.D. administrators that they "fire Dr. Ravenholt."

A determined attempt at my removal was made by then deputy administrator John H. Murphy [a Catholic] and others during 1975, when they created a task force for the purpose of reorganizing and thereby decapitating the Office of Population, but this action was abandoned after six months when committee chairmen Senator Hubert Humphrey, Senator Daniel Inouye, and Congressman Otto Passman all registered strong support for me.

But following the election of President Jimmy Carter in November 1976, a much more thoroughly programmed action aimed at my removal was launched and implemented approximately as follows:

Shortly after the election, John H. Sullivan, former staff assistant to Congressman Zablocki and staff consultant to the House International Relations Committee, moved into A.I.D. where he had a strong hand in the selection and appointment of staff by the Carter Administration.

The position of administrator of A.I.D. was initially proferred to Father

Theodore Hesburgh [a Catholic], president of Notre Dame University, and when he turned it down it was given to John J. Gilligan [a Catholic], graduate of Notre Dame and former governor of Ohio.

While considering the appointment of Jack Sullivan as assistant administrator of the Population and Humanitarian Assistance Bureau (which would have made him my immediate superior), it was recognized that such placement would make the religious [Catholic] connection of "Right to Life"—Zablocki, Gilligan, Sullivan—exit Ravenholt too obvious; and so instead Jack Sullivan became assistant administrator of the Asia Bureau and Sander Levin, defeated candidate for governor of Michigan, was chosen as assistant administrator of the Population and Humanitarian Assistance Bureau.

Repeatedly during January and February 1977, when interviewing candidates for key positions in the Bureau of Population and Humanitarian Assistance, Jack Sullivan made it clear that they would not be seriously considered for such positions because they were "too close to Ravenholt." But in Sander Levin he found someone well suited by need and temperament for the task at hand.

Motivations are often complex: Jack Sullivan, despite a positive interest in population and development assistance, has during many years manifested a particular aversion to the most effective means of fertility control and has strongly criticized A.I.D.'s population program for its emphasis on contraceptive services.

During 1973, he was a leader in the development of the Helms (anti-abortion) Amendment to the Foreign Assistance Act, and throughout the last decade he has worked to diminish emphasis on contraceptive services in population assistance programs.

The main mechanism invoked for the latter objective has been to press for "integration" of family-planning programs into health programs—deliberately ignoring the fact that virtually all A.I.D.-assisted family-planning programs always have been, as a first order of business, integrated with existing rudimentary health structures and programs. But by the shiboleth "integration," Jack Sullivan and other adversaries of forthright contraceptive service programs have sought to divert funds and to prevent the rapid extension of contraceptive services beyond the reach of existing health programs to entire populations by the mechanism of village and household distribution of contraceptives—a key initiative of the Office of Population during the seventies.

That the "integration" of family planning and health programs as proposed by Congressman Zablocki and Jack Sullivan was aimed at weakening rather than strengthening A.I.D.'s family-planning program was clearly stated by Mr. Zablocki during hearings of the House International Relations Committee on July 18, 1975:

Our purpose in combining the two is that more of this money, or as much as possible, be used for health programs rather than for contraceptives.

If, as proposed by Congressman Zablocki, Jack Sullivan, and other adversaries of family-planning programs, contraception services must be limited to those "integrated" with broad gauge health clinics and services, then contraceptives would not become available to the rural masses of much of Asia and Africa during the twentieth century.

Not only did Congressman Zablocki clearly state his antipathy to contraceptives and family planning during the hearings on July 18, 1975, but he also discussed my removal with Randy Engel, executive director, U.S. Coalition for Life, as follows:

> Mr. Zablocki: "I am sure you will agree that Dr. Ravenholt is the wrong person to administer this particular program."
>
> Mr. Engel: "Most certainly."
>
> Mr. Zablocki: "I would hope we could find a way of removing him."

Sander Levin, on the other hand, was not personally opposed to birth control nor any of its modalities but had opportunistic need for a new political vehicle and the most likely vehicle in A.I.D. was the powerful population program we had built during more than a decade. Thus, a collusion was formed between those who for religious or other ideological reasons resented A.I.D.'s strong focus on contraceptive services and several political appointees whose primary motivation was increased political and fiscal power.

But for the population program to serve as a satisfactory political vehicle for Mr. Levin, I, its director, with whom it was closely identified, would obviously have to be removed, despite my Civil Service status and accomplishments.

To this task Sander Levin devoted a considerable portion of his energies. Within a few days of the time he commenced work as assistant administrator (March 18, 1977), it became evident that Mr. Levin had a hidden agenda.

Rather than working closely and cooperatively with me and key Office of Population staff to strengthen the program as previous assistant administrators had done, he immediately engaged in a series of actions aimed at building a case against me and sidelining Office of Population leadership of the population program.

To this end he interposed several "special assistants" between his office and the Office of Population and shifted responsibility for certain key program functions from the Office of Population to his office and other Bureau units.

Without pausing to look, listen, and learn despite lack of previous relevant training and experience, Mr. Levin immediately grasped for the controls of the population program, and we were off on a lurching course which severely threatened the integrity and effectiveness of many projects—and programs in various stages of implementation.

The difficult task for me and Office of Population staff was to somehow meld the impulsive directives and actions of an inexperienced but highly assertive new assistant administrator with ongoing program strategies and projects representing investment of tens of millions of dollars, which would be wasted by abrupt change in program direction and configuration.

This task, difficult enough under ordinary circumstances, was made much more difficult by Mr. Levin's basic adverse motivation and activities aimed at my removal.

Almost immediately following his confirmation by the Congress as assistant administrator, May 25, 1977, Sander Levin on June 8, 1977, requested that I vacate my position as director of Office of Population and "move on to another challenge."

When asked his reasons for this request, he commented that, although I had done outstanding work in building the population program to its current state, our "policies" were different. When asked which policies he was speaking of, he avoided specifics but reiterated that it would be timely for me to move on and leave the population program to him.

Again, on July 21 and August 18, 1977, Mr. Levin requested that I resign; and when I brought Mr. Levin's demands to the attention of administrator Gilligan on August 23, he stated that he supported Mr. Levin.

In August 1977, at the IUSSP Conference in Mexico City, Mr. Levin's special assistant, Pat Baldi, confided in a contractor that Mr. Levin and company had compiled a "hit list" of key population staff they proposed to remove from their positions, including myself; Dr. Willard Boynton, deputy director; E. Randall Backlund, associate director; Dr. Harald Pedersen, chief, Family Planning Services Division; Dr. Gerald Winfield, chief, Information and Education Division; and Elizabeth MacManus, then deputy assistant administrator of the Population and Humanitarian Assistance Bureau.

On September 28, Mr. Levin again pressed me to resign; and when after discussion of alternative opportunities, I stated my intention to remain as director of the Office of Population, Mr. Levin lost his cool and stated that he would "destroy" me.

Since then he and others have colluded to scrape together every incident and pseudoincident that could possibly be used for their destructive purpose, including events and communications taken out of context and activities alleged to have occurred before Mr. Levin joined the Agency. This activity gained formal expression in a letter from Mr. Levin to me, dated October 25, 1977, in which he began the wearisome process of trying to create a justification and mechanism for adverse action against me.

To this effort he and his partners in this destructive enterprise have devoted many months of Agency work time seeking to somehow develop adequate justification along the way for this action clearly decided upon before most of the alleged incidents upon which it is claimed to be based had actually occurred.

Surely this violates usual federal merit system standards of fairness and provides no sound basis for this adverse action.

Nowhere has Mr. Levin or Mr. Nooter contested the fact that the population program, which I have directed virtually since its inception, is actually the Agency's strongest program and clearly the dominant program in the international population program assistance field. And despite their considerable animus they make no allegations of mismanagement or malfeasance by me or my staff during the many months we programmed $1.3 billion of population funds.

Rather, by their assertions and allegations of minor misstatements and policy differences, they have attempted to create a case for adverse action, ignoring the fact that even under such duress Office of Population staff and I have continued to implement the Agency's strongest program. Indicative of the specific perversity of their adverse actions is the fact that they have moved to decapitate the strongest program under their general aegis, not the weaker programs which have been operating unsatisfactorily for years.

Surely it would be unrealistic to expect that any creative and massive global program in a new and sensitive field such as population program assistance could be driven rapidly over A.I.D.'s rocky bureaucratic terrain without a few protests from some persons whose turf or equanimity was somehow disturbed by this extraordinary activity.

To propose, as Mr. Levin has, that I should be removed from my position as director of A.I.D.'s population program mainly because adversary forces have criticized me, especially as crucial actions were taken to make voluntary sterilization services more fully available in the developing world, is analogous to General Halleck requesting that General Grant be removed from his command of the Union Army during the Civil War because Confederate leaders and sympathizers bitterly complained about his attacks on Richmond.

During the last two years, while primarily aiming to remove me as director of the Office of Population, Mr. Levin has taken many ancillary actions which have weakened A.I.D.'s established population program leadership: by removing Elizabeth MacManus as his deputy, by supporting dispersal of responsibility for bilateral programs to the Geographic Bureaus, by supporting transfer of certain population monies and responsibilities to the Bureau for Program and Policy Coordination, by reduction in Office of Population staff, and by removal of Randall Backlund from his position as associate director for Operations in the Office of Population—a position he had exercised with outstanding distinction for a decade.

These have been three wearisome years for Office of Population staff. If they had been less experienced and less dedicated the program would have foundered. But it is a tribute to their experience, tenacity, and skill that they have steadfastly continued to implement the program despite extensive harassment from Mr. Levin's office, and the program has continued to move forward with considerable though diminishing strength despite the many administrative distractions and obstacles. But the program could be moving far better, especially in Africa and the Middle East, if Mr. Levin and others were providing solid support rather than discombobulation.

In accord with his vow to "destroy" me, Mr. Levin has since then (September 28, 1977) taken the following actions to limit my operating freedom and to sully my reputation:

• He interposed another bureaucratic layer above me consisting of Dr. Stephen Joseph, deputy assistant administrator, and staff who have repeatedly taken flagrantly destructive actions to disrupt my leadership of the population program.

• While urging improved coordination with other organizations, Sander Levin and Steve Joseph have blocked my participation in numerous working population conferences of the United Nations, the World Health Organization, the International Planned Parenthood Federation, the Department of State, and other federal agencies and in hearings before several committees of the U.S. Congress.

• In January 1978, Mr. Levin ordered destruction of 55,000 copies of an important *Population Report* on "Oral Contraceptive Use and Circulatory Disease Mortality," the preparation of which I had directed and coauthored. This destructive action was taken without consultation with me and despite Mr. Levin's lack of relevant technical training. Whether he took this action for political reasons or because he resented my thus communicating with professional colleagues is uncertain. But his impulsive and ill-considered action wasted considerable funds and blocked our communicating new and valuable data to family-planning colleagues at the time most needed. The accuracy of our observations and conclusions was affirmed by the findings of independent investigators published more than a year later.

• Despite my earnest and repeated pleas that for the good of the program and Agency we settle our differences and combine our strength to move the population program forward, Mr. Levin each time refused and continued on his course aimed at my removal.

• He specifically and repeatedly directed that I not communicate with the administrator of A.I.D., despite it being my fundamental right to do so; and thus limited my capacity to defend against his inaccurate assertions and allegations.

• In May 1979, he denied me official travel to participate in the Fourth International Conference of the Association for Voluntary Sterilization in Korea, which congregated 462 family-planning leaders from eighty-six countries in Seoul. To fulfill my professional commitment as a keynote speaker, it was necessary for me to use a week of annual leave and $2,000 of my personal resources.

In these and other ways, as many colleagues can testify, Mr. Levin has worked for three years to denigrate my accomplishments and reputation and to remove me as director of the Office of Population.

Instead of dedicating his energies to those tasks which are the natural function of an assistant administrator, Mr. Levin has assiduously worked to usurp my role as director of the Office of Population—with unfortunate results both for the population program and the Bureau for which he is responsible.

On February 28, 1979, after two years of harassment, and misusing a provision of the Civil Service Reform Act which went into effect in January 1979, Mr. Levin formally proposed that I be demoted.

I appealed this proposed action to the then acting administrator, Robert Nooter, during several months without much hope of success because, by his own statement, Mr. Nooter had been a biased participant in this action since at least April 1977. Finally, on July 2, 1979, Mr. Nooter issued the above letter [deleted as noted on page 116].

Reflections and Conclusions

In the social and bureaucratic fields, as in the physical, action begets reaction and it is difficult if not impossible to take powerful and effective program action without polarizing reactive forces among those whose status or aspirations are somehow negatively altered or threatened by the actions taken.

This has been especially true in the population field where reactionary elements of certain religious and educational disciplines [namely, the Catholic Church] have long opposed direct action toward solution of problems of excess fertility and population growth by means of fertility control service programs.

Adversary forces are not much troubled as long as population and family planning activists devote their energies to peripheral and rhetorical exercises. But if one firmly grasps the nettle of decisive action to make the most effective means of fertility control fully and readily available to entire populations, then one becomes the lightning rod for adversary wrath.

An interesting footnote to this: In 1982, it seems that the Roman Catholic Church rewarded Sander Levin for his "assistance" in fulfilling the Church's agenda to remove Ravenholt by providing their "support" in his bid to become the congressman from the seventeenth district of the state of Michigan. Four-term Congressman William Brodhead, a Catholic, pro-abortion, and pro-international population assistance, in a surprise move, decided not to run again, although he was only forty years old, competent, and had a bright future ahead. With Catholic hierarchy support, Sander Levin beat Republican candidate Gerald Rosen by a margin of 66 percent to 32 percent in the

1982 general election.[1]

Dr. Ravenholt continues to work for the government today, but in cancer research. There were many other Catholics involved in Ravenholt's dismissal from the Office of Population. He only identified the most visible ones in his memo. Many held postgraduate degrees. Some were physicians. They viciously and without just cause attacked him. I myself have heard them do so. Not all were Catholic. Among them were Protestants and Jews as well, some of whom looked for personal gain through "cooperation." We will return to this topic later. Most important is the fact that the U.S. National Security Council had already determined that world population growth is a serious threat to our national security and all of the actors Ravenholt names knew this well.

No doubt this memo fell into the hands of at least a few members of the press, but they remained silent. Ravenholt considered forcing the issue: that the Catholic hierarchy was behind his demise into public view. However, some "friends" strongly discouraged him from doing so, saying that he could not possibly win. He was thus effectively coopted into silence. However, there was certainly no guarantee that the press would do anything with the story. Consider the following:

In the June 3, 1983, issue of *Science*, an article appeared entitled "Universities Find Funding Shortcut," written by staff writer Colin Norman and summarized below:

> The Speaker of the House, Thomas P. (Tip) O'Neill, Jr., [a Roman Catholic] received a call recently from his archbishop, Humberto Cardinal Medeiros of Boston. As a result, Catholic University in Washington, D.C., may soon get a new $13.9 million research facility, courtesy of the Department of Energy (DOE).
>
> In a highly unusual move, the House voted on May 12 to remove $5 million from the budget of the National Center for Advanced Materials (NCAM) at the Lawrence Berkeley Laboratory and directed that the money be spent instead on a vitreous state research lab at Catholic U. The vote, which came as an amendment to a DOE authorization bill, was the result of an impressive lobbying campaign by some of the nation's bishops.
>
> Catholic was not the only university to indulge in some successful pork barrel politics. Columbia University also raided DOE's authorization bill for a $5 million downpayment on a $32 million chemistry building. In this case, the House decreed that the funds be taken out of a variety of basic research programs in DOE.
>
> What makes both these moves unusual is that neither facility

has been reviewed by DOE or by the House Committee on Science and Technology, which authorizes DOE's budget. The proposals bypassed the usual peer review and authorization process and were sent straight to the House floor, where they arrived with a good deal of political momentum.

The proposals "came out of left field," says one DOE official, who complains that the department had no chance to determine whether they should have a high priority claim on the federal budget. "I would have no way of knowing whether these proposals are more meritorious than others," he said. "This could be a very bad precedent. . . ."

Help was sought from Catholic U.'s board of trustees [by Catholic University president, Father William Byron]. Cardinal Medeiros, who recently left the board, contacted O'Neill, and Archbishop Philip Hannan of New Orleans contacted Representative Lindy Boggs (D–Louisiana) [a Catholic], who occupies a key spot on the appropriations subcommittee that deals with DOE's research budget.

O'Neill sent a letter, dated April 28, to Science and Technology Committee chairman Don Fuqua (D–Florida), saying he hoped Fuqua could find some money in the authorization bill for the facility. Representative Norman Mineta (D–California) agreed to sponsor an amendment on the floor diverting money from NCAM. When the vote came up, House Majority Leader James Wright, Jr. (D–Texas), spoke in favor of the amendment, and, according to one aide, "Members were notified it was the Speaker's amendment." It was approved by 261 votes to 113. Opposition was led by Representative James Sensenbrenner (R–Wisconsin). *According to an aide, he got a call shortly before the vote from Archbishop Rembert Weakland of Milwaukee.*

The Columbia University proposal did not have any divine connections. . . .

Representative Charles Rangel (D–New York) [a Catholic], whose district included Columbia, was approached [probably to lay a smoke screen to mask otherwise obvious Catholic corruption] in late April and he agreed to sponsor an amendment to the DOE bill. . . . The amendment was passed by 215 votes to 150. [Note: Material in brackets is that of this author.]

What makes this article so incredible is that no mention of this act of corruption ever appeared, to my knowledge, in any newspaper or newsmagazine or on television or radio. That it did not appear elsewhere shows the considerable power of censorship held by the Catholic hierarchy over the U.S. news media. The skill with which this act of corruption was executed by the nation's top bishops suggests that such acts are frequent occurrences in America. This act also reveals the contempt the Catholic hierarchy has for American democracy.

Furthermore, despite the disclosure in *Science* of this act of corruption, the bill was passed, an indication of the impunity with which the Catholic hierarchy acts. It also suggests that this sort of action is frequently undertaken by an experienced hierarchy and is a reminder of its political sophistication.

The implications of this *Science* article for Ravenholt's case are considerable. The hierarchy apparently has an iron grip on what is published and broadcast regarding hierarchy activities and are highly effective in their censorship of the press. Whether Ravenholt could have broken their iron grip in order to get his story told is uncertain.

Obviously, these two corrupt acts are vastly different in importance. The Catholic actors fully intended to cripple the AID population program and everyone agrees that they have. This was their intention despite the fact that this program is of vital national security interest. Why would so many university-trained Catholics agree to participate in the corruption of the AID population program despite the obvious security implications as delineated by the National Security Council in two recent reports? Why would some Catholic scientists be responding to the population problem differently from non-Catholics although they are exposed to the same data?

Catholic Higher Education and "Truth" or Intellectual Honesty

Consider the following paragraphs:

> It is only when some famous "liberal" like the late Monsignor John A. Ryan of the National Catholic Welfare Conference talks frankly about his past that the non-Catholic can appreciate the nature of Catholic academic freedom. Monsignor Ryan admitted in his autobiography that he resigned from the national board of the American Civil Liberties Union "simply and solely because the organization had gone into the field of academic freedom. I called attention to the absurdity, for example, of my membership in the national committee of an organization which might undertake to defend a professor at a Catholic university who has been discharged for teaching heresy."[2]

Redden and Ryan in their standard Catholic work for teachers,

Freedom Through Education, defines the conception of freedom in unmistakable terms:

"Freedom to worship God implies in its correct meaning and application that every man should acknowledge God as his Creator, submit to His divine rule and will, and, through the proper use of faith and reason embrace the eternal truths which alone insure salvation. This is true freedom. It is opposed to that so-called 'liberty of conscience' which a 'seditious and rebellious mind' dominated by man's lower nature and blinded to truth and goodness employs to undermine, overthrow, or destroy the infallible authority of religion to guide and direct all the individual's conduct in terms of the moral law."

Under this interpretation of "freedom" no teacher in a Catholic school is free to disagree with the hierarchy on any social [for example, overpopulation] or religious policy that the hierarchy cares to include in its modicum of "eternal truths." As Father Wilfred M. Mallon, S.J., phrased it in criticizing the American Association of University Professors before the National Catholic Educational Association in 1942 [and later published in the National Catholic Educational Association bulletin]:

"Freedom to teach what is true is without practical applicability unless we have a norm. . . . The Catholic college norm must be not only natural knowledge but the deposit of divinely revealed truths immeasurably more certain than any truth arrived at by mere human deduction or experiment because we have for them the guarantee of the infinite knowledge and veracity of God. . . . We reserve the right to dispense with the service of the staff member whose life or utterances on the campus or off of it undermines the purposes for which we exist. . . . In view of the very nature and fundamental purposes of Catholic education, violations of Catholic doctrine or Catholic moral principles or of the essential proprieties of Catholic life, on the campus or off the campus, render a man unfit for service in a Catholic college."[3]

It is evident that academic freedom in the Catholic system is freedom to *receive* what the hierarchy considers truth.[4]

But the Catholic hierarchy still does not accept either the method or the conclusions of science when the results of scientific inquiry conflict with priestly belief and practice, and every Papal endorsement of science is made with this spoken or unspoken reservation. In fact, the mechanism of priestly control over science, and the fundamental theory on which the mechanism works, are essentially the same today as they were in the

Middle Ages. The technique for disciplining a rebellious scientist has changed; the principle has not.

The theory behind the Church's control of science is that all truth is divided into two grades, divine and human. Divine truth comes from God via the Roman Catholic Church; human truth comes from finite reason, experience, and observation. Divine truth is per se infallible; human truth is always subject to correction by divine truth. If the two conflict, that conflict *ipso facto* proves that the supposed human truth is not truth at all but falsehood.[5]

The penalties imposed upon Catholic professors for departure from orthodox dogma almost never reach the level of public revelation because the dissident Catholic has no real forum for the discussion of grievances. College faculties are dominated by priests who are themselves dominated by bishops. Their lines of promotion are all within the hierarchy or the Catholic educational system. There is no reward for independence and there are very severe penalties for defiance. Priests and religious teachers who leave the Church because of a change of views usually avoid publicity because, as "renegades," they expose themselves to vindictive reprisals by their former Catholic brethren.[6]

Catholic scientists who work in the population field are exposed to, and many respond to, this repression of thought and intimidation. The boycott of books by the hierarchy is far more extensive than most Americans realize:

Actually the Catholic boycott includes all books which specifically oppose the major social policies of the Church even when those policies have no direct bearing on worship or theology. No book favoring sterilization of the feebleminded, birth control, euthanasia, artificial insemination, therapeutic abortion, cremation, state operation of all colleges, divorce, complete separation of church and state, and other subjects, can be deliberately and knowingly read by a good Catholic.

Even in the field of social policy [such as, population growth control], the Church rejects the right of all persons to criticize its fundamental doctrines. It teaches that a Catholic sins who reads the side of a public discussion that contains direct attacks upon the Catholic position. If the Catholic hierarchy could extend to all American literature the system of censorship that it has developed in Catholic countries, the rule would be applied to all books and magazines that expressed any criticism of the Church.[7]

But the censorship operations of the hierarchy have gone far beyond religion and decency. They have extended into the world of politics, medicine, and historical truth. They have impaired the integrity of the media of information serving non-Catholics as well as Catholics. Most important of all, the hierarchy has stifled self-criticism among its own people by refusing them permission to read both sides of vital controversies on matters of social policy. Such repression is directly contrary to the American conception of freedom of thought.[8]

For non-Catholic Americans, this organized deliberate repression of the freedom of thought in Catholic universities is just about beyond comprehension. The above paragraphs were written thirty-five years ago, but very little has changed. One would think that, because of the Church's official opposition to population growth control, Catholic campuses in America would be hotbeds of debate and inquiry into the population problem with extensive press coverage. Yet, there is total silence! Total silence! Discussion of one of the two most serious problems facing humanity is prohibited. Freedom of thought is prohibited.

On the whole, the Church is less charitable to heresy in the social sciences than in the physical sciences. No matter how overwhelming the evidence may be, no Catholic social scientist is permitted to declare publicly that birth control, socialism, civil marriage, remarriage after divorce, or sterilization of the feeble-minded is a scientific solution for a social problem. All these solutions, of course, have been specifically denounced by the Popes.

The limitations imposed upon the social scientist by Catholic discipline are usually stated with considerable moderation in order to avoid ridicule. The Right Reverend Francis J. Haas, dean of the School of Social Science at the Catholic University of America, describes these limitations suavely (italics supplied):

"In the Catholic institutions of higher learning, *due regard being given to the requirements of the natural and divine law,* there are no restrictions on the biologist, chemist, or physicist in *assembling* data or in *proposing* new formulas, regardless of how novel his discoveries may be. The social scientist enjoys the same freedom in *gathering* data on all subjects, no matter how unpalatable such data may be to those who would not want them brought to light in assembled form. . . . More than this, he is entirely free, *within the framework of the Church's social teaching*—which rests on the common good and which in turn is based on human needs—to *propose* any formula or remedy which he can demonstrate will advance human well-being."[9]

More specific is a sociology professor from the same university, Father Paul H. Furfey, in a chapter on "Supernatural Sociology" in his *Fire on the Earth:*

"The Catholic sociologist, then, enjoys complete freedom of investigation in the social field, but he is not allowed to rely upon merely human science as the sole means of procuring individual and social well-being. . . . It is dangerous, then, for a Catholic sociologist to deal with social problems by the methods of purely natural science if, in doing so, he conveys the impression that this purely natural treatment of social questions represents the complete mind of the Church. . . . We ought constantly to emphasize the fact that no important problem can be solved without taking the supernatural into account."

The effects of priestly limitations upon scientific thinking are evident in nearly all Catholic textbooks on sociology and in the voluminous pamphlet literature of Catholic organizations. Perhaps the most serious limitation is evident in the analysis of population problems. I have already quoted the declaration of the *Catholic Encyclopedia* on this point: "With supplies increasing in proportion to population, there is no such thing as overpopulation."[10]

Although all Catholic scientists are subject to this Congregation of the Holy Office without recourse or appeal, they are, in practice, allowed great liberty as long as they do not encroach upon priestly preserves. Then the Holy Office may become firm and even vindictive. The penalty of excommunication and expulsion faces any scholar in a Catholic institution who dares to disagree openly. Usually Catholic scholars do not disagree openly. Either they submit quietly or slip out of the Church quietly, since the penalties of public defiance are painful in the extreme.

The general effect of this supervision of all science by priests is to create a special kind of ecclesiastical anti-science in the Church which the educated Catholic does not dare to evaluate candidly and openly. The special effects of this anti-science may be summarized briefly under six heads: (1) the system permits the continued exploitation of the poorer and more ignorant Catholic people by practices which have been discarded as medieval superstitions by nearly all other religious groups in the West; (2) it limits the physical scientist not so much by thwarting his research as by preventing him from drawing logical deductions from his data; (3) it imposes dogmatic restrictions upon Catholic social science, especially in the analysis of family and population problems; (4) it shades history in order to exalt Catholic accomplishments and conceal the devastating effects of clerical control in the past; (5) it makes the Catholic philosopher an underling of the theologian; (6) it reduces the Catholic universities to the lowest scientific level in American education.[11]

Catholic scientists are not alone in this repression of freedom of thought. All other university-trained Catholics have been subjected to the same repression, including lawyers, journalists, administrators, accountants, and others.

It should come as no surprise that many Catholics who have trained in Catholic universities reject the reality of a population problem and *all* information substantiating this fact. Yet it is no accident that a number of these people, including some who have trained as demographers, have gravitated to the population growth control field.

Catholic Action and Population Growth Control in America

In chapters four and five, I discussed Vaillancourt's extensive studies of Catholic Action in Italy. Catholic Action is a Vatican-controlled lay organization whose purpose is primarily to create a political environment favorable to the Vatican's needs. This same organization exists in the United States and, as discussed in chapter four, serves as the Church's front line lobby in all 435 congressional districts. Catholic Action was largely responsible for the defeat of the ERA and for the anti-abortion movement in this country. Consider the following:

> The Catholic hierarchy proposes to . . . [enhance its power] by infiltrating and penetrating non-Catholic organizations with faithful Catholic laymen who will act as soldiers and missionaries for the Church. This latter activity is the special task of the overall coordinating organization of Catholic laymen, Catholic Action.[12]

> "Catholic Action itself," says *The Catholic Action Manual*, "is an army involved in a holy war for religion." The military symbolism is not accidental; the whole emphasis of the organization is upon a crusading faith, inspired with militant confidence that the Catholic Church can conquer the earth if its followers obey their priests with military precision.[13]

> Although its techniques are sometimes conspiratorial rather than democratic, there is nothing particularly secret or sinister about Catholic Action, unless the goal that it seeks is considered sinis-

ter. Catholic Action is a "lay apostolate" working for a totally Catholic civilization—political, medical, cultural, economic, and religious—a civilization in which the Catholic Church will be "the mistress and guide of all other societies."[14] It is completely subordinate to the hierarchy, being described by Pius XI as "the participation of the laity in the apostolate of the Church's hierarchy." In the United States, in a sense Catholic Action is simply the total network of Catholic lay organizations, inspired by a set of militant shibboleths. It has a separate department in the overall organization of American Catholicism.

The cell technique employed by communism to infiltrate other bodies is frankly used by . . . Catholic Action. The chief role of Catholic Action is in politics, where it serves as a general denominational pressure group. . . .[15]

(Note: in chapter eleven, we will discuss the fact that Catholic Action heavily influences both the Republican and Democratic Parties.)

Its [Catholic Action's] techniques of penetration into non-Catholic organizations are not always candid. The priests choose Catholic laymen from Catholic Action to infiltrate non-Catholic organizations in much the same manner that communists were chosen to infiltrate labor unions and political parties for the Kremlin. Says the *Catholic Action Manual:* "The layman is not surrounded by that net of prejudice and distrust that secularism has woven around the sacred person of the priest; he is not suspect of pleading his own cause, or fulfilling a professional job; and so he can penetrate into areas where the priest can never set his foot; and can gather great sheaves where the priest would find nothing but dry and prickly stubble."[16]

The International Fertility Research Program Experience

This author joined the International Fertility Research Program (IFRP) on October 9, 1977. This organization was founded by Dr. Elton Kessel in 1971. Its purpose was to perform Phase III clinical trials (intermediate size field studies) on new and improved methods of contraception and to assist in transferring new and improved contraceptive technologies to Third World countries. The organization, funded by AID, had met with considerable success, growing from a staff of one to a resident staff of 135 and working in forty countries by the time I joined. It had already developed an excellent reputation for itself and consequently became an obvious target for the Catholic Church, in the same way that Ravenholt had. Like the Ravenholt assistants who appeared on the hit list attributed to Sander Levin, Elton Kessel appeared on the hierarchy's master hit list.

A few weeks after I arrived at IFRP, the medical director, Dr. Leonard Laufe, a key international leader in this field, read my recently published book, *Population Growth Control: The Next Move Is America's*. It makes the case that world population growth is a serious threat to national and global security. One chapter discusses the Catholic Church's success in thwarting population growth control. Dr. Laufe asked me to give an in-service training lecture on the contents of this book, and seven weeks after arriving I gave this lecture. One of the attendees, Peter Donaldson, became agitated during the course of the lecture and, shortly before it ended, walked out, obviously distressed. Later that day he asked for a copy of the book, which I provided. The next morning our paths crossed. He had finished the book. He was very upset. When I asked his opinion, he fired back, "This book is very poorly written. If I had written this book, people would have read it. As it is, nobody is going to read it." I was surprised, perplexed. His comment was an obvious attempt to discourage me from promoting the book. I did not understand why he was reacting in this way. Within days, I discovered that he was working very hard to undermine my IFRP position and undermine my working relationship with other IFRP staff members. He succeeded in creating a very hostile work setting for me. (Some colleagues later discussed his actions and statements with me.) I still did not understand why. Then one day, I learned that he is Irish Roman Catholic; he probably did not relish hearing that the Catholic hierarchy, by thwarting population growth control, was threatening the security of the United States. In retrospect, Donaldson exhibited the kind of reaction you might expect from a Catholic who is working to fulfill the kinds of duties described in *The Catholic Action Manual*. Very understandably he did not want to view his personal acts in thwarting population growth control as threatening U.S. security.

Peter Donaldson obtained a bachelor's degree from Catholic Fordham University and a doctorate at Brown University in demography. He had previously worked at the Population Council and the Ford Foundation. He had joined IFRP only two months earlier than I. About the time of my first encounter with him, or about four months after he had arrived, he began to recruit staff members to form a coup to oust the founder and executive director, Elton Kessel. One evening when alone in the building, Peter Donaldson approached a new employee, Dr. Charles Ausherman, an ordained Reformist minister, and told him of the coup plans, inviting Ausherman to join the coup. Ausherman was shocked and assumed that Donaldson was unaware of

Ausherman's previous close relationship with Kessel, with whom he immediately discussed the conversation. Kessel dismissed any suggestion that a coup at this time, especially one led by a thirty-three-year-old newcomer, was even remotely possible. Donaldson also approached Dr. Roger Bernard, a distinguished epidemiologist, with the same request, and he, likewise refused the offer to join. They never approached me. However, I did recognize that Donaldson was achieving considerable success at being divisive. He spent much of his time pitting individuals against each other and nurturing factions. A number of staff members had more than the average amount of lust for power, and they could see their power enhanced by throwing in their lot with Donaldson. By March 1978, the coup actors were lined up and reasons for the action concocted. In March 1978, it was carried out, evidently with the close collaboration of the Agency for International Development. No doubt, some of the same actors who were undermining Ravenholt wished to rid themselves of Kessel. Three weeks after the action, all of the concocted reasons were suddenly dealt with easily. A Reduction in Force (RIF) was planned and executed. About thirty-five of the 135 staff members were forced out, including most of those who owed their loyalty to Kessel. No single strong person emerged from this takeover.

Dr. Malcolm Potts was hired to replace Kessel in July 1978. I later learned that he had had extensive discussions with Donaldson before being offered the job, and, according to a close friend of Potts, Donaldson had put forward his views of what it would take to make the organization "successful" and what it would take to ensure Potts's continuation in the job. No doubt Potts had concerns from previous posts held. Several of his closest friends had told me that they felt that Potts's abrupt resignation as medical director of the International Planned Parenthood Federation in London was due to the influence of the Catholic hierarchy from within the organization. Also, at this time Potts was working for the Population Crisis Committee which had been (and continues to be) racked by divisiveness, prompted, in large part at least, by certain Catholics working for the organization. There is little doubt that Potts was quite aware that those obedient to the hierarchy could do him more than their fair share of harm.

I remember the first time that I talked to him about the problem of overpopulation. It was over lunch, and there were several others present. The conversation drifted to the negative influence of the Catholic Church on world population growth control efforts. Potts sharply defended the Catholic Church and claimed that the Church was having no significant negative effect on population efforts. I was really taken aback. He just flatly dismissed one bit of evidence after the other. A few months later, we had our second general conversation, a repitition of the first. Potts ardently defended the Catholic Church, simply rejecting all criticisms of it. Except on one occasion, throughout my six years of working as his subordinate, he never failed to defend the Church when I criticized it.

In its November 1981 issue, *Mother Jones* magazine attacked the work of Potts and IFRP on the injectable contraceptive, Depo-Provera. After reading the article in late October, I went to Potts's office to bring to his attention several items of information that could only have come from a "mole" within IFRP. He said that he agreed and that he believed that "there are two moles at IFRP." I asked him to name them, but he refused and said, "I do not wish to discuss this any further." He was obviously angered by the article.

It was on my very last day at IFRP, at 4:30 PM, August 19, 1983, that I understood what I had witnessed for the past six years. Dr. Nancy Williamson, a Harvard-trained sociologist, and one of the most competent people I have worked with, had just returned from the Philippines to learn of my sudden departure. She said that she was concerned that I might act to hurt the organization and wanted to know my plans. She had understood that "policy differences" prompted my departure. I responded that I was not aware of any policy differences. She informed me that "there is a major organizational commitment to *collaborating and cooperating* with the Catholic Church." I was not surprised but nevertheless was stunned to hear this confirmation from this very level-headed woman. I had worked at IFRP for six years, and such a plan had never been verbalized! I responded that no enemy of the Church (and certainly the Church perceived that IFRP was its enemy) *ever* successfully collaborates or cooperates with the Church; that it is either *coopted by the Church* or it is destroyed and that anyone familiar with Church history knows this. Williamson, in this short exchange, explained many events of the past six years that, at the time of their occurrence, had appeared to be inexplicable.

When Potts arrived to assume the position of executive director, Donaldson immediately became his closest ally and near constant companion. Soon Donaldson was perceived by the staff to be the second most powerful person in the organization and, as director of the Field Division, he had considerable influence on policy and direction of the organization. What had been an organization concerned with the biomedical aspects of contraception and the dissemination of contraceptive technologies saw its emphasis changed to health surveys and social science research. Under Donaldson's leadership, the Field Division, responsible for communicating with physician collaborators around the world in clinical medicine terms, saw the departure of all its physicians and a shift to sociologists and other nonphysicians. Both the organization's ability to do clinical research and its technology dissemination activities seriously deteriorated under his leadership, probably by design. Finally after several months, it became apparent that things could not continue as they were. He was replaced by a competent physician, and the Division improved considerably.

Under Potts, and with considerable help from Donaldson, Potts's first two years saw the organization undeniably decline, again apparently by design. The board of directors recognized this decline and decided to create the position of deputy director and, according to the job description, fill the position with an administrator experienced in contraceptive research and family planning programs.

Just prior the hiring of a deputy director, chapter one of this book was quietly published by the IFRP. It had been commissioned by Georgetown University's Center for Strategic and International Studies and prepared in collaboration with the Center, which saw its publication there blocked by the Church. Knowledge of this endeavor was deliberately withheld from Donaldson by my design. In late October, using IFRP private funds, nearly seven thousand copies were distributed by Werner Fornos of the Population Action Council.

Within the week, Donaldson stormed into my office, demanding a copy of the monograph. "All right, where is it? Where is it? What have you been hiding from me?" he said in great excitement. The next day, he was visibly agitated. The monograph, all the more significant because it had been prepared at CSIS, made the irrefutable argument that population growth is a serious national security threat and that the Catholic hierarchy is likewise a serious national security threat because it is thwarting population growth control.

A few days later, Donaldson had posted on bulletin boards throughout the building an announcement of three one-hour lectures he would give:

The First Annual
Talcott Parsons Memorial Lecture
presenting
Peter J. Donaldson

Topic: "What Karl Marx and Steve Mumford Have in Common"
Dates: November 11–13, 1980
Time: 3:30 PM — 4:30 PM, Conference Room A

I was surprised to see the announcement, but I was even more surprised to learn that he was deadly serious. I took a copy of the announcement to Potts and voiced my strong objections. I informed Potts that I was aware through first-hand accounts from other staff members of Donaldson's repeated attempts over the past three years to force me out of the organization, and he acknowledged this. I offered my reasons for having become convinced that Donaldson was playing on the other team and urged him to dismiss him. I also made the case that my monograph activities were completely extracurricular, as we had agreed, and that any "lectures" concerning that monograph should be extracurricular as well and asked him to inform Donaldson that there would be no lectures during normal duty hours. However, I, along with many others in the organization, doubted whether Potts had any influence over what Donaldson did at this point.

On November 11, 1980, a second notice appeared announcing that the lecture had been "postponed due to staff absences in the International Projects Department." Then on November 26 a notice was posted setting the date for December 1. At the lecture, an outline of his lecture was handed out. One of the topics of his lecture was, "Why the real problem is not the Catholics but the Jews."

Donaldson had reacted to this monograph as any well-trained Catholic Action devotee might. If a person threatens a Catholic Action mission, call them "anti-Catholic." If that does not check the threat, call them a "communist." Donaldson had been screaming "anti-Catholic" for three years but at least most staff members had dismissed this charge because it was obvious to everyone that several of my closest collaborators and colleagues and friends were Roman Catholic.

That he would try to label me a communist in this way in an attempt to discredit me and the monograph was stunning. He gave the impression of being quite stupid, which he most certainly is not. It appears that he was getting his signals from a much older and less perceptive person who had had successes in an earlier era when priests ran around at will charging anyone they disliked with being a communist sympathizer.

In November 1980, the IFRP board hired the organization's first deputy director to relieve Potts of the "day-to-day" administrative activities of the organization. This hiring went almost unnoticed by me as I was exceedingly busy at the time. I was aware that the man hired, John L. Ganly, was grossly overqualified for the job in every respect except that he had had no experience in contraceptive research or family planning. He had served as a senior staff member in the Office of the Secretary of Defense in the 1950s, had been director of Program Management and Purchasing for AVCO Corporation, negotiating over $300 million of contracts in the early 1960s, and was general manager of Weston Instruments in the mid-sixties. From 1971 to 1973, he was the deputy assistant secretary at HUD, responsible for the operations of the FHA which included eighty-seven offices and nine thousand employees. In 1973 and 1974, he was auditor general of the Agency for International Development (AID), heading a professional staff of four hundred, operating in forty countries. From 1974 to 1976, he was deputy director of ACTION and chief executive officer with a staff of eighteen hundred and a budget of $200 million. In the late 1970s, he returned to private industry as a group vice-president of the Safetron Systems Corporation. What was he doing at IFRP?

Two weeks after Ganly's arrival, he invited me to lunch with him just to chat. His responses to my questions about his interests and background came as a shock. He was rabidly anti-abortion, showed a strong bias against international family planning programs, and was generally opposed to contraception. I remember that I could not imagine how someone with those strongly held opinions would move from Louisville, Kentucky, to work for the world's most outspoken advocate of abortion, Dr. Malcolm Potts. Ganly also stated that he would have to live separated from his wife so that she could work the one more year needed before retirement, which he agreed was quite a sacrifice.

Upon returning to the IFRP building, I approached Dr. Kessel about this conversation. He said that he had heard very little about Ganly except that he had been very hostile toward the International Planned Parenthood Federation (IPPF, London) during an audit in the early 1970s and that he was a good friend of John Murphy, one of the key figures in the firing of Ravenholt. I asked Kessel, a board member, how closely the board had questioned Ganly before his appointment. I learned that there were only three people significantly involved in his hiring: Potts, Donaldson, and the chairman of the board, Dr. Sharon Camp, who had always been an ardent defender of the Catholic Church and a firm believer in "collaboration" and "cooperation" with it. No other board members had much to do with this selection. In retrospect, after my talk with Williamson three years later, it appears that Potts and Camp, both committed to "collaboration," may have felt that the organization (and their positions) was more likely to survive if a known intimate of the Church anti-abortion/anti-family-planning mafia was providing leadership in the organization. A few days later I learned from another staff member that Ganly, like Murphy and Donaldson, is Irish Roman Catholic.

About this time, Ganly asked me for a copy of the Georgetown monograph. The following day, he called me into his office to say that he had "read the monograph not once but twice." He said that, while he did not agree with everything in the monograph, he thought it was solid work and well-written.

We did not speak any more until December 19. At 11:00 AM Ganley called and asked me to report to his office. He was enraged! He had apparently gotten a call from someone who had taken him to task. He told me that if I ever wrote anything attacking the Church again, whether on my own time or on company time, he would fire me. He repeated this threat four times in this conversation. Then, fellow staff member Dr. Pouru Bhiwandiwala, accompanying a visitor, interrupted our conversation, and I left his office. I decided that I would return to his office later to determine what had prompted his outburst. During the second meeting, Ganly repeated his threat at least five additional times. He refused to give me any reasons. Once, he attributed the complaint to the State Department, but, when I said that I would call my friend Dick Benedict (ambassador for Population Affairs), a relationship of which he was unaware, and get to the bottom of this, he quickly changed his story. He was obviously attempting to deceive me.

Potts was out of the country at the time and returned the first week in January. I met with him at the home of Bhiwandiwala to describe this unusual set of circumstances. I made my case, and Potts's angry response was, "I hired this man, and he will do whatever I tell him to do." In effect, that was the end of the conversation.

Ganly and I did not talk again for two months when he called me into his office. He asked me to resign, saying that it would be better for both the IFRP and me. I rejected the suggestion adding that the only great advantage to me under those circumstances would be complete freedom to write about the Church.

Our next encounter was alone in the canteen in August 1981. The conversation dealt with the fact that, if abortion is completely eliminated by the anti-abortion lobby, then the IUD will be the next to go. Until our meeting, Ganly did not understand that the probable mode of action of the IUD, in most cases at least, is really abortion of the very early embryo. He was obviously really taken aback by this revelation! By this time, most people in the organization recognized that he was rabidly anti-abortion, and some were asking why he was working at IFRP, given these strong feelings.

Ganly spent much of this year convincing people of two things: first, that "family planning is dead" and that we must change the function of the organization to health research; and second, that AID money was going to dry up and that we must get private grants and private contracts if we were to survive. He discussed these arguments with Kessel privately and with various staff members in group meetings. I argued against this because of the growing awareness in Washington of the serious national security threat of overpopulation, but it was to no avail. Funds continued to increase throughout, however. Nevertheless, Ganly succeeded in striking terror into the hearts of the staff by constantly pounding on the theme that "family planning is dead" and on the need to switch to health research if they were to survive.

In January 1982, I approached Potts again about Ganly's performance and offered additional reasons why I was concerned about his motivations. His only comment was, "I have complete faith in Mr. Ganly." I walked out quietly. I discussed this meeting that day and later with another staff member, a close friend of Dr. Potts, and told her of my concerns and frustrations. Later she told me, "Even if Potts knew that Ganly and Donaldson were moles, he would not do anything differently. He would just play out the scenario." I dismissed her statement completely and did not recognize the significance of it until Williamson dropped the information concerning "cooperation and collaboration" with the Church. He knew.

By early 1982, most of the senior research staff were committing a large part of their time to proposal writing, looking for non-AID funds without much hope of substantial returns. Many support personnel were devoting even more time to these fundraising activities. I became concerned that not only were our AID contract activities (clinical trials research and technology dissemination) suffering from such a large commitment to fundraising but also that I was not familiar with the legality of using hundreds of thousands of tax dollars to write grant and contract proposals for private funds. I approached the IFRP contract officer Bob Hughes, an impeccably honest and sincere man, to ask if he were aware of the extent to which our resources were being committed to fundraising. He assured me that it was perfectly legal, but about that time Ganly walked into Hughes's office and he repeated the question to Ganly. Ganly was visibly angered by the question and responded, "I have an unblemished record in my thirty years of administration and I can assure you that I would not take a chance on blemishing it to help out a bunch of God-damned IUD pushers!" With this response, Ganly let his true sentiments toward the IFRP staff and its mission be known. We did not discuss how much this fundraising effort had detracted from our family-planning work.

The most telling event in my interactions with Ganly occurred in early 1982, when he was the guest speaker at the weekly "scientists" meeting, which included about ten senior staff persons. We had just learned that we would be awarded an additional million dollars in funds from AID to study so-called natural family-planning methods. The discussion concerned this natural family-planning activity. Toward the end of the meeting, Ganly made a completely revealing statement in an angry tone: "The AID Population Office has spent $2.1 billion since it began in 1966, and every dime of it has been a waste! Now we have an opportunity to do something really good, something really important with this natural family-planning work." Several of us were amazed that he was so blatant about his intentions. You would expect to hear only representatives of the Vatican speak so critically of population assistance and so favorably of natural family planning. The average number of years of employment by IFRP among those present exceeded five. He was in effect saying to each of us, on the average, that we had totally wasted five years of our professional lives. Several present saw any remaining doubts about Ganly's intentions disappear with that statement. This meeting was still being discussed when I left the IFRP eighteen months later.

In August 1982, it was decided that the name of the organization should be changed. One was chosen that would be less offensive to the Church—Family Health International (FHI)—removing the identification of the organization from family planning, a move not well-received by the most committed people at AID and throughout the population establishment. For the next year, the policy of cooperation and collaboration with the Church continued to be implemented.

The last few years of this policy have witnessed the de facto forced departure of most of the organization's most competent and dedicated people, including Elton Kessel, Roger Bernard, Kay Omran, J. Y. Peng, Winston Liao, Irene Rosenfeld, and F. Curtiss Swezy, to name a few. To diminish the dissemination of information ("evil family-planning information"), the superb publications unit of four editors and three-and-one-half graphics personnel was eliminated leaving only a single graphics person. It is no accident that Donaldson, despite access to a very substantial amount of IFRP data and a gift for writing, has not published a single paper advancing family planning based upon IFRP data, while others have published twenty-five to fifty papers or more since he joined the staff. The organization's willingness to forego the study of the use-effectiveness of the natural family-planning methods in order to satisfy the needs of the Vatican is a blatant exercise in intellectual prostitution. These are but a few of the many examples of what "cooperation and collaboration" has meant to this organization. The more accurate term is *cooptation.*

Cooptation and the Family-Planning Field

The IFRP is not alone. Many of the organizations involved in international family-planning work have been coopted by the Church. Some of those more discussed are the Population Council, the Ford Foundation, the Rockefeller Foundation, the IPPF in London, UNFPA, and the Population Crisis Committee. The Population Association of America has been criticized as being too heavily influenced by the many Catholic demographers in its ranks.

Organizations can be coopted by Church representatives acting within, but individuals can be coopted as well, and they may then contribute to the cooptation of one or more organizations. One of the key ways in which this is accomplished can be described as follows.

There are two men who stand out as the Church's leading thinkers on overpopulation: Father Arthur McCormack, whose work was discussed earlier, and Father Francis Murphy. They were among my most important teachers and have considerably influenced my thinking. They are highly esteemed by most population establishment people—and herein lies the problem. The presence of these two men in the population field greatly blunts the criticism of the Church, especially because they are constantly sending out signals praising the pope and the Church.

For example, in a recent article written for the *Draper Fund Report*[17] published by the Population Crisis Committee, McCormack states, "In 1965 Pope Paul VI made an appeal at the United Nations, *based on the Church's overriding concern about world poverty . . .*" (emphasis added). But does the Church have this overriding concern? If it did it would be placing this concern first; instead the Vatican's first concern seems to be the maintenance and enhancement of its power. McCormack's article continues:

> In a recent message sent to the Second International Conference on the Family of the Americas, Pope John Paul II demonstrated his realization and compassionate understanding of this dilemma. After praising natural family planning methods and those who promote them, his message continues:
> ". . . We cannot conclude these considerations without recalling that there are, in spite of everything, many families living in such circumstances—we think, for example, of the vast sectors of acute poverty in the Third World—that the putting into practice of moral law expressed in the Christian ideal may appear impossible. While continuing to maintain its validity, a great pastoral effort should be made to strengthen the faith of these persons, while leading them 'gradually to the knowledge and the putting into practice of the the Gospel ideal *according to the possibility of their strength*. It is necessary as well to work hard to overcome the living conditions that are characteristic of underdevelopment and which *make well nigh impossible* a cultural, human, and spiritual development such as God wished for his children. The general norms of morality must be applied in order to illuminate individual cases in the light of truth and mercy, according to the example of Jesus."[18] [emphasis added]
> The compassion, common sense, and realism of Pope John Paul II have managed to blend adherence to papal doctrine and concern for those whose living conditions make it virtually impossible to practice it.

Compassion, common sense, and realism are three attributes that can never be ascribed to this pope. These comments by McCormack are terribly destructive in two different ways. First, McCormack gives a false sense of hope that the Church is going to change its position, allowing the reader to postpone the acceptance of the fact that it is not. We have been seeing these deceptive signals for thirty-five years, and the Vatican is more reactionary than at any time during this period. Second, McCormack is, in effect, saying to population field personnel, "I think my pope is wonderful and don't you say anything negative about him. If you do, you will make me angry and I won't be your friend anymore." In other words, he is coopting his population field colleagues.

Father Murphy also similarly misleads and coopts: "John Paul knows that he is not a monarch, even within the Church. . . . Early on, the pope saw himself as 'the voice of the voiceless' and he has grown increasingly confident in that role."[19] I have seen scores of similar praises of the popes by McCormack and Murphy, and I have observed scores of my population colleagues coopted exactly in this way. "We don't want to do anything to hurt their feelings or make them mad at us," is the ultimate response of many of my population colleagues to their writings.

Obviously the Vatican sees this special value of McCormack and Murphy and allows them to exist for this purpose. If their work were of no benefit to the Vatican, they would have been crushed like Hans Kung, who was recently subjected to a vicious campaign to discredit him, led by the Catholic hierarchy.

Murphy has been known to use the influence he has gained through this kind of cooptation. I once received a copy of an article by Lyndon La Rouche, Jr., which included a paragraph that attacked both me and Murphy. I showed it to Potts, who asked for a copy to give to Murphy. Several months later, Potts returned the article to me apparently without showing it to Murphy. He may have forgotten that he had underlined my name and written a note in red ink to Murphy which read, "That's the member of my staff you said was sick!" When Potts fired me for publishing articles on population and the Church, he commented that he probably should have done this long ago because people had been urging him to do it for some time. No doubt, Murphy was one such person.

The Population Apologists for the Church

It is true that Murphy and McCormack contribute significantly to suppression of criticism within the population establishment, but there are Catholic and non-Catholic population specialists working in most population organizations, both in the United States and abroad, who are constantly apologizing for the Church, suppressing criticism of it, and spreading the word about how wonderful the Church, bishops, priests, and the pope really are. More often than not, these apologists are not identified as Catholics. Non-Catholic apologists are often nurtured by the Church, particularly if they are in positions of influence. They are rewarded for these activities, and I have seen some of them in action that justifies these rewards. This strategy for the cooptation of the population establishment has been highly effective.

There is almost no significant criticism of the Church to be heard from population specialists. Their comments and discussions are limited to private conversations; all too many of these exchanges I have heard myself, involving literally hundreds of population specialists around the world. Their silence allows the Church to act in secrecy or without review as it goes about undermining most population activities.

Population organizations as such also contribute to this atmosphere of secrecy to the benefit of the Church. Their literature actually misleads readers regarding the nature of the opposition to population activities. Nearly all population organizations, including those attempting to stop illegal immigration, are guilty of this, as are ERA organizations, environmentalists, and others working to achieve objectives that the Church is trying to thwart. For example, "ZPG [Zero Population Growth] has also met with strong opposition toward our efforts to create an effective national population policy" and "ZPG has also met with vigorous organized opposition from those who would block efforts to create an effective immigration policy" are two comments from a fundraising letter. It never identifies *who* this vigorous opposition is! From another fundraising letter, "From within our federal government . . . allies of the 'New Right' have launched an insidious, behind-the-scenes campaign of harassment against Planned Parenthood." But *who is* the "New Right"? I have a file of examples such as these, and most population and related organizations are represented in that file. These organizations (except Planned Parenthood on a few occasions) *never* identify the Catholic Church as their opposition.

Publications of population organizations are devoid of criticisms of the Church. *INTERCOM*, during its first two years of publication (August 1973 to July 1975), under the direction of Philip Harvey and Timothy Black, for Population Services International, showed their courage in frequently publishing items that the Church would have much preferred to have been kept secret. For example, the August 1974 issue contained the following article, "Population Booklet Draws Catholic Ire":

> A Roman Catholic group has threatened to sue the school board
> of Birmingham, Michigan, if it refuses to discontinue classroom
> use of a controversial booklet on population control by Septem-
> ber 15. The Catholic League for Religious and Civil Rights
> charges that the booklet, published by Xerox Corporation, asks
> questions which amount to a defamation of the pope and the
> Catholic Church.
>
> "Most of the authors represented in the booklet are from the
> Zero Population Growth movement," stated Stuart Hubbel, ex-
> ecutive director of the Catholic organization. "I won't quarrel
> with that, but it's just not a balanced booklet." He charged that
> it contains anti-clerical passages from the diary of a South Ameri-
> can woman, questions the ethics of Catholic doctors who refuse
> to perform sterilization operations, presents a petition signed by
> three thousand scientists attacking Pope Paul VI for immoral
> world leadership, and suggests—through a study question—that
> grounds exist for bringing the Catholic Church before an inter-
> national tribunal to be tried for crimes against humanity. The
> booklet, Hubbel charged, infringes on students' "constitutional
> rights to have the public schools kept free from religious discrimi-
> nation."
>
> An earlier threat by the group to sue Xerox Corporation for
> distributing the controversial booklet to public schools was with-
> drawn when, according to Hubbel, Xerox agreed to discontinue
> its circulation in response to the threatened legal action.

This article draws attention to an important act of censorship by the
Church. This Xerox sponsorship was one of the last corporate contributions to population growth control activities. American corporations, during the early 1970s, were so intimidated by Church threats of
boycotts that they halted contributions to population activities. There
has been almost no corporation initiative in this regard since this
Xerox incident. This is Vatican censorship in America in action.

Then in July 1975, *INTERCOM* was taken over by the Population
Reference Bureau, and criticism of the Church all but disappeared.
However in January 1976, *INTERCOM* in an uncritical manner did
publish an article covering an announcement by the Bishops' Pastoral
Plan for Pro-Life Activities of their creation of the lobbying organization that was later to become Moral Majority, Inc., and proposing the
formation of interdenominational pro-life groups in all 435 congressional districts.[20]

By the time the Catholic Church recruited Jerry Falwell to be the
nominal head of the Moral Majority, this organization was already
fully developed by the Vatican. However, no population publication

has ever revealed this. The most sinister act of secrecy thus far under-taken by the Church in population matters has been met with the most disturbing act of silence by the population establishment. While it is true that population apologists outside population organizations, both Catholic and non-Catholic, have crippled efforts to publish arti-cles which expose the Church's acts of corruption affecting the popula-tion growth control effort, there are people who work within these organizations who owe their loyalty to the Vatican and who personally thwart the publication of such articles. There are hundreds of ex-amples of these actions.

A Request for a United Nations Fund for Population Activites Book Review

Since the inception of the United Nations Fund for Population Activi-ties (UNFPA), its executive director has been Rafael Salas, a deeply committed, honest, sincere, and courageous man. Salas has long recognized the national and global security implications of over-population. In September 1980, he invited a group of scholars to discuss the relationship between population and conflict. Out of this meeting came a conference on this topic which was held one year later at the Massachusetts Institute of Technology. The report of that con-ference, "Population and Conflict," was prepared at Salas's request by Nazli Choucri, professor of political science at MIT.

Salas was aware of my long standing interest in the population-security relationship and my work in this area. I received a letter dated September 6, 1983, from UNFPA requesting that I review Choucri's monograph for their *Populi* magazine, which I immediately agreed to do. The deadline was set for October 3, 1983. The following is the review I submitted.

Review of *Population and Conflict* by Nazli Choucri, United Nations Fund for Population Activities, 1983

On February 28, 1977, accompanied and introduced by former priest and close friend and supporter, Dr. E. J. Farge, I met George Bush, now vice-presi-dent of the United States. He had recently left the directorship of the Central Intelligence Agency (CIA) and returned to Houston. As we sat before him, he read a two-page synopsis of a book I had completed a year earlier on the relationship between population growth and national and global security. His response was, "I agree with everything you are saying here and I can assure you that the people in the CIA agree with you also." He readily agreed to assist in obtaining funding for a project designed to advance the discussion of this emerging national security threat. A few months later, William Colby, also a former CIA director, appeared in a television news interview stating that, "I believe that world population growth is the most serious threat to U.S. security." Six-and-one-half years have passed since it became apparent that the U.S. security establishment had acknowledged this new major threat to security.

By the time these two CIA directors made their pronouncements, Professor Choucri's book, *Population Dynamics and International Violence* had been available for three years and her book with R. C. North, *Nations in Conflict: National Growth and International Violence* for two years.

In *Population and Conflict*, Professor Choucri summarizes her studies of 307 explicit conflicts between 1945 and 1980. The link between population issues and conflict is indisputable. She closely examines the related world forum since 1974: major international conferences; conferences dealing with population and development; and major reports prepared by the international community.

Major world conferences since the 1974 Population Conference in Bucharest have dealt with food, the role of women, employment, human settlements, desertification, technical cooperation among developing countries, agrarian reform and rural development, and others. Major conferences dealing specifically with population and development that have taken place since 1974 include the International Conference of Parliamentarians on Population and Development, Columbo, Sri Lanka, 1979; the Latin American Conference on Population and Development Planning in Cartagena, Columbia; the 1980 International Conference on Population and the Urban Future in Rome, Italy; the 1981 Asian Conference of Parliamentarians on Population and Development in Beijing, China; and the 1981 International Conference on Family Planning in the 1980s in Jakarta, Indonesia. Major reports include: *World Population and Development: Challenges and Perspectives* (1979); the *Global 2000 Report to the President* (1980); *North-South: A Program for Survival* (1980); and *National Agenda for the Eighties* (1980).

These activities collectively represented the world forum for the discussion of population issues since 1974. *Nowhere have the serious national and international security implications of rapid population growth been discussed;* mentioned possibly, but never discussed. "In sum, the most notable international assessments during the latter part of the 1970s, and the early 1980s, show a singular disregard for the conflict-producing dynamics engendered by rapid demographic change both within and across nations."

Professor Choucri examines annual world military expenditures and international population assistance expenditures over the past decade and rules out any hope that, even in this silence, international donors had sharply increased population assistance relative to military expenditures. In 1979, the last year included in her analysis, population assistance amounted to only 0.18 percent of the world military expenditure ($800 million and $446 billion respectively). Clearly, there has been no significant response to the realization that population growth is a serious security threat that had obviously occurred in the U.S. intelligence community prior to the comments made by Mr. Bush and Mr. Colby as a result of their extensive U.S. CIA experience.

Professor Choucri states that, "There is a continual lack of awareness by both policy-making and academic communities of the close links between population and security. It would be the height of myopia to continue to disregard the increasing evidence concerning the relationship of population variables to conflict dynamics." With her second statement, I completely agree. However, with the first statement, I disagree.

I believe that there is no lack of awareness among policy-makers or academic communities of the population-security relationship. It is not lack of awareness but rather the *profound* conflict of massive proportions that immediately becomes apparent as soon as this relationship is recognized. Immediately, one realizes that the powerful religious institutions that actively oppose modern methods of birth control on the international, national, and local levels are themselves threats to national and international security and peace. Only a few have had the courage to speak up and then only briefly. In the meantime, this great threat to security and peace continues to increase and remains unattended, but recognized.

Population and Conflict is a major contribution to the world population literature. It should be considered required reading by all concerned with either population policy or security policy, though, admittedly, the writing style may make it a little difficult for persons who learned English as a second language.

Stephen D. Mumford

I anticipated that there might be trouble with the next to the last paragraph. But to offer any other explanation would be merely misleading the reader and an exercise in intellectual dishonesty. Within this paragraph lies the heart of the world population problem.

On October 10, 1983, I received a call from a person who identified himself as Hugh O'Hare, an editor with *Populi* magazine. Approximately 70 percent of the Catholic component of the anti-abortion movement in the United States is Irish as is the proportion of U.S. Catholic bishops. The leadership of the anti-abortion movement is almost entirely Irish, despite the fact that only 20 percent of the Catholic population in the United States is of Irish descent. As soon as I heard the name, I thought to myself, "This book review is dead." I asked him if there was a problem with the book review. He replied that he only needed to clarify how I had made the calculation that population assistance amount to only 0.18 percent of the world military expenditure. This I did. I also offered that I was a little concerned that the next to last paragraph might give somebody a little problem. He responded that he thought that the review was just excellent and that he did not think there would be any problems.

Two weeks later, I got a second call from O'Hare. I thought to myself, "This is it. It's dead." However, he said that he only wanted to reword one sentence and wanted my approval for the change, which I gave. He again said that he thought it was an excellent review and that he anticipated no further problems. He said that a book review was a set of opinions, that I was asked for my opinions, and that I have the right to express them.

On November 7, 1983, Hugh O'Hare called for the third and final time—with some bad news. He said that there had been a mix-up. UNFPA has two publications—*Population*, the UNFPA newsletter, and *Populi* magazine—with the same readership and mailing list. He had discovered that another editor, unknown to him, had asked someone else to review the Choucri book for *Population* and that this review had been published just the day before (September 1982, 9:9:4). It would be inappropriate to publish a second review even though it was to appear in *Populi*. He mentioned that he had read my articles on population and the Catholic Church (chapters four and five) and that he could understand how I might be suspicious of the turn of events. He wanted to "assure" me that this was mere coincidence.

I read the published review. Written in the style used by Monsignor James McHugh or writers at the Catholic League for Religious and Civil Rights, the techniques for deprecation were clearly recognizable. The anonymous reviewer was able to find a few sentences and phrases in the work of some forty-eight pages that, when taken out of context, support the Vatican position. To fully appreciate the extent to which the reviewer went to mislead the reader concerning the link between population and conflict, one must read Choucri's serious and profound book. The attempt to undermine and make light of Choucri's work is not subtle. The reader is actually discouraged from pursuing the author's argument. There is no suggestion of how a copy might be obtained. The entire review reads as follows:

> There are no simple connections to be made between population and conflict, as Professor Choucri is quick to point out:
>
> "Population size, growth, and density do not in themselves lead to conflict. Population increase is not in itself the source of crowding, stress, and conflict. Although there is some relationship between crowding and pathological conditions, there initially must be a "critical mass," [that is] a population "at risk" amenable to violence or using violence as a preferred strategy."
>
> So much for laboratory rats. Professor Choucri, professor of political science at MIT and the acknowledged leader in the

study of population and conflict, takes her conclusions about the roots of conflict from the evidence of the conflict themselves—191 of them between 1945 and 1980. The evidence is very patchy, as she admits, and the conclusions are therefore tentative, but some demographic connections can be determined. Among them are the effect of population composition and distribution, which seem to be more important than mere size. Change tends to exacerbate the effects of size, but "size and change factors seldom have more than background significance because their effects are long-term and indirect." Nevertheless, rapid change "invariably generates problems that go beyond those derived from an increase in numbers alone."

Hence Professor Choucri's conclusion that "thorough consideration of the consequences of rapid and pervasive demographic change is essential to the formulation of viable domestic and international, social, and economic policies. . . . The incidence of peace, and peaceful resolution of conflict situations, rest most profoundly on an initial understanding of conflict-producing dynamics."

The heart of the booklet—which is itself only a short summary—is contained in ten "central propositions," which set out tersely the state of knowledge in the field. Readers will look forward to Professor Choucri's forthcoming collection, *Multiple Dimensions of Population Conflict: Theory and Evidence.*

This was but one of innumerable acts of censorship of population information carried out by those Catholics obedient to the hierarchy within the population establishment during the past two decades. They are free to do this because the lay press submits to censorship by the Catholic hierarchy and is unwilling to print stories such as this one. Thus the Church is allowed to act with impunity.

The Murphys, Sullivans, Zablockis, Gilligans, Donaldsons, Ganlys, and O'Haras all appear to be responding to the call of the Catholic bishops in their 1975 Pastoral Plan of Action (*see,* appendix two) for laypersons to undertake action to ensure "adoption of administrative policies that will restrict the practice of abortion as much as possible." The ultimate goal is to eliminate all effective contraception practices as well.

Notes

1. M. Barone and G. Ujifusa, *The Almanac of American Politics 1984* (Washington National Journal), p. 612.

2. Paul Blanshard, *American Freedom and Catholic Power* (Boston: The Beacon Press, 1950), p. 77.

3. Ibid., pp. 75–76.

4. Ibid., p. 77.

5. Ibid., p. 213.

6. Ibid., p. 77.

7. Ibid., p. 185.

8. Ibid., p. 209.

9. Ibid., p. 230.

10. Ibid., p. 231.

11. Ibid., p. 214.

12. Ibid., p. 270.

13. Ibid., p. 271.

14. Father James J. O'Toole, *What Is Catholic Action?* (Paulist Press, 1940). Imprimatur Bishop of Toledo.

15. Blanshard, *American Freedom and Catholic Power*, p. 271.

16. Ibid., p. 272.

17. Father Arthur McCormack, "Roman Catholic Perspectives on Population Ethics, *The Draper Fund Report* (1983), 12:22.

18. *Osservatore Romano* (December 6, 1982).

19. J. Mann, "Globetrotting Pope: What Drives Him?" *U.S. News and World Report* (March 21, 1983), p. 22.

20. *INTERCOM* (January 1976), 4:1:13.

9.

The Catholic Hierarchy and Freedom of the Press in 1984: The Example of the Durham Morning Herald

As the old saying goes, "secrecy is power." Secrecy is the Roman Catholic Church's single greatest source of political power, and great care is taken to protect this source of power. For population growth control, this secrecy is of major importance.

Censorship of the American press by the hierarchy is extensive. Almost never does an American see a negative comment about the Church. Not that the Church is all goodness, though we have all developed this image to some extent, and this image is certainly nurtured by the Church. We are under a constant barrage of positive comments about the Catholic Church and are protected from negative information by the Church. This is not by accident.

Research conducted by James G. Stewart, Jr., for his master's degree in radio, television, and motion pictures at the University of North Carolina produced some rather astounding results.[1] He reviewed the transcripts of the three national networks for the eleven-year period from 1972 through 1982 to identify, count, and analyze stories about religion in the United States. He discovered vast disparities in the amount of coverage given the different denominations. He found that Roman Catholics, who comprise 44 percent of the national church membership (and about 22 percent of the church-going membership)[2] received 56.4 percent of the network reports. On the other hand, Baptists, Methodists, Presbyterians, and Lutherans, who together represent about 33 percent of the American church-going population, all together attracted only 2.3 percent of the coverage.

This twenty-five to one ratio, despite the fact that these four Protestant denominations collectively have about 50 percent more church-goers (as opposed to members) leaves little doubt that this arrangement is by design. The coverage of the Roman Catholic Church by these three networks is clearly being manipulated, no doubt from within. Virtually all of the coverage is positive. This grossly unbalanced cover-age gives a disproportionate amount of power and influence to the Catholic Church. This, likewise, is no doubt by the design of the Catholic hierarchy.

It is not so much this extensive effort by the Church to accentuate the positive that threatens America, though this does create a gap between perception and reality that is never healthy. Instead, it is the repression of the publication of the negative that is threatening. The *Durham Morning Herald*, a newspaper published in my home state of North Carolina, offers a good example of this censorship in regard to chapters one through five of this book, an example repeated a thou-sand times or more every year all around the country. While the *Herald* is spotlighted here, its behavior is no different from virtually all other newspapers in the country. This series of letters is most revealing.

My first encounter with the *Herald* followed the mailing by Werner Fornos of my monograph (appearing here as chapter one) to the *Herald*. An editorial, "The Population Challenge," by staff writer Jerry Gentry (October 27, 1980), was prompted by that mailing. This editorial was very positive and of a kind that I had hoped the monograph would generate.

The Population Challenge

Dr. Stephen D. Mumford is a Research Triangle Park scientist who worries about demographic disaster. He says it will take great effort from a "highly influential and respected organization" to avoid the cataclysm, according to *Popline*, the monthly publica-tion of the Washington-based Population Action Council.

Dr. Mumford suggests creating a superagency, one on the order of the National Aeronautics and Space Administration, to attack the problem of global overpopulation. Such an organiza-tion would need "unwavering commitments from other coun-tries" and be able to "command whatever resources deemed necessary to achieve its final goal."

The reality of population pressures is scarcely disputable—yet the solution is highly controversial for it touches basic human emotions. Dr. Mumford says, "The inevitability of widespread social and political chaos in the face of continued unprecedented 2 percent population growth for the next two decades makes population growth the single greatest threat to world peace. . . .

The effective opposition to population growth control activities by the Roman Catholic Church has clearly been the single greatest deterrent."

Anti-abortion and pro-life advocates are not to be dismissed. Their religiously based objections to birth control are known—their energy demonstrated.

While the opposing sides argue, the problem persists and grows ever more salient and irreversible.

Dr. Mumford has thrown a challenge to the United States for leadership in this field. From his office in the International Fertility Research Program in the Park, he sounds the alarm and calls for action.

It behooves each of us to reflect and respond.

Three years passed before any reference to my work appeared again. Then on October 3, 1983, John Adams, editorial page editor, in response to the article appearing as chapter four of this book, wrote the following editorial:

A Classic Failure to Understand

Is God liberal, conservative, or apolitical? You can hear all three views from within Christendom—sometimes sitting side by side in the same pew. Likewise, the non-church world, as St. Paul says, eagerly awaits the revelation of the sons of God—particularly as they line up in political camps. But more often it reaches conclusions without revelation.

Such is the case with *The Humanist*, the unabashedly anti-Christian magazine of the American Humanist Association. In its July/August edition, the magazine dredges up old scare tactics—similar to those used by the Ku Klux Klan—to warn of the power of the Vatican.

The article's most ridiculous assertion is that the Vatican seeks to repress birth control measures to increase its proportionate population in the United States and thereby "exercise much greater, if not complete, control over the American democratic process."

The Humanist further says that Jerry Falwell's Moral Majority is simply a Vatican front, despite Falwell's claims of autonomy. The magazine says the Vatican seeks not to settle moral issues but to soak up power, and that issues like abortion are not moral at all—that consensus determines morality.

With that notion, *The Humanist* fails completely to understand the fabric of Protestant, Catholic, Jewish, Islamic, or any great religion. Religion is by nature rebellious to human consensus. Indeed, matters of urgency are not matters of choice but predetermined by the God religious people worship.

That their interpretations and actions vary perhaps exemplifies the fuzziness of their understanding or their unwillingness to be obedient to the faith they profess. But it should not—and does not—suggest that political power is their goal, as *The Humanist* says.

The pew is the sometimes searing seat of those who seek righteousness—not by consensus but by divine imputation. That they would leave the same pews and sometimes clash in the political playground is not evidence of a power grab but frequently of the seriousness with which they seek to make their faith come alive.

This editorial is decidely religious in orientation. I would have ignored it had I not been seriously misrepresented in the third paragraph. I immediately prepared a response and mailed it. After two weeks, my reply had not been printed. I called the newspaper and learned that no one had seen it. It was apparently "lost."

To ensure that this did not happen again, I hand carried it to the paper and I stopped in to see Gentry while in the editorial office. We discussed recent events in my life, and then I was introduced to Adams. He made it very clear that he was strongly opposed to abortion. He indicated that he was pro-Moral Majority and not Catholic.

Adams made one completely revealing statement, "I disagree with everything you are saying." Adams did not like being told that world population growth is a national security threat and that abortion is a national security issue. He did not like to draw the obvious conclusion that a person who works to restrict the availability of abortion threatens the security of the United States. In order to avoid facing up to this dilemma, he chose to reject *everything* I was saying. By doing so, Adams now serves as a censor, in effect, for the readers of the *Durham Morning Herald*. When he sees something that supports what I am saying, he rejects it, and his readers are deprived of the information. This is done to reinforce his own decisions against abortion. Unfortunately for Americans and truth, hundreds of his fellow journalists who are anti-abortion behave similarly. A whole body of information is rejected outright because it threatens this religious belief.

The Catholic hierarchy, in part through the Moral Majority organization, encourages this sort of conduct or censorship by news media personnel, whether or not they are Catholic. The hierarchy has gone to great lengths to make this sort of censorship acceptable.

During my meeting with Gentry and Adams, we also discussed my recent firing due to Catholic political pressure. Gentry showed a strong interest in doing an editorial on the firing and Adams approved. Adams did seem completely sincere regarding the obvious First Amendment violation of my dismissal. Gentry's editorial on my dismissal appeared November 6, 1983, and read as follows:

An Unconscionable Muzzling

A controversy of major proportions boils behind the firing of Dr. Stephen D. Mumford, population scientist of Chapel Hill. Until recently, he was on the staff of Family Health International, formerly the International Fertility Research Program in the Research Triangle Park.

Dr. Elton Kessel, founder of the Fertility Research program and a present board member, characterizes Dr. Mumford as "one of the most valuable people in the organization."

Yet Dr. Mumford was summarily fired. His presence on the staff was detrimental to the organization, he was told.

Dr. Mumford contends that the U.S. Agency for International Development threatened to cancel its contract with Family Health International unless he were fired. Since most of the Family Health International's budget comes from AID, the threat was no small consideration.

Dr. Mumford's "sin" apparently was his off-hours authorship of an article published in *The Humanist* magazine—an article in which Dr. Mumford accused the hierarchy of the Roman Catholic Church of subverting efforts at population control the world over.

The confrontation was predictable. Abortion and preventive pregnancy measures are not in line with official Catholic thinking even though many Catholics practice birth control.

The issue here is not whether a private organization can or should be able to fire whom it pleases. That is a given. Rather, it is a question of free speech without repercussions and, just as important, a matter of where the United States stands on population issues.

AID, a branch of the State Department, provides most of the money for international population work in this country, and half of the population money spent around the world comes from the same source.

This government, cognizant of the devastating global ramifications of overpopulation, committed itself years ago to seeking solutions.

But groups like the Moral Majority and the U.S. Coalition

for Life are pressuring the Reagan administration, as are Catholic bureaucrats within the government, to reverse itself.

Dr. Mumford is one who sees the dangers of such a course and speaks up. He lost his livelihood for his efforts.

It isn't fair.

Three days later, my reply to Adams's editorial of October 3 was published and read as follows:

Editorial's Facts Out of Context

To the Editor:

Your October 3 editorial, "A Classic Failure to Understand," attacked an article appearing in the July/August edition of *The Humanist* magazine, "The Catholic Church and Social Justice Issues."

You stated, "The article's most ridiculous assertion is that the Vatican seeks to repress birth control measures to increase its proportionate population in the United States and thereby 'exercise much greater, if not complete, control over the American democratic process.' "

The second half of this sentence was taken completely out of context. This phrase is found in the illegal immigration control section.

It is a major fact that 90 percent of all illegal aliens are Catholic. In October 1979, in a major address in New York, Pope John Paul II proclaimed that all aliens have the right to illegally immigrate to the United States. He made his stand clear to American politicians and labor unions, the American Catholic hierarchy, and the news media.

An estimated 10 to 15 million illegal aliens live here and their presence accounts for most of our unemployment.

In a recent article [en]titled, "Illegal Immigration, National Security, and the Church," I estimated that during 1980–2000, 161 million aliens would attempt to illegally immigrate here, seriously undermining our national security. Almost 90 percent will be Catholics, giving the church a near majority.

As a long-time close observer of the anti-illegal immigration control movement, I am certain the energy, organization, and direction of this movement is the Catholic Church.

Early [last] week, a top lobbyist estimated the chances of passage of a good law at eighty/twenty. Then in a brilliant move, the Church called on their faithful, "Tip" O'Neill, who smoothly killed this legislation for this year and the next, allowing 5 to

6 million more in to take jobs from Americans.

On your other point, Falwell's claim not to be a front for the Catholic Church doesn't make it so. I wish you would have attacked the facts presented in evidence.

Stephen Mumford

At this point, I thought that my interaction with the *Herald* was finished. Then on November 26, 1983, the following character assassination appeared, written by William F. Hunt, Jr., a Catholic:

Anti-Catholic Article Was Distortion of Facts

In contrast to Stephen Mumford, I strongly agree with your editorial of October 3, which criticized an anti-Catholic hate article in the magazine, *The Humanist*.

Your characterization of the magazine as anti-Christian could not be more accurate.

In the January/February 1983 edition of *The Humanist*, John Dunphy, in discussing the role of the public school teacher, says, "The teachers must embody the same selfless dedication as the most rabid fundamentalist preachers, for they will be ministers of another sort, utilizing a classroom instead of a pulpit to convey humanistic values in whatever subjects they teach. The classroom must and will become an arena of conflict between old and new— the rotting corpse of Christianity, together with all its adjacent evils and misery, and the new faith of humanism."

Their anti-Christian values are clear, but what's extremely frightening is their stated intention to use the schools to impose their beliefs.

Mr. Mumford's assertion that the Catholic Church is a threat to the national security of the United States is both ignorant and insulting. Interestingly enough, his letter was published very near to Veteran's Day, which serves as a reminder to all Americans of those who have fought and died for their country.

Catholics have fought and died for our country in every war we have fought in. For these fine patriots to be slandered by Mr. Mumford is an outrage to their memory and to our country! Think of the Catholic Americans serving in our armed forces who have died in Lebanon and Grenada. Are they a threat to our national security or are they an important part of it?

In his letter, Mr. Mumford presented what he called facts. His so-called facts, however, are an exercise in distortion. He fails to present the truth because he is blinded by his rabid anti-

Catholicism. He refers to a so-called good immigration law, which he says was defeated by the Catholic Church. He fails to say that the bill was cosponsored by a Catholic, Congressman Romano Mazzolli, and that official Catholic spokesmen said the bill had both good and bad features. A Catholic in good conscience could either support or work toward the defeat of his bill.

He blames Pope John Paul II for the illegal immigration from Mexico and has taken out of context a statement made by the pope concerning the rights of people to seek a better life and safer environment when their basic freedoms are denied—witness the Jews in Nazi Germany or in the Soviet Union today or the boat people from Vietnam. Would Mr. Mumford deny them the right to emigrate?

His suggestion that the Reverend Jerry Falwell is a front for the Catholic Church is laughable. The fact that the Reverend Falwell and Catholics both believe in Jesus Christ as the Son of God, the importance of the family, their country, and that abortion is wrong does not make one a front for the other.

In summary, Mr. Mumford's diatribe against the Catholic Church is reminiscent of the scare tactics of the Ku Klux Klan with echoes of Bob Jones.

William F. Hunt, Jr.

Frankly, I was surprised that the *Herald* would publish this obvious hate letter. Adams, in a phone conversation several weeks later, told me that in Hunt's original letter there were five different statements that were obviously slanderous and that he had helped Hunt rewrite it in order to remove these statements. Hunt's letter offers nothing but character assassination, and Adams wanted to make clear his position by publishing it. The Hunt letter does not identify Hunt as Catholic, a fact that would have helped *Herald* readers understand his motivation.

I immediately wrote a reply to the Hunt letter. After a month, it had not yet appeared, and neither had a letter written by William Harnack, associate editor of *The Humanist*. I contacted Adams who said that he was not going to publish any more letters from me or about my work. I strongly objected to his publishing an assault on my character and then refusing to allow me to respond to this diatribe. I reminded him of the paper's own editorial on fairness and balance in the press that had appeared a few days earlier. He refused to reconsider. A few days later, I took my argument to Michael Rouse, managing editor of the *Herald*, who agreed that my argument for publication of my reply was reasonable and sound. Because of vacations, he would not see Adams for ten days. He told me to contact Adams on the following Monday and that he would leave a note for Adams. When I talked with Adams, he agreed to publish my reply but he wanted to make it very clear that he was only doing it under duress, reading Rouse's entire note to me over the phone as a form of protest. Both my reply and Harnack's reply appeared on January 5, 1984, as follows:

Attack was "Psychic Terrorism"

To the Editor:

William F. Hunt, Jr.'s, November 6 letter directs vicious hate propaganda at me personally, not a very Christian act.

However, his letter is more than this. It is an act of psychic terrorism directed at all readers. It serves to terrorize newspaper reporters and others so that they dare not take a critical look at Catholic Church positions in American and world affairs that the Church prefers go unexamined. It reminds all that, if they do, they are under the threat of being branded as rabidly anti-Catholic.

I have chosen to disagree with the Catholic hierarchy because of its positions on population growth control issues. For this, Mr. Hunt labels me as rabidly anti-Catholic.

Consider the fact that despite the Catholic hierarchy position against abortion and effective contraception, American Catholics and non-Catholics are using abortion and contraception equally. Then, using Mr. Hunt's definition, are not most American Catholics anti-Catholic, since they are not only speaking against the Catholic hierarchy, they are acting against it?

It is a fact that the best interest of the United States and the best interest of the Vatican are not always the same. Likewise, it's a fact that our National Security Council (NSC) has determined through extensive study that world population [growth] is a serious threat to U.S. security and the security of all other nations. Their findings were published in NSC reports in 1979 and 1980.

It is also a fact that the Roman Catholic hierarchy is seriously thwarting world population growth control. The obvious conclusion is that the Catholic hierarchy is seriously threatening the security of the United States.

The NSC dropped the study of this new threat when Mr. Reagan took office. I am concerned because his three national security advisers are all Catholics, as have been his two secretaries of state. His CIA director, his attorney general, and his HHS secretary likewise are all Catholics. These are the key people in the Reagan administration most responsible for the population security issue. The odds that this arrangement happened by chance are nil. There has been some "divine" guidance.

The American realization that overpopulation does seriously threaten U.S. security is a threat to the Catholic hierarchy itself. For this reason, this new threat to our national security is being covered up. Many reputable people believe the threat of overpopulation is greater than the nuclear threat, a view your "Day After" [November 21] editorial suggests that you agree with. Labeling me as rabidly anti-Catholic for pointing out these facts is a sham.

Stephen D. Mumford

"Humanist" Favors Student Freedom

To the Editor:

William F. Hunt's intemperate remarks about *The Humanist* and Dr. Stephen Mumford [November 26], a courageous man who has suffered personally for his concern for millions of starving children and for the future of the world, are unfortunate and, indeed, contradictory to the *Morning Herald*'s fine and accurate editorial, "An Unconscionable Muzzling," in which is mentioned "free speech without repercussions." Mr. Hunt's comments comprise not criticism but personal attack. Dr. Mumford can and has ably answered for himself; I just wish to clear up some of Mr. Hunt's misconceptions concerning *The Humanist*.

First, in answer to the oft-quoted-by-fundamentalists quote of John Dunphy concerning teaching humanism in the schools: As quoted, this is Mr. Dunphy's view, not necessarily that of the editors or of most humanists. It has been repeatedly taken out of context by fundamentalist writers.

The Humanist supports not indoctrination but just the opposite—incorporation of humanistic values in the classroom—that is, freedom of the student to learn in an unfettered and nondogmatic environment. Mr. Dunphy's phrase "teaching humanism" to describe this was perhaps unfortunate, but Mr. Hunt's stooping to the level of fundamentalist propagandists is deliberate and, I feel, far more offensive.

Also, his description of Dr. Mumford's articles as hateful and his bringing Catholic patriots into his argument is beneath the standards of the *Herald*. Neither Dr. Mumford nor *The Humanist* is anti-Catholic or anti-Christian per se—we are pro-rationality and a livable and secure future for humankind.

William J. Harnack

Once again, I thought that my interactions with the *Herald* were finished. However, on January 16, 1984, the Catholic hierarchy officially responded to my reply. The response was penned by Stephen Settle of the Catholic League for Religious and Civil Rights in Milwaukee, Wisconsin, the hierarchy's "anti-defamation" office. It was another hate letter aimed at character assassination and very similar to the first one. Like Hunt's letter, it was strictly a personal attack and did not address any significant issues.

Try Annihilating the Poor to End Their Problems?

To the Editor:

In his letter of January 5, Stephen Mumford takes William F. Hunt, Jr., to task for committing "psychic terrorism." As a friend of Bill for several years, I can personally assure the readers that Mr. Hunt is no terrorist, either of the "psychic" variety or otherwise.

Moreover, having been an avid if not sympathetic witness to Dr. Mumford's zealous Catholic-baiting ever since his career with *The Humanist* began, it seems obvious that whatever bombs are going off in his head are self-detonated, the product of his own fevered imagination.

On the same page, Mumford's defender and co-communicant in the humanist faith, William J. Harnack, castigates Hunt for "stooping to the level of fundamentalist propagandists." Yet it is Mumford and his humanist cronies, not Hunt, who reflect the ultimate in sectarian fantasies, the spectre of Vatican conspiracy and takeover.

Mumford's tirades evince little more than that old-time backwoods paranoia given a modern secularist twist. Indeed, he has pursued his anti-Catholic witch hunt with a homiletic fervor to rival and surpass the Bob Joneses.

Finally, Harnack's reference to Mumford's "concern for millions of starving children" is insipid at best, on par with Hitler's "concern" for millions of displaced Jews. In their advocacy of massive sterilization and abortion as a cure for the world's ills, we are privy to the sordid world view of the social-Darwinist humanist elite.

Theirs is a campaign to eliminate the problems of the poor by annihilating the poor themselves. Though Mumford's single-minded obsession with the activities of the Catholic Church may not tell us much about the church, it does expose the shameless fanaticism with which some promote what they call "population control" as a veritable holy war against the world's unwanted.

Stephen Settle

Again I prepared a reply and sent it to Adams. Again he refused to publish it and again told me that he disagrees with *everything* I am saying in my publications. My unpublished reply read as follows:

To the Editor   January 17, 1984

In his letter of January 16, Catholic Church official Stephen Settle of Milwaukee provides another example of "psychic terrorism" as discussed in my January 5 letter. In his five paragraphs, Mr. Settle calls me no less than eighteen bad names and implies that I am crazy before my family and community. He directs his message to newspaper reporters and readers who might be inclined to recognize the logic and truth in what I am saying and dares them to repeat the truth. Psychic terrorism—except this time it comes from the official Church.

Mr. Settle's vicious hate propaganda is so similar to Mr. Hunt's letter (November 6) that one might suspect that both letters were written by the same person. Both are devoid of discussion of the issues and both attempt character assassination.

Mr. Settle reinforces two of the points I make in my January 5 letter which he attacks. The first is that the Catholic Church uses "psychic terrorism" to counter any criticism of the Church no matter how valid. The second point is that the Church is actively opposing population growth control.

In my January 5 letter, I state that it is a fact that the best interest of the United States and the best interest of the Vatican are not always the same. Likewise, it's a fact that our National Security Council has determined that world population growth is a serious threat to U.S. security and the security of all nations. It is also a fact that the Catholic hierarchy is seriously thwarting world population growth control. The obvious conclusion is that the Catholic hierarchy is seriously threatening the security of the United States.

These are the issues. Yet, Mr. Settle ignores them. I would assume because he fears that my statements are true. Instead, he chooses to follow the usual Catholic hierarchy response and flatly dismisses reality. He elects "psychic terrorism" to frighten newspaper editors and readers who might think about these issues which concern our national security and who might wish to write a response. We can join the Vatican and ignore these vital issues, but for how long and at what price?

Again I called on Michael Rouse. We talked at length about the official Catholic response. "Fairness" and "balance" seemed to be of lesser concern this time. He firmly believed that the Settle letter did not constitute character assassination.

Then I showed Rouse a letter I had received from Robert F. Butz, a local scientist, dated January 17, 1984, as well as a copy of a letter-to-the-editor sent by Butz to the *Herald*.

Dear Mr. Mumford   January 17, 1984

Accompanying this note is a copy of a letter which I intend to send to the editor of the *Durham Morning Herald* on January 18, 1984.

As I mentioned during our telephone conversation this evening, Messrs. Hunt's and Settle's approach is inappropriate and embarrassing to me personally as a member of the Catholic Church. I'm glad you realize that theirs is a position which to my knowledge is not shared by the majority of the people at Holy Infant Catholic Church.

I applaud your courage and professionalism in addressing this important topic in such a thorough manner and hope that your critics will from now on aim their salvos at your points rather than at your person. For the record, please consider that Bill Hunt is a decent, concerned fellow whose objectivity has been hampered by an unfortunate bout of emotionalism. I've suffered from that ailment myself on occasion.

Sincerely,
Robert F. Butz, Ph.D.

cc: James Behan, O.S.F.S.

Rouse was deeply impressed with Butz's letter-to-the-editor. Adams had not shared this remarkable letter, also dated January 17, with him. It reads as follows:

Dear Editor, *Durham Morning Herald*   January 17, 1984

I note with concern and dismay the recent responses in this column by Messrs. William Hunt and Stephen Settle to a *Humanist* magazine article by Dr. Stephen Mumford entitled "Population Growth and Global Security." In this article Dr. Mumford expresses his views on the relationship between population growth and national security, the role of American leadership in resolving the problem, and the purported impact of Roman Catholic doctrine with regard to the matter.

I hold no brief for Dr. Mumford and feel that a thoughtful reader may legitimately take issue with some of the views expressed in the article. Clearly, this controversial article has stimulated lively discussion, a result which I would guess was anticipated and welcomed by Dr. Mumford. However, while the article is critical of the policies of the Roman Catholic Church regarding population issues and political influence, I find in it no basis for Messrs. Hunt's and Settle's charges of rabid anti-Catholic sentiment on the part of the author. Rather than addressing the points in *The Humanist* article with which they disagree, both Mr. Hunt and Mr. Settle unfortunately have chosen to attack the motives and integrity of Dr. Mumford. Such an *ad hominem* approach serves neither to rebut Dr. Mumford nor support the position held by Messrs. Hunt and Settle, but rather merely reflects unfavorably on those who adopt it.

As a member of the church attended by Mr. Hunt, whom I have come to know and admire, and previously attended by Mr. Settle, I urge these well-intentioned gentlemen to adopt a calmer and more thoughtful approach in their increasingly public debate with Dr. Mumford.

Yours truly,
Robert F. Butz

cc: William Hunt
Stephen Settle
Stephen Mumford, Ph.D.
James Behan, O.S.F.S.

I believe that there are millions of thinking Catholic Americans just like Butz, who have retained freedom of thought and do not blindly follow Vatican teaching. However, members of the hierarchy are promoted into and up through the hierarchy because they are the most obedient and they blindly follow commands, having surrendered their freedom of thought. The Hunts and Settles, who have acted in like manner, rely upon the higher ranking hierarchy to do their thinking for them, victims of a successful Catholic educational system and its "programming" practices. The hierarchy then uses them to attack anyone who attempts to thwart its agenda so that the clergy are not identified with these attacks and their hands remain clean. From outward appearances, the Hunts and Settles are merely the tip of a great Catholic uprising, when in fact they no doubt represent less than 5 percent of the Church membership. As mentioned in chapter seven, great care is taken by these activists to give the appearance that they represent far greater numbers than they really do in order to terrorize the American press.

When I left Rouse that evening, he told me that he did not think that I should have a chance to respond to Settle's attack and that he would not publish my reply. However, he did indicate that he would publish Butz's letter to the editor and that he would speak with Adams about it the next day. After two weeks, Butz's letter had not been published, and, indeed, it never was. Unfortunately, the Butzes have absolutely no influence within the Church because the Church is in no way a democratic institution. The only way that the Butzes can influence the course of events is through the Rouses. However, if the Rouses are so intimidated that they will not let the Butzes speak, then we are at an impasse—exactly where the Church hierarchy wants Protestant America to be.

Notes

1. O. Williamson, "Network Religious Coverage Disporportionate," *Chapel Hill Newspaper* (January 1, 1984), p. 9A.
2. G. Gallup, "The Gallup Poll," *Chapel Hill Newspaper* (January 1, 1984), p. 5A.

10.

Influence of the Catholic Hierarchy on Government Policy

The Reagan administration is the most Catholic administration in American history. Yet few Americans are aware of this. Why all the secrecy? Why has this fact never been mentioned in the press, particularly in light of the Reagan agenda?

About 4 percent of Americans are of Irish Roman Catholic descent. Ronald Reagan's father was and his brother is Roman Catholic. The president has never been very active in any faith; however, all but two of Reagan's key appointees concerned with the national security/population growth control issues have been Irish Roman Catholics. They include: his three national security advisers, Allen, Clark, and McFarlane; CIA Director Casey; Secretary of State Haig; Health and Human Services Secretary Heckler; and Attorney-General Smith. One exception is Schultz, who is a Roman Catholic of German extraction; the other was Schweiker, not a Catholic.

What of other critical positions in the administration? At the cabinet level, other Catholics are Secretary of the Treasury Donald Regan and Secretary of Labor Raymond Donovan. Also, Reagan appointed Sandra Day O'Connor to the Supreme Court and Ann Gorsuch to the post of EPA administrator. Both are of Irish descent.

Since only 4 percent of Americans are Catholics of Irish descent, it would seem that this particular ethnic group is grossly overrepresented in the seats of power. The odds of this happening by chance are nil.

Making this disturbing is the makeup of the Church hierarchy. Although descendants of Irish immigrants to this country constitute only 20 percent of the nation's Catholics, the roots of American Catholic bishops are mainly in Ireland. They are unquestionably the most politically aggressive element of the Church. Their ethnic group was strongly favored by the person who put the Reagan team together. My concern is that this person was not Mr. Reagan. What makes this arrangement so troubling are the marked similarities between the Reagan agenda and the Vatican agenda.

The Vatican Agenda vs. the Reagan Agenda

Few Americans realize that the Vatican and Reagan agendas are, despite minor disagreement, virtually identical. Let us look at the record.

Table I shows the Vatican and Reagan Administration positions on twenty-four of the most controversial issues of the past three years. It is difficult to find a single example of disagreement between them. The president has made no secret of the fact that he calls on the pope for guidance in the governing of America. In chapter four, I have quoted his incredible statement before the National Catholic Education Association in April 1982: "I am grateful for your help in shaping American policy to reflect God's will . . . and I will look forward to further guidance from His Holiness Pope John Paul II during an audience I will have with him in June."[1] After this one-hour private meeting at the Vatican on June 7, he said that the Catholic Church "pursues the same goals of peace, freedom, and humanity." Reagan added that he wanted the U.S. government "to work closely with the Church in Latin America . . . to prevent the spread of repression and godless tyranny." He also invited the pope to visit the United States again, saying, "There is a great need for such a visit."[2] In May, they met in Alaska. In his March 8, 1983, speech before the National Association of Evangelicals, Reagan expressed himself in terms normally reserved for use by Catholic clergy: "I urge you to beware of the temptation . . . to ignore . . . the aggressive impulses of an evil empire, to . . . thereby remove yourself from the struggle between right and wrong, good and evil."[3] During a speech to a group of conservatives on February 18, 1983, Reagan made the statement that the attempted assassination of the pope was "an assault on God." Can it be that the president receives the words of the pope as if they were actually words or instructions direct from God?

On August 6, 1984, columnist Mary McGrory offered that Mr. Reagan comes on as more Catholic than the Pope:

Catholic issues seem to consume him. . . . Reagan's motivation

TABLE I

The Vatican and Reagan Administration Positions on Selected Issues

Issue	Position of Vatican	Position of Administration
1. Abortion	anti	anti
2. Equal Rights Amendment	anti	anti
3. School prayer	pro	pro
4. Domestic family planning	anti	anti
5. International population assistance	anti	anti
6. Constitutional convention	pro	pro
7. Tuition tax credits (parochiaid)	pro	pro
8. *Global 2000 Report*	anti	anti
9. Kahn/Simon Report	pro	pro
10. Environment	anti	anti
11. Communism	rabidly anti	rabidly anti
12. Sex education	anti	anti
13. Family planning for teenaged youth	anti	anti
14. Grenada invasion	pro	pro
15. U.S. military support for El Salvador and other Central American governments	pro	pro
16. U.S. military involvement in Lebanon	pro	pro
17. American hard line against the Soviet Union	pro	pro
18. United Nations and its agencies	anti	anti
19. Support of repressive governments in Latin America	pro	pro
20. Population growth as a national security threat	anti	anti
21. Gay civil rights	anti	anti
22. Federal aid to public education	anti	anti
23. Illegal immigration	pro	given the administration's neglect, must assume pro
24. Strict separation of church and state	anti	anti

now seems to be his inability to tolerate the "oppression of the Church" to which the Pope has attested. . . . John Kennedy may be smiling somewhere at the sight of an American president wrapping himself in the arms of Holy Mother Church. . . . By contrast, Reagan is going out of his way to show that *with him there is no separation of church and state.* He wants it known that *there is a direct line between him and the Pope,* that he seeks counsel from the Vatican City. Reagan took the extraordinary step of inviting the Pope's ambassador, Pio Laghi, to his Santa Barbara ranch for consultation on delicate foreign policy questions.[4] [emphasis added]

In a prepared address to an ecumenical prayer breakfast attended by twelve thousand religious leaders and delegates to the Republican National Convention, Mr. Reagan challenged the constitutional premise of separation of church and state. "The truth is, politics and morality are inseparable, and as morality's foundation is religion, religion and politics are necessarily related." A report on this speech stated that "his remarks put him squarely in the camp of the funda-mentalist religious right," implying that this is not consistent with the Vatican camp. However, the Reverend Virgil C. Blum, president and founder of the Milwaukee-based Catholic League for Religious and Civil Rights, endorsed Reagan's church and state sentiments.[5]

The truth is that Mr. Reagan is just giving his blessing to a reality. The Vatican has for decades ignored the constitutional premise of separation of church and state though this situation has worsened since the publication of the Pastoral Plan for Prolife Activities in 1975. Columnist Mary McGrory, in an article on the unprecedented chal-lenge to the archbishop of New York by Governor Mario Cuomo, frankly stated that for a Catholic politician to publicly oppose the wishes of an archbishop is political suicide. She pointed out that Cuomo is the first Catholic politician to pick a fight with a prelate and that "it is the conventional wisdom that no politician wins in a fight with the Catholic Church."[6]

The Major Difference Between the United States and Latin American Countries

The vast disparities between Latin America and the United States should not exist. Both were settled by Europeans at about the same time. Both are rich in resources. But where a democratic form of government grew out of the British experience, and among its North American possessions the principle of separation of church and state had been fostered, Latin America reflected the authoritarian Spanish and Portuguese conquest of the countries to the south. The nature of these settlements was particularly distinctive in regard to religion. Many in the North had come to seek religious freedom, which they guarded jealously, insisting on separation of church and state. In Latin America, the new land was explored for its wealth and for conversions to Catholicism. The modern Catholic Church adheres to this day to this prerogative, this close alliance of government and religion. It acts in this country as if it has a moral obligation to influence, in whatever way it can, issues that are at variance with Catholic priorities. The Catholic Church disregards the fundamental American concept of separation of church and state, claiming a "divine right" to do so. I am deeply concerned about this state of affairs as it concerns over-population.

As a result of the Vatican's position and actions, our government is not dealing with the realities of overpopulation, including illegal immigration. Should the Vatican agenda be followed for even the next fifteen to twenty years, there will be no turning back for the U.S. The United States of North America will become a part of Latin America.

The Church and Divisiveness in America

Because the Catholic Church ignores the principle of separation of church and state, it is the most divisive force in America. The March 19, 1984, issue of *U.S. News and World Report* examined two secret Catholic elite religious societies in this country: the Knights of Malta with one thousand U.S. members who are prominent in government, business, or professional life and Opus Dei with three thousand members of widely varied backgrounds. The Knights of Malta organiza-tion dates back to the time of the Crusades; its members include some of our nation's most prominent Catholics: CIA Director William Casey; William Wilson; Vernon Walters; Senators Denton and Domenici; Alexander Haig; William Sloan; and William F. Buckley, creator and leader of Young Americans for Freedom, from which a large proportion of the Reagan administration team were drawn. Because many Knights and recipients of the Order's honors have worked in or around the CIA, critics sometimes suggest a link between the two. The CIA has been dominated by the Catholic hierarchy.

According to members, the order serves *"as an international defend-er of the Church."*[7] In June of each year a ceremony is held in Rome for Knights of Malta which includes the "swearing of allegiance to the defense of the Holy Mother Church."[8] Herein lies the problem for population growth control and its recognition as a national security issue. Population growth control seriously threatens the survival of the Vatican, as discussed in chapters one and four. Knights are committed to defending the Church. Only the most devout and obedient are invited to join the Knights and Opus Dei (which its detractors have compared to mind-controlling cults).[8] If the Vatican has determined that population growth control threatens the Holy Mother Church, the members of these societies are obliged to counter this threat by thwarting the development of population growth control government policies and their execution. It is inevitable that the best interests of the Vatican and those of the United States are not always going to be the same. For this reason, no one can possibly swear complete allegiance to both and mean it. The acts and attitudes of the Knights of Malta in the Reagan administration seem to reflect this complete allegiance to the Catholic Church rather than to our country.

This deep conflict has serious ramifications for population growth control. As long as it exists, it is not possible to effectively deal with the population problem. The real population problem is not convincing people that they must have small families or delivering the family planning services to them. *This we can most certainly achieve in just ten years for 95 percent of the world's population and at a price we can afford.* The real population problem is this conflict between the needs of the Church and the desperate needs of humanity to control its proliferation.

Consider the intensity of the commitment of these secret society members as "international defenders of the Church." It is hardly a secret that one of the most important American advances in "defending the Church" by Catholic elitists was the creation of the Central Intelligence Agency (CIA). The activities of the CIA go far beyond intelligence gathering of an international nature.[10] The CIA serves as an agency through which secret "assistance" to the Holy Mother Church can be provided by secret American society members acting as her defenders:

> During the CIA's formative years, Protestants predominated. . . .
> Somehow, however, Catholics wrested control of the CIA's
> covert-action section. It was no coincidence that some of the
> agency's more grandiose operations were in Catholic countries of
> Latin America and the Catholic regime of South Vietnam.[11]

For creating the Office of Strategic Services (OSS), the wartime predecessor to the CIA, and this special arrangement with the Vatican,

General William "Wild Bill" Donovan was decorated in July

1944 by Pope Pius XII with the Grand Cross of the Order of Saint Sylvester, the oldest and most prestigious of papal knighthoods. This award has been given to only one hundred other men in history, who, "by feat of arms or writings or outstanding deeds have spread the faith and have safeguarded and championed the Church."[12]

Donovan did more to safeguard and champion the Church than any other American, and he was rewarded for his services with the highest Catholic award ever received by an American. No doubt, thousands of others have striven with their deeds for similar recognition.

What has this meant in terms of the issues cited in Table I? Communism is the greatest threat faced by the Church. The Catholic Church and communism cannot coexist. They are both rival absolutists. Both indoctrinate their children so as to ensure complete rejection of the other. Columnist Robert Blair Kaiser who covered the Vatican for *Time* magazine had a conversation with Pope John XXIII in August 1962. "For too long, he [the pope] said, the Church had been waging a so-called holy war against the forces of communism. That was getting us nowhere."[13] This holy war continues in Central America today!

It is believed by some historians that the reason the Vatican aided Hitler in his rise to power was so that he could destroy Russian communism. When this failed, the Vatican through its defenders called upon the United States to stop the spread of Russian communism in Europe and elsewhere. A Vatican-inspired hate campaign against the Russians, the greatest hate campaign ever endured by Americans, was launched. To this day, like most other Americans, I am a victim of this campaign launched during my childhood.

In August 1984, President Reagan showed his intense hatred of the Russian people in his infamous radio microphone test, "My fellow Americans, I'm pleased to tell you today that I've signed legislation that would outlaw Russia forever. We begin bombing in five minutes." No doubt, this Vatican-inspired hate campaign has influenced Mr. Reagan.

By this theory, at a cost of hundreds of billions of American dollars, we built a war machine for the protection of Catholicism. For this same reason have we built a nuclear arsenal powerful enough to destroy the world five times over and have we seen the Russians match it? This is, I feel, in great part the origin of the other great threat to civilization—nuclear war. Hundreds of millions of dollars were spent to protect Catholicism from communism, and one can only conjecture about the ways in which the world would have been different if this money had been spent differently and if the first requests to the World

Health Organization by India for population growth control assistance had not been blocked by the Vatican thirty-four years ago.

Our commitment to saving the Catholic government in South Vietnam from communism (only 5 percent of the people of South Vietnam were Catholic,[14] causing some observers to refer to it as a Vatican colony) can be thought of as a result of the activities of the "U.S. Catholic defenders of the Church," largely members of the CIA. The French provided this same service to the Vatican for eighty years before they gave up on the holy war in Vietnam.[15]

A number of issues cited in Table I, including U.S. military support for El Salvador and other Central American governments, the Grenada invasion, and maintaining the status quo in Latin America can be seen as Vatican-inspired actions to prop up Catholic (Vatican-dominated) governments against popular uprisings. They are the "holy wars against communism" mentioned by Pope John XXIII. During a May 1984 fundraising visit to New York, the archbishop of Managua, Nicaragua, Miguel Obando y Bravo, said his campaign represented the best-organized opposition in Nicaragua to popular Sandinista government efforts.[16]

Another example is Lebanon. Most Americans are not aware of the closeness of the Gemayel government to the Vatican. "Maronite Christians," a minority group in Lebanon, are the Eastern Catholic Church. "The Maronites are in communion with Rome and have a college for the education of their clergy in Rome. In the year 1181, at the time of the Crusades, the Maronites . . . made peace with Rome and became attached to the Holy See."[17] Gemayel, like his politician father, was Jesuit trained in a Catholic university.[18] The Vatican wishes to see the Maronites continue to be the dominant power in Lebanon so that the only country in the Middle East in the Vatican sphere of influence will remain so. In all of these cases the Vatican, to maintain and expand its geographical control, seems to be calling upon the services of the U.S. Defense Department to serve as an instrument of Vatican foreign policy in much the same way it has in Cold War Europe.

My purpose in presenting this brief discussion of selected foreign policy initiatives of the Vatican is to show the lengths to which "defenders of the Church" in the Reagan administration are willing to go in order to "safeguard" the Church. To these "defenders," Vietnam, El Salvador, Grenada, and Lebanon are viewed in part as "holy wars for the preservation of the Church." They are unquestionably willing to go to similar lengths to protect the Church from population growth control activities.

Population scientists, field workers, and, more importantly, journalists must acknowledge the magnitude of this obstacle to solving the population problem and deal with this problem in its entirety—and without delay.

In the meantime, the Vatican is enhancing its political power through generating domestic divisiveness. The abortion issue is clearly the most important to the Church and one of the most contentious issues in American history. It has allowed the Church to mobilize (under the guise of an emotional or "moral" issue) many Catholics, though a minority of those in this country, for political purposes. But it has also given the Church the opportunity to mobilize a large number of non-Catholics, mostly Protestant fundamentalists, to serve the needs of the Vatican.

Just after the Reagan administration announced the radical change in U.S. population assistance policy, Senator Bradley of New Jersey sent out a press release dated August 8, 1984. He sharply condemned the Reagan administration policy change in the name of abortion restriction. "I cannot comprehend the logic of this new policy. It is not about abortion. What the policy is about *is denying support for family planning services*. . . . The administration's new policy will do a great deal to suppress family planning efforts . . ."[19] (emphasis added). The Vatican's real target here was family planning, and it expects Americans to be fooled by its strategy. *Most Protestant fundamentalists have no problem with family planning, but they have been used here by the Vatican to accomplish Vatican goals.*

Few fundamentalists are opposed to family planning, international population assistance, or illegal immigration control. Yet the Vatican uses its "Moral Majority" and the political force of the fundamentalists to undermine family planning, international population assistance, and illegal immigration control through this organization of lobbyists.

Federal aid to public education has always been opposed by the Church. Between 1925 and 1945, it was blocked by the Catholic lobby[20] because it enhances the disparity between Catholic education and public education and shifts some decision-making to the federal level where it is less susceptible to Church influence than at the local level. The Vatican is opposed to the United Nations and its agencies because it sees them as a competitor for the role of international arbitrator and peacemaker. Parochial school aid is viewed by the Church as vitally important. Only 30 percent[21] (about three million[22]) of Catholic children attend Catholic schools. While these schools produce enough obedient Catholics to advance the Vatican agenda, tripling this proportion would substantially enhance the power of the Church. School prayer is important because, the more religious the public schools are made, the easier it is to justify government assistance to parochial schools. Other issues appearing in Table I have been discussed elsewhere in this text and need not be dealt with here.

What is important is that the Church picks up non-Catholic support on each of these issues. For example, non-Catholic private school parents who send their children to nonreligious schools support the Church's political initiatives because they stand to gain from them. The Vatican has elevated fundamentalist leader Jerry Falwell to a position of power and status of which he never dreamed. He is enabled to have frequent meetings with President Reagan and given an opportunity to be one of the nation's foremost "moral leaders," delivering "Moral State of the Union" speeches on nationwide prime-time telecasts. In return, Falwell provides the Church with a constituency of millions of fundamentalists to mask as a "Christian" effort the Vatican's lobbying effort against abortion, the Equal Rights Amendment, family planning, and population assistance issues.

The Vatican's extensive intrusion into American policy-making is causing considerable national divisiveness. The Vatican gains considerable political advantage from its allies among non-Catholics and uses it to heavily influence government policy (or to thwart the making of policy altogether in some areas). Their manipulation has frustrated mobilization in this country to deal with the nation's most pressing problems, such as population growth control, nuclear disarmament, illegal immigration control, environmental degradation, including the pollution of our nation's waters and soil, soil erosion, and the "greenhouse effect." Our country is finding itself in a position similar to those in Latin America which are literally being buried under their problems because their national interests sometimes differ from Vatican interests.

Decisions on Three Issues Which Would Allow a Rapid Expansion of Vatican Power in the United States

Three issues which will be decided upon in the next year or so could radically enhance Vatican power. The first is the creation of a constitutional convention. Few Americans realize that its creators are those people who served as front men for the creation of the Moral Majority. The actual creators are Catholics Richard A. Viguerie and Paul Weyrich.[23] Most of the thrust is coming from the National Taxpayers Union (NTU). Its executive director was a leading anti-abortion activist. NTU bankrolled a tuition tax-credit initiative for Catholic schools in the District of Columbia in 1981.[24]

The convention would be formed for the purpose of passing an amendment to balance the federal budget. But many experts believe that nothing would stop it from considering other changes in the Constitution. Such a convention has not been held since the writing of our current governing document in 1789. Already thirty-two states have voted to call this body to order—just two states shy of the thirty-four needed.

It seems clear that the institution standing to benefit most from this convention is the Roman Catholic Church. It could arrange for the rewriting of the Constitution in such a way as to provide tax support for Catholic schools, to ban all abortions, to put government-mandated prayer back in the schools, to ban government support for family planning, to legalize unrestricted immigration, to mandate intensified anti-communist hate propaganda, to eliminate support for the United Nations, and to reduce sharply First Amendment rights such as the right to criticize the Catholic Church. Award-winning columnist George Will, almost an official spokesperson for the Reagan administration, has already called for a reduction in First Amendment rights.

It is almost inconceivable that thirty-two of the thirty-four states have already voted for the calling of the convention without more media and public attention being drawn to this movement headed by NTU. No such effort has ever progressed with so little attention.

> The drive for a convention was moving smoothly and swiftly until California Governor Jerry Brown raised the banner of the NTU, calling publicly for a convention to balance the national budget. Brown's political opportunism put the issue on the front page of national magazines and newspapers, out from the protective obscurity it had quietly enjoyed. Once it was exposed to the light, people began to get informed, and they soon developed legitimate concerns.
>
> Unhappy with this turn of events, NTU Treasurer William Bonner acknowledged that NTU would have preferred to get all the required thirty-four states lined up before the national media began examining the issues. "It would have been better to let a sleeping dog lie," he observed. "There is no point in heating things up. When Brown announced, we had to go more public."[25]

The lobbying effort at the state level has been finely honed and orchestrated and is truly fantastic. People who have worked in movements like the ERA and the environmental movement can appreciate the amount of effort that has gone into this massive lobbying campaign.

Only the secretive hierarchy of the Catholic Church is capable of orchestrating such massive lobbying effort so quietly. No doubt it has used the political lobbying organization it set up to ban abortion—the Moral Majority—to achieve this near miracle. The convention movement should be a matter of great concern. It is certain to at least cause a constitutional crisis and considerable national divisiveness. The greater the divisiveness, the greater the political gain for the Catholic Church. Population growth control is certain to lose.

A second opportunity for government policy manipulation is through influencing the selection of Supreme Court justices by the reelection of Mr. Reagan to a second term. Of the six sitting pro-abortion justices, five are now more than seventy-three years old. Sandra Day O'Connor, a conservative and obedient Irish Roman Catholic, has been Reagan's only appointment thus far. If he is reelected, the odds are fairly good that he would have occasion to appoint four additional justices, and they could all be conservative and obedient Catholics just like his first selection. Then we would have a majority of the Court appointed with the same kind of "divine guidance" Reagan has been getting all along and have a Court no doubt responsive to the needs of the Vatican. This end is already within reach of the Church if Reagan is reelected.

The third opportunity for government policy manipulation comes with the continued influx of illegal aliens. John Tanton, chairman of the Federation for American Immigration Reform (FAIR) and leading thinker on illegal immigration, summarizes the findings of studies of the beneficiaries by saying that the only *Americans* who benefit are business interests that employ illegals at low wages.[26] That is all![27] In this country, 75 percent of Hispanics approve of illegal immigration control and of national identification cards.[28] This is the group that the Catholic hierarchy said opposed control. (Of course, the Church was only speaking "on behalf of" Hispanics all along.)

No one benefits except some often unscrupulous business interests and the Catholic hierarchy (90 percent of all illegal aliens are Catholic). No illegal immigration control organizations *ever* mention opposition by the hierarchy—another example of the power of censorship.

If illegal aliens were comprised of other religious groups, we probably would have little illegal immigration control problems in the United States. How does the Church justify this blatantly anti-American activity of creating a sanctuary in America for Catholic illegal aliens from Latin America?

Officially one-quarter of the people in the Catholic Church in the United States are Hispanic. However, according to Church spokesman the Reverend Raymond G. Schutte, a Benedictine, in reality almost 40 percent of our country's Catholics are Spanish-speaking, and their number will rise to 50 percent by 1990[29]—only six years from now—due mostly to illegal immigration. The justification:

The principle [of sanctuary] . . . a part of Catholic canon law, which states: "A church enjoys the right of asylum so that criminals who flee from it are not to be removed from it, except in the case of necessity, without the assent of the ordinary or the rector of the church." Thus, when Milwaukee Archbishop Rembert Weakland welcomed four families into a church in December, he said he was only obeying the law of his church.

In greeting the refugees on the day St. Benedict the Moor Catholic Church became a public sanctuary, Archbishop Weakland said, "To many, the concept of sanctuary may seem to be one that Catholic tradition forgot since the Middle Ages. This is not true."

"Sanctuary is not really a way of avoiding justice," the archbishop added, "but a holy respite so that true justice can eventually be done."[30]

Obviously Archbishop Weakland defies American law, placing the law of the Vatican, a foreign power, above American law. Of course, he has a "divine right" to do so, because the Vatican has sovereignty over the United States in matters of faith and morals, as we discussed before, and, of course, morals include illegal immigration since it enhances the power of the Church.

The real meaning of the hierarchy's interests in illegal immigration can be gleaned from a recent monograph on illegal immigration and national security. No doubt the most important ever published on this subject, it was written by Dr. George Fauriol and produced by Georgetown University's Center for Strategic and International Studies:

> The viability of the nation depends upon an informed electorate and the absence of deep cultural or lingual divisions among its people. Illegal immigration, to the extent that it fosters the establishment of communities of persons unable or unwilling to converse in English, can foster just such divisions. The problem of a large ethnic group repeatedly fueled by massive immigration—whether legal or illegal—detached from the main stream U.S. population by language and custom, "could affect the social stability of the nation," says William A. Henry, III. "The disruptive potential of bilingualism and biculturalism is worrisome: millions of voters cut off from the main sources of information, millions of potential draftees inculcated with dual ethnic loyalties, millions of would-be employees ill at ease in the language of their workmates."

According to a study prepared by the Twentieth Century Fund, bilingual education, on which the U.S. government spends nearly $200 million annually, does not assist in creating a better society, but just the opposite. "Anyone living in the United States who is unable to speak English cannot fully participate in our society, its culture, its politics," says the Fund's task force.[31]

Unfortunately, an end to illegal immigration, and the curtailment of legal immigration to reasonable levels, may be perceived in the future as a threat by the beneficiaries of this growing political clout. Illegal immigration, to the extent that it fuels an increasing number of insular ethnic groups, becomes a tool with which to persuade government policymakers to look favorably upon the demands of ethnic organizations, which could include the maintenance of open borders.

The political implications of such activities have not received the attention or critical examination they deserve. The obligations of the U.S. government, to the citizens of this country, should not be determined by the number of petitioners before the government. By including illegal immigrants in the census, the U.S. government legitimizes the use of illegal immigration itself as a political tool for the advancement of certain interests in American society, which are certainly not without significant implications for the future of American democracy. The political use of illegal aliens has included attempts by certain states, particularly California, to make major efforts to register illegal aliens to vote. During the Carter administration, the Justice Department informally ruled that it saw no legal reason why illegal aliens could not vote even in federal elections![32]

Fauriol never mentions the Catholic Church. Yet, he could not be more on target if he were aiming at the Catholic hierarchy. The Vatican is the chief "beneficiary of this growing political clout." It obviously seeks the "use of illegal immigration as a political tool for the advancement of its interest in American society" at the expense of American democracy.

The Vatican promotes social and ethnic political power blocs in this country to foster divisiveness within American society. Then it uses these ethnic power groups—such as Poles, Irish, Mexicans, and Salvadorans—to manipulate U.S. domestic and foreign policy. Though an enormous influx of immigrants is required, the strategy is simple: divide and conquer.

The major support for bilingual education was the Catholic hierarchy. No doubt the Church recognized that bilingualism divides the country culturally and politically and destroys the critical linguistic cohesion. Yet it succeeded in getting $200 million per year in taxpayers' dollars to fund this activity—a sum equal to the entire U.S. population assistance budget!

The Vatican is not concerned about the best interests of the United States. Nor does it seem to care about the people in developing countries. Increasing the number of Catholics in the United States to increase their power in the United States, regardless of the expense to the Third World, is its major concern.

If the Church had a greater compassion for the developing world, it would be doing whatever possible to encourage their educated and skilled people to remain at home where they are desperately needed. As John Tanton notes:

> What of the plight of the millions of unseen countrymen left behind to live with conditions that the emigrants might have helped to change? Open immigration policies in the U.S. contribute significantly to what the *Christian Science Monitor* has called the "brain, brawn, and gumption drain" of less developed countries. Contrary to popular belief, it is not the destitute who emigrate. More often it is the energetic, the talented, the skilled, and the educated who have the means and the initiative to leave their native lands.[33]

For example, desperate Kenya has three thousand of its professionals living in the United States. In Sudan, an African country in which I have worked for some time, only 10 percent of its twenty million people are literate. An estimated one million of its citizens, including most of the intelligentsia and skilled laborers, have emigrated to more comfortable environs, particularly to Western countries. A case in point: the 1980 graduating medical school class was 103 strong. Only three of these doctors remained in the country long enough to pick up their diplomas on graduation day. Another case: each year the government sends three physicians to Great Britain to become obstetrician-gynecologists. In 1973, there were seventy-eight of these specialists to serve a nation of twenty million. After supporting this program for eight years, the country finds itself with only seventy-three. Most of the others have left for the United States. All professional and skilled personnel groups of that country have been similarly affected by out-migration.

Perhaps even more important is the immigration of policy-makers from developing countries.

> With the United States acting as a "safety valve," the elites in these nations are able to avoid seeking solutions to their problems of underdevelopment and overpopulation. The result is continuing poverty, misery, and hopelessness for the masses of people who will never be able to emigrate.[34]

Examples number in the thousands, some of which I can cite from personal experience. A policy-maker sends his children to the United States or Europe for training; by design, they remain and are joined several years later by the "retiring" policy-maker, his domestic decision-making having all along been influenced by his personal long-term plans. This kind of out-migration of policy-makers must stop.

The hierarchy's claim that their interest in illegal immigration is a result of compassion for Third World peoples simply does not hold up under close scrutiny. Lust for increased political power in the United States more accurately reflects the Vatican's interest; increased numbers of devouted followers increase political power.

Recently the Vatican offered its own immigration bill after successfully thwarting the Simpson-Mazzoli bill. To introduce this bill they called upon Catholic Congressman Edward Roybal (D–California) who, coincidentally, is pro-abortion, pro-family planning, and pro-international population assistance—in short, a man who would be the least likely suspected of cooperation with the Church. This bill is a blatant attempt to maintain the status quo. The Roybal bill would:

- Amnesty [grant Permanent Resident Alien status] to illegal aliens who entered the U.S. prior to January 1, 1982.
- Amnesty children and spouses of legalized aliens who entered the U.S. after January 1, 1982, and were present in the United States at the time of amnesty.
- Ease the identification requirements for amnesty and provide several levels of appeal to applicants who are turned down.
- Allow amnesty applicants to work until final determination of their status.
- Eliminate the current exclusion of aliens likely to require welfare or other public assistance.
- Strike employer sanctions in favor of increased enforcement of Department of Labor wage and hour laws.
- Authorize $65 million for start up of a legalization program and for increased enforcement.
- Increase legal immigration by 100,000 a year for five years.
- Make it illegal for state and local police to hold illegal aliens for the Immigration and Naturalization Service.
- Create another four-year immigration commission.[35]

The tide will only be stemmed by a law that includes an unforgeable national identification card, severe employer sanctions for all employers, rejection of any liberal amnesty, and a vastly expanded Immigration and Naturalization Service. Any law without these provisions is doomed to failure, a fact well known by those who drew up the Roybal bill. Every item of this bill is designed to thwart illegal immigration control.

Where does Mr. Reagan and his administration stand on illegal immigration control? According to Texas Governor Mark White, in a speech to the seventh annual Conference on Immigration and Naturalization at the University of Texas Law School:

> President Reagan told the American people . . . he's serious about immigration control and a secure border. But at the same time, this administration has turned its back on its responsibilities to stem the tide of illegal immigration by refusing to adequately fund the Border Patrol to do its job. . . . They are reluctant to adequately enforce existing laws, which makes you question how actively they would enforce the new law. . . . I think it's time for the administration and the federal government to put some money where the mouth is.[36]

The Reagan administration and the Vatican both stand for maintaining the status quo. This is not a coincidence.

The constitutional convention, Supreme Court appointments following a Reagan reelection, and the status quo on illegal immigration control all offer opportunities for quick gains in Vatican political power in the United States. However, just conducting "business as usual" is producing substantial gains.

Vatican Influence on Domestic and Foreign Policy-making in the United States

Most of the Vatican's political influence in this country has been developed within this century. To achieve this end, it is undeniable that the Vatican has taken advantage of the fundamental fair-mindedness of the American people, and the hierarchy continues to gain strength in the genial and tolerant climate of America. Though it is apparent that the Vatican is influencing U.S. policy in other areas, such as the defense and military, we shall concern ourselves only with population growth control at this point.

The Vatican began its opposition to birth control in 1914; in 1930, the hierarchy became the world's leading opponent of contraception.[37] Since then, the hierarchy has been methodically crippling, prostituting, or destroying population growth control institutions around the world. With its "divine authority," the Church has exercised its sovereignty over the United States in matters of "faith and morals" and politically opposed those activities at variance with "Catholic morality," including all activities related to population growth control.

As late as September 20, 1983, the pope stated in the clearest of language the Church's implacable position on contraception. Speaking at Castel Gandolfo to fifty bishops attending a seminar on responsible parenthood, the pope condemned artificial contraception in unprecedentedly severe terms. "Contraception," he said, "is so illicit that it can never, for any reasons, be justified."[38] If there was any remaining doubt about this pope or the Church changing its position on contraception, it disappeared with this and other recent proclamations.

In December 1983, the Vatican's Congregation for Catholic Education issued "Educational Guidance in Human Love." The document reaffirmed the Church's teaching on sexuality. However, paragraph sixty-five of the document states, "It is the task of the state to safeguard its citizens against injustice and moral disorders such as the . . . improper use of demographic information." The purpose of this paragraph is plain. The 1980 Synod of Bishops on the Family had decried "improper" use of demographic statistics to cause "hysteria" or other "emotional reactions" of despair. According to a report in Population Today, "This new warning against employing 'improper' demographics was based on the same concern, and—like the 1980 statement—was aimed squarely at governments. Preventing the 'misuse' of demographics is, according to the guideline, a government's responsibility."[39]

In other words, it is the responsibility of governments to censor demographic information that suggests the existence of a population problem. Shortly after Reagan was elected, this "misuse" or "improper" use of demographic information all but stopped flowing from our government. Not since the Global 2000 Report was published in 1980 by the Carter administration has there been any significant information on overpopulation published by our government, no doubt in response to the 1980 Synod statement. It is as if the Reagan administration expects the problem of overpopulation to go away if it is ignored.

More recently, the Vatican has issued a new proclamation, Charter of the Rights of the Family (see, appendix five). According to this proclamation, governments and international agencies are obligated to: perform their duties in accordance with the "objective moral order" which excludes recourse to contraception, sterilization, and abortion; ban the concept of population growth control; ban incentives and disincentives for having small families; and provide big families with adequate public welfare (Article 3). Human life must be protected from the moment of conception (Article 4). Parents have the right to educate their children, and the Vatican will tell them what's in the best interest of the children—not the federal Department of Education. Parents should receive tuition tax credits, and the government has a responsibility to subsidize church schools. Governments should ban sex education in schools. School prayer should be in all public schools. Government must control information and entertainment, favoring censorship in order to ensure public morality (Article 5). Public authorities must not grant divorce (Article 6). Families have the right to form "New Right" organizations to protect the family, undertake censorship, and so forth, and to lobby the government (Article 9). Governments must make it possible for mothers to have as many children as they choose and to be able to stay home and raise their families (Article 10).

"The Vatican is sending copies of its Family Charter to *all* governments and international agencies to serve 'as a model and a point of reference for the drawing up of future legislation and family policy,' according to Archbishop Edouard Gagnon, the Vatican's family expert."[40] Futhermore, in a blatant show of bigotry and arrogance, the Holy See distributed copies of this document at the World Population Conference in Mexico City in August 1984.

We can expect to soon see these new pronouncements reflected in Reagan administration policy. In December 1981, it made one serious attempt to completely eliminate the international population assistance program by leaving the program out of the budget.[41] It is apparently complying with the Vatican request to "protect the public morality" by censoring demographic information. Only one month later, *Population Today* reported the following:

"Demographic trends of the last two decades have greatly influenced major institutions in American society and have caused significant changes in public policies. . . . Future trends will be at least as influential."

That quotation comes not from some data-making guru but from a Reagan administration report—one that the public will not see. Prepared last fall, the internal study was written for the Cabinet Council of Economic Affairs—one of about ten such groups of cabinet secretaries that meet on a frequent basis to consider future national policy.

Though their study was made for internal consumption only and is unobtainable, the *Washington Post* typically gained access to a copy and in January published excerpts that make intriguing reading. . . .[42]

How does the Vatican influence U.S. policy? In hundreds of ways. Most important in creating many of these opportunities is the Church's almost unimaginable wealth. Recently Luigi Di Fonzo, a Harvard professor, published an extensive study of Vatican wealth. "The Vatican's total assets—not including the assets of the Roman Catholic Church, but including stock it controls on the New York and American stock exchanges, and property, gold reserves, and paintings —are probably $50 billion to $60 billion. . . ."[43] The Catholic Church in the United States, with "assets of more than $100 billion, today possesses more than ten times the combined wealth of IBM, Exxon, General Motors, and U.S. Steel."[44] There is no accountability for these funds to anyone except the Vatican. Everything is done in complete secrecy.[45] It is simply mind-boggling to see Vatican claims of compassion for the poverty-stricken in Latin America in the face of this fantastic accumulation of wealth.

Given our tax laws, and in the continued absence of any kind of redistribution of this wealth, the Church will continue to amass wealth indefinitely. Mexico was witness to the behavior of the Church that we are seeing in the United States today. By the time of its independence, the Church in Mexico had acquired perhaps half the land and capital wealth of the country. This is the reason that in Latin America "priests have become identified in the minds of the people with exploitation, superstition, and tyranny."[46]

One of its most important accomplishments is instilling children in its school system with the idea that Catholics are persecuted, that non-Catholics are determined to injure them, that all criticism of the Church and its hierarchy is directed against them personally. Children are taught to reject all criticism of the Church as being unjust, to be angered by this criticism, to hate the individuals at the source of the criticism. Catholic children who are active in the Church are "programmed" to respond this way. The thought process is blocked in such a way that negative information about the Church cannot be received and evaluated by using one's intelligence. Instead, it is automatically rejected no matter how truthful or justified it may be.

The hierarchy is a master at capitalizing on the anger and hatred generated by this criticism, capturing it, and channeling it in ways to make it productive for the advancement of its own agenda. This generates the considerable human energy that drives Catholic Action and many individual Roman Catholics.

The hierarchy avoids most direct attempts to influence policy. These activities are restricted to vociferous support for a public policy or announcements that they will lead a defiance movement if a certain policy is enacted.

As Congressman William Clay (D–Missouri) found (*see*, note

twenty-six, chapter one), whenever any issue arises in Congress that affects Catholic interests, a seasoned lobbyist in priestly garb is likely to appear in a Congressman's office reminding the legislator that 52 million Catholics in America feel thus and so about this matter. Even when the legislator knows full well that the opinion is actually that of a handful of top-ranking bishops, acting on orders from Rome, he may swallow his convictions and say, "Yes, yes," because he is aware that in America the powerful bishops speak for American Catholics. Should he not comply, Catholic pressures can be mortally effective in swinging any close election against him.[47]

The hierarchy has learned to act indirectly through Catholic laypersons. The hierarchy acts through Catholic politicians such as Lindy Boggs (D–Louisiana) and Charles Rangel (D–New York). There are many similar examples directly affecting population growth control. Ravenholt, in his memo, pointed to several acts of Clement Zablocki (D–Wisconsin). Other obvious examples include Tip O'Neill (D–Massachusetts), who killed the Simpson-Mazzoli bill in a thinly veiled act in December 1983, Henry Hyde (D–Illinois), and Jeremiah Denton (R–Alabama). They act through hundreds of bureaucrats such as John H. Murphy and John H. Sullivan, as Ravenholt pointed out in his memo. They act through Catholic laypersons not associated with the government, such as Paul Brown, executive director, Life Amendment Political Action Committee (LAPAC), Phyllis Schlafly, executive director of Eagle Forum, and Peter Donaldson and John Ganly of Family Health International.

The hierarchy has also learned to act indirectly through political, bureaucratic, and religious "independents"—non-Catholics who have something to gain by cooperation. Examples include Jesse Helms (R–North Carolina), Robert Kasten (R–Wisconsin), and Mark Siljander (R–Michigan), who were elected with considerable assistance from the hierarchy and are dependent upon its continued support, financial and otherwise, for reelection. The Helms Amendment that has blocked international population assistance for abortion activities for a decade was written by John H. Sullivan, a Catholic. Examples of non-Catholic bureaucrats who have "cooperated" with the Church include Sander Levin and Dr. Stephen Joseph, two key figures mentioned in Ravenholt's memorandum. Examples of nongovernment non-Catholics who have "cooperated" with the Church include Malcolm Potts and Sharon Camp. I can name scores of non-Catholics in these categories just from my own experience in population and I am sure that population is only the tip of the iceberg. In a sense, the non-Catholics are the most important to the Church for influencing policy. They allow the hierarchy to keep their hands perfectly clean.

There are thousands of examples of Vatican influence of foreign and defense affairs—national security issues—including population growth control. Of the hundreds of cases in the area of population growth control, we will concern ourselves with a widely mixed selection of eleven examples here.

1. Government approval for "new" contraceptive drugs. The best known case regards blocking FDA approval of the injectable contraceptive, Depo-Provera. This contraceptive drug is approved in eighty nations, including Great Britain and Canada, and is used by more than ten million women.[40] Approval was first blocked by FDA Commissioner Donald Kennedy. Before this and since, the hierarchy's interests were maintained by the staff at the FDA. In 1983, the Reagan administration was called down for trying to place on the Fertility and Maternal Health Drugs Advisory Committee a Catholic woman psychiatrist whose resume identified her as a founder of the California Pro-Life Council, which lobbies for anti-abortion legislation. She had no qualifications for the position, but she did support the hierarchy's position on Depo-Provera. Under fire, her nomination was withdrawn.

I wrote to Ralph Nader in 1983 asking him to reconsider the negative position of his Health Research Group which had reported about the contraceptive in the July 30, 1982, issue of *Science*. I pointed out the historical Catholic influence on FDA policy and the fact that his organization was the only reputable organization opposed to Depo-Provera. Virtually every professional advisory committee concerned with contraceptive drugs has approved of Depo. It carries the approval of advisory committees to the FDA, the Agency for International Development and the British Minister of Health, the National Association of Family Planning Doctors in Britain,[49] the World Health Organization,[50] and the American College of Obstetrics and Gynecology. The International Planned Parenthood Federation (IPPF) has supplied millions of doses. The drug is safer and more use-effective than contraceptive pills, and it has never been associated with a single death.

It is unquestionable that blocking of FDA approval of this drug has resulted in tens of thousands of deaths of mothers in the developing world who died in unwanted childbearing, victims of these Catholic American activists who are sometimes unaware that they are fighting a "holy war" for their Vatican. Furthermore, literally millions of unwanted children have been born in the developing world in the past decade as a result of this FDA disapproval. For example, Zimbabwe, which has the highest birth rate in the world at 4.3 percent, is experiencing a wave of "baby dumping." Even though the prime minister said that the practice was immoral and evil, the bodies of twenty-two babies were found abandoned in Harare in the first five months of 1983. Since then dozens more have been dumped. Doctors say that the banning of Depo-Provera is a contributing factor. The former health minister banned the drug, saying that it was part of a colonialist plot to oppress blacks.[51]

2. In a policy formulated and imposed by the Catholic hierarchy that began during the period described by Ravenholt, the AID population program has been increasingly decentralized, substantially decreasing its effectiveness. Decentralization inevitably reduces both a program's visibility and its accountability. Under the Nixon and Ford administrations, for example, AID's population assistance program was administered almost entirely by a single bureau devoted exclusively to population and humanitarian affairs. Today, parts of the population budget are administered by the Science and Technology Bureau, the four regional bureaus, and the Bureau for Program and Policy Coordination. To this, the administration proposes to add the Bureau for Private Enterprise. Similarly, the population program was administered ten years ago by an agency official who reported directly to the administrator. Today, the director of the central office of population reports to the director of health and population, who is, in turn, responsible to the assistant administrator for science and technology, whose chief is the AID administrator.[52]

3. The Catholic Church and its Protestant allies in the Moral Majority are currently attempting to impose a policy to deny all federal funds to various private agencies that provide abortions with their own funds while receiving federal funds for services such as family planning. "Anti-abortion legislators (and, reported-ly, the Reagan administration) for some years now have been seeking ways to 'defund' various domestic [family planning] organizations, notably local Planned Parenthood affiliates, but apparently have not yet found a constitutional way to do so."[53] Thus, although the Vatican uses abortion as a target in common with its allies, its real target is family planning.

4. With the Catholic Church's strong support, Senator Robert Kasten (R–Wisconsin) defeated Gaylord Nelson in the 1980 general election by a margin of 50 percent to 48 percent. Now Kasten is paying his dues to the Catholic hierarchy.

> On June 9 [1983], Senator Bob Kasten (R–Wisconsin), chairman of the Foreign Operations Subcommittee of the Senate Appropriations Committee, filed an "objection" with the Agency for International Development (AID) to its plans to continue granting several million dollars annually to the Pathfinder Fund. The Pathfinder Fund, a private, nonprofit agency, receives federal funds for international family planning assistance but uses its own, nongovernmental funds to finance several abortion-related activities, including some training of medical personnel to perform abortions overseas. Senator Kasten based his objection

on a belief that Pathfinder's use of private funds for abortion-related activities violates the spirit (though not the letter) of the Foreign Assistance Act, which prohibits the use of federal population assistance for abortion. Faced with the possible loss of its AID funding, which amounts to 90 percent of its budget, Pathfinder had to divest itself of its abortion-related activities in an attempt to retain its eligibility for AID funding.[54]

After this, international family-planning agencies receiving AID funds all operated under this *de facto* U.S. policy formulated and implemented by the Catholic Church with the "assistance" of a non-Catholic.

5. In part to give the impression that abortion is wrong, the Church attempted to impose (and was partially successful) their "Baby Doe" policy.

Abortion opponents [the Catholic Church] along with President Reagan have sought to portray the denial of medical care to severely ill newborns as an outgrowth of legal abortion. On March 7, the Department of Health and Human Services (DHHS) issued its controversial "Baby Doe" regulations, effective fifteen days later, requiring that severely ill newborns be given all medical care possible, establishing a hotline for reporting suspected cases of abuse, and requiring that a notice be posted in all hospitals giving the hotline number.[55]

The press that the Church enjoyed from their imposition of this policy was invaluable to their cause—and nobody was the wiser. It was more than "an outgrowth of legal abortion" issue. This was an attempt to impose the "absolutism" essential to the Vatican's control discussed in chapter seven.

6. In an attempt to get a policy adopted that would advance its "absolutism" in matters of reproduction, the "politics of abortion" were extended into an unrelated area during the summer of 1983. This involved an attempt to restrict the use of federal biomedical research funds.

During consideration of legislation affecting the National Institutes of Health (NIH), abortion opponents have proposed amendments to block the use of NIH funds for virtually all research involving human fetuses. Despite the proven benefit of fetal research for the health of infants and children, the amendment's sponsors claim that researchers are using living fetuses that either will be or have already been aborted for grotesque experiments.

Such an amendment passed the full House last year but died when the bill was not considered by the Senate.[56]

The use of "abortion politics" to fulfill a need of the Vatican speaks to its sophistication in manipulating U.S. policy at the expense of the American people.

7. The management of appointments of personnel who are obedient to the hierarchy and its allies in the Moral Majority and anti-family planning to key family planning positions can vastly influence government policy and the implementation of policy. For example,

> Marjory Mecklenburg was appointed last spring [1982] as director of the HHS Office of Adolescent Pregnancy Programs and as acting deputy assistant secretary for Population Affairs. Prior to her government positions, Mecklenburg was president and cofounder of American Citizens for Life and a former chair of the National Right to Life Committee.[57]

She has carried out the Vatican agenda to the maximum extent politically possible. There are scores of other examples that I can cite from my own experience.

8. Under the leadership of "ideologically correct" Richard Schweiker, HHS decided that the Utah Department of Health would be the sole Title X grantee (federal family planning funds recipient) because that state required parental consent for minors to have access to family planning services. HHS defunded the Planned Parenthood Association of Utah and Park City Community Clinic because they refused to impose the requirement on teens. The purported reason advanced by HHS was "to enhance management efficiency."[58] Policy actions of this nature under hierarchy influence have numbered in the thousands in the past decade alone.

9. In 1983, the Vatican successfully blocked the Simpson-Mazzoli bill for the control of illegal immigration. For the second time in less than two years, the Senate overwhelmingly passed the bill (seventy-six to eighteen). Then, with Peter Rodino (D–New Jersey) at the helm, the House Judiciary Committee, before reporting the bill to the floor, *gutted the original bill!* It was reported that Chairman Rodino received some coaching from the archbishop of New Jersey just prior to sending the bill to the floor. In any case, the congressman played a significant role in weakening the bill, including the elimination of a ceiling on legal immigration. A national poll of black and Hispanic attitudes toward immigration showed that *overwhelming majorities favored strong illegal immigration control.*[59] These findings caught everyone by surprise —including the Catholic Church. After an excellent educational effort

in the House of Representatives by the Federation for American Immigration Reform (FAIR) and other organizations, Roger Connor, executive director of FAIR, informally surveyed the House. One of the Vatican's principal strategies at blocking illegal immigration control for years has been to convince everyone that Hispanics in this country do not want immigration controlled and, because of this, control was politically sensitive. When many congressmen, who had been opposed, learned about these poll results, they switched their positions. Connor's survey showed that the control proponents had the votes not only to pass the weakened bill but also strengthening amendments, close to the Senate version. At this point, Connor told me that he estimated the chances of passage of a good law at eighty/twenty. Then word got back to the Vatican office in Washington concerning this rapid change in the vote distribution. The hierarchy apparently panicked and called on their Catholic faithful, House Speaker Thomas "Tip" O'Neill, who killed the bill for 1983 and 1984. O'Neill offered ridiculous reasons for killing the bill and was subsequently taken to task by the press. One of the reasons given was that immigration reform has "no constituency."[60] Since O'Neill's main concern here was the Catholic hierarchy (and certainly among them there is no constituency for it), he was unconcerned about criticism.

10. In an act that potentially has major national security and foreign policy implications, the Catholic hierarchy presented to the White House on January 22, 1984, a demand for the elimination of all family planning funds for Central America in the administration's five-year $8 billion legislative proposal developed from the so-called Kissinger Commission. The administration did not honor that demand, and now the Catholic American Life Lobby has written to the House Foreign Affairs Committee, stating that it will lobby against the Central American legislative package in its entirety if it includes population aid.[61]

It is ironic that this act by the hierarchy would concern the nation of El Salvador. Consider the fact that the Soccer War between El Salvador and neighboring Honduras in 1969 was formally attributed by the Organization of American States to Salvadoran migrants being pushed into Honduras by El Salvador's skyrocketing population—the first time population pressure received official mention as a cause of war. At that time, it had a population of less than four million. In sixteen years from now—the year 2000—the projected population is nine million, more than doubling in the thirty-one-year period.[62] For El Salvador, its own population growth is its own greatest national security threat. Is the Catholic hierarchy concerned about the security of the Salvadoran people? Obviously not! Is the hierarchy concerned about the threat to our security imposed by El Salvador's insecurity? Obviously not! The survival of the Vatican and the advances of its power are its main concerns.

11. In its most important foreign policy manipulation of all, the Vatican is successfully blocking consideration of the reality that population growth is the most serious threat to the security of all nations. For fiscal year 1985, the Reagan administration is requesting a 4.8 percent increase in development aid, including population assistance, while asking Congress for a 240 percent increase in military aid financing.[63] This in addition to the budget in fiscal year 1984, which had a $9.2 billion worldwide military assistance program juxtaposed to a $212 million population assistance program—a fifty-fold difference![64]

In 1979 and 1980, under President Carter, the National Security Council (NSC) published results of their studies which concluded that world population growth seriously threatened this country's security. With the arrival of the Reagan administration, however, this new reality was rejected outright and in a most frightening way. During Richard Allen's tenure as national security advisor, the hierarchy launched a letter-writing campaign directed at the national security advisor. Hundreds of letters from Catholics all over the country informed him that the senders believed the Council had erred in concluding that world population growth was a serious security threat to the United States and asked the council to reconsider its position. However, before this initiative could be completed, Allen was forced to resign. William Clark then became the national security advisor. Not long after joining the staff, Clark walked into a NSC meeting with a bundle of these letters under his arm. He commented that Americans all over the country believe that the NSC made an error in deeming world population growth a serious security threat. Clark offered the bundle of letters as evidence. Then he said, "We are here today to begin correcting this error." I learned of this from someone well known to me who sits on the Council and who was stunned by this action.

This is probably the most devastating act of interference in government policy formulation committed by the Church during the Reagan administration. It brought to a halt all discussions by the NSC of population growth as a security threat, seriously undermining the security of all Americans.

The Vatican, through the Reagan administration, succeeded in negating the Carter NSC position on population growth and national security on May 30, 1984, when the NSC sent out to a number of agencies the working draft of the U.S. statement presented at the U.N. Conference on Population in Mexico City. This said, in effect, that there is no world population problem.[65] By choosing the NSC to circulate this draft, which otherwise made absolutely no sense, the administration reversed the NSC position on population growth as a security threat *without debate*. It was exceedingly important to the Vatican that this action be completed; without such a statement, it would have been obvious to everyone that the Vatican is a serious threat to U.S. security.

In contrast to the U.S. government's radical shift to the Vatican position on population growth, United Nations Fund for Population Activities Director Rafael M. Salas stated in his opening remarks in no uncertain terms that world population growth has serious implications for global security. This theme was repeated many times throughout the conference by governments which are apparently less under the control of the Vatican.[66]

At the Mexico City meeting, James Buckley reiterated that the United States no longer would contribute funds to private organizations that "perform or actively promote" abortion as a means of family planning and that it would require assurances from governments to which it sends funds that its aid would not be used for abortions.[67] In effect, the U.S. Agency for International Development is being used as an instrument of Vatican foreign policy.

Of the 149 states represented at the Mexico City meeting, only the Vatican, Costa Rica, and Chile voiced their support for the American position! As *Newsweek* magazine pointed out, "If the administration continues to put its money where its mouth is, the international consensus on population control could yet be shattered,"[68] *the Vatican's openly professed goal.* The Vatican could never accomplish this goal without using the United States government as an instrument of Vatican foreign policy.

Vatican Influence on Policies of Other Nations

Vatican influence on domestic and foreign policy of the U.S. is not unique. *All* governments except China are victims of this Vatican manipulation of government policy. In 1971, *Time* magazine reported their interception of a confidential document issued by Pope Paul. In his book which was discussed in chapter seven, Waldo Zimmermann writes:

> An article in *Time* [February 1, 1971, p. 54] entitled "The Rhythm Lobby" told about Pope Paul's covert attack. In a fifteen-page confidential document issued through his secretary of state, Cardinal Villot, and sent to all papal nuncios [including the one in Washington, D.C.] and apostolic delegates and the Vatican's permanent observers at the U.N., Paul stressed the

secrecy of the new *lobby effort* and was sharply critical of the U.N. for supporting population control programs in the Third World.

In his instructions, Cardinal Villot said that world governments must be persuaded to take positions that "favor *Catholic morality*"; that papal diplomats should press bishops in each country to build up relations with local representatives of international organizations, key men who are able to influence the secretariats to which they report. Such relations, said Villot, will facilitate the choice of delegates to international conferences "who possess Catholic convictions." Predominantly Catholic countries should be pressured further, said the Cardinal, "to give their delegates *unequivocal* instructions, and if necessary suggest that those delegates make contacts with representatives of the Holy See.[69]

The impact of such a document can have no equal in causing hopelessness, tragic death, poverty, and sickness—misery for human beings and destruction of our fragile life-giving ecosystem. Few, if any, acts have so threatened the security of so many people in so many ways.

By these acts, the needs of the Vatican were placed above the needs of the people of all nations. Processes were initiated in all nations to undermine population growth control activities and corrupt policy-making processes. All of these initiatives emanate from Rome. There is no "American Church" or "Chilean Church" or "Sri Lankan Church." The Church is strictly "Roman" and has strictly "Roman" leadership.

One of the most notable events in population growth control history was the fall of Indira Gandhi after allegations of forced sterilization were made against her government. When Mrs. Gandhi accepted the first annual U.N. Population Award in New York in 1983, she restated that these allegations were without foundation.[70] Too few people are aware that her downfall was initiated by a Catholic American journalist and a Catholic-inspired world press. A couple of years ago, during a dinner conversation in Colombo, my Indian colleague, Dr. Datta Pai, a family planning leader for more than two decades, recounted what had happened. He was an acquaintance of the journalist and had watched the scenario unfold. The Catholic reporter made the allegations in an article, and, without any verification of these allegations, the world press exploded. Gandhi's government quickly fell. During the sterilization campaign, 10.8 million sterilizations were performed.[71] After the new opposition government was installed, it offered government compensation to the "millions of victims." What seems never to have reached the world press was that fewer than one hundred people out of 10.8 million were found to have been documented as coerced into sterilization, or one per 108,000 persons. It is likely that the rate was higher in some states. It was the Vatican and its press manipulations that destroyed the Gandhi government and made fools of her opposition government. But the real tragedy was the death and suffering experienced by millions of Indians as a result of this setback in the Indian population growth control program. The tragic effects went far beyond India. The Vatican terrorized politicians the world over with the news of particulars of the downfall of the Gandhi government. Virtually all countries have seen their population programs grow at a slower pace as a result.

In December 1983, I met with another Indian family planning leader and colleague, Dr. C. L. Jhaveri, at a population conference in the Dominican Republic. He told me of a keynote speech he had given on November 27, 1983, to the Fourth World Congress on Human Reproduction in Bombay, in which he reported on his analysis of the opposition to population growth control in India. He said that religious opposition to family planning was the major obstacle to population growth control in his country. The opposition only comes from two minority religious groups, Moslems and Catholics. I suggested to Dr. Jhaveri that, while there are far more Moslems than Catholics, and some Moslems are opposed to control, they are not sufficiently organized to significantly influence the government. However, Catholics in India are highly organized, have considerable "outside" influence, and the Catholic Church has an impressive history of such action. I asked him if, carrying his analysis further, the Catholic Church is the major obstacle to population growth control in India. He agreed.

We should not be surprised. After all, the Vatican had installed a Catholic government in South Vietnam while only 5 percent of the population of South Vietnam is Catholic. It takes only a small group of highly organized and well-led people, operating in secrecy, to completely dominate a government such as South Vietnam. India has many times the number of Catholics required for the Vatican to be in a position to have great influence. Certainly there are several examples of African countries with Catholic-trained government leadership and even smaller Catholic populations.

At the same meeting I saw Dr. Ben Viel. He told me of an example in his country, Chile. In 1979, with approval from the minister of health of Chile, Dr. Viel began setting up a female sterilization program with $1 million worth of sterilization equipment provided by the International Planned Parenthood Federation in London. When the equipment arrived in Chile, a Father Ibanes Langlois, serving as a messenger for the Vatican, met with the president of Chile. There was then and continues to be a disagreement between Chile and Argentina, almost bringing the two countries to war over a strategic waterway located at the tip of South America, that may prove to be rich in oil. It is called the Beagle Channel. Chile and Argentina had agreed to let the pope mediate the dispute. Langlois informed the president that, if this sterilization equipment was not removed from Chile, the pope would favor Argentina in the settling of the Beagle Channel dispute. The president called in the minister of health and ordered him to get the sterilization equipment out of the country. Viel was so notified by the minister of health, and it was shipped out. Sterilization remains strictly against the law in Chile.

If the Vatican had its way, all governments on earth would adopt the Ivory Coast sterilization law as a model. In that country, which is inordinately influenced by the Vatican, performing a voluntary sterilization on a woman or man is a *capital crime*. Chile has not gone to this extreme, but it is only one step away. The influencing of government policy by the Vatican, shown by Dr. Viel's example, is a daily occurrence the world over.

Vatican Population Policy Manipulations Seriously Threaten U.S. Security

On May 25, 1983, U.S. Navy Lt. Cdr. Albert Schaufelberger, III, was slain in San Salvador, the first U.S. military man to die in the war there. Three days before his death, Schaufelberger was interviewed on Cable News Network (CNN) News. He had a powerful and profound message for America. *"There is no military solution here in El Salvador. The country is overpopulated. Population growth must be stopped. There must be literacy programs and schools built and agricultural development and jobs created and health care. This is the only solution."* Unfortunately, when Schaufelberger was killed, only CNN reported what this man had to say. The newspapers reported only on the intrigue surrounding his death. Schaufelberger's message, vitally important to the security of our country, went unreported.

In an August 30, 1983, *Washington Post* article, General Maxwell Taylor, U.S. Army Retired, stated in no uncertain terms that overpopulation is a serious threat to the security of the United States. Consider the following excerpts:

> Irked by the charge of over-concentration on military aid, President Reagan of late has been demonstrating a greater interest in political, economic, and social conditions in El Salvador, which, unimproved, will tend to nullify the accomplishments of the military programs. . . .

These nonmilitary obstacles to American policy have been often discussed by the press in recent months. However, in the heated debate over the merits or demerits of this policy, I have never heard mention of the existence of a seminal cause that is responsible, wholly or in part, for most of the difficulties being encountered by our officials. I refer to the overlooked factor: excess population and its consequences.

Since the warning of Malthus some two centuries ago, demographers, sociologists, ecologists, and thoughtful generalists have speculated as to the likely consequences of overpopulations and their future effects on the ecology, human society, national governments, and their interrelations in peace and war. Unfortunately, their conclusions over the centuries have had no visible effect on the present-day politicians, diplomats, and policy-makers in Washington responsible for our policy in Central America. So it is worth the time to consider how population growth may affect the policy they have adopted.

. . . Their hopelessness may be expected to express itself in domestic turbulence, frequent overthrows of government, and expanded migration to greener pastures beyond national boundaries. . . .

The hard fact is that unchecked population growth alone creates problems so difficult and so costly to solve that the United States can never afford to take so ambitious a target. It is not merely that the regeneration of Central America is beyond any sum Congress is likely to appropriate for the purpose. We must remember that concurrently these same conditons that frustrate us in Central America today are present in virtually every other country in Latin America, many of which, like Mexico, Venezuela, and Brazil, are far more important to our national interests than Central America.

This list could be lengthened by adding countries in Asia and Africa which, because of their importance as trading partners, lessors of military bases, or formal allies, also deserve a higher national interest rating than Central America. Such funds as we have for foreign aid, if allocated with due priority, will be exhausted long before the basic needs of Central America can be met. . . .

Such an appraisal should lead them to limit our objectives in Central America to something relatively modest, such as the restoration of order in war areas, an end to identified communist troublemaking, and the first steps of a realistic social-economic program in which aid for family planning would be a lead item.

Finally, we might hope that these future policy-makers would henceforth recognize overpopulation as a perennial enemy of our national interests throughout the underdeveloped world and consider it in their global planning.[72]

Both unchecked population growth and illegal immigration threaten U.S. security. Former CIA Director William Colby, a Catholic, stated in 1978: "The most obvious threat to the United States is that there are 60 million Mexicans and there are going to be 120 million of them by the end of the century."[73] Gordon J. MacDonald, retired deputy chief of the U.S. Border Patrol, recently stated, "Based on my experience in the Border Patrol, I must tell you that this tidal wave of illegal aliens poses the most serious long-term threat to the survival of the United States."

George Fauriol concluded his December 1983 monograph on illegal immigration with the following paragraph:

> The national security of this nation depends upon its domestic strength and international stability. This strength requires an ability to control national borders, the maintenance of an independent foreign policy, a prosperous economy, and a cohesive domestic politic environment. As this essay has attempted to outline, uncontrolled migration is undermining this strength. Unchecked immigration, whatever its impact on labor and wage rates, does not just affect the unskilled and marginal job market. Its impact, because of its sheer numbers and because of its illegality, affects the very fabric of American society, U.S. national security, cultural, political, and linguistic unity, economic well-being, and international standing.[74]

It is undeniable that the thwarting of both population growth control and illegal immigration control by the Vatican seriously threatens the security of the United States. It is likewise undeniable that Americans and others who assist the Vatican in these activities seriously threaten the security of the United States.

Notes

1. A. Menendez, "Of Presidents and Popes," *Church and State* (1982), 35:6:11.

2. "Reagan Says U.S., Catholic Goals the Same," *Church and State* (1982), 35:7:17.

3. B. Peterson, "Reagan's Use of Moral Language to Explain Policies Draws Fire," *Washington Post* (March 23, 1983), p. A15.

4. M. McGrory, "Irishman in White House Now Says 'Ciao,'" *Raleigh News and Observer* (August 6, 1984), p. 4A.

5. O. Ullmann and E. Warren, "'Government Needs Church' Reagan Says," *Raleigh News and Observer* (August 24, 1984), p. 1.

6. M. McCrory, "Cuomo's Rule: Discuss Difficult Issues," *Raleigh News and Observer* (August 10, 1984), p. 4A.

7. J. Mann and K. Phillips, "Inside Look at those Elite Religious Groups," *U.S. News and World Report* (March 19, 1984), p. 60.

8. M. A. Lee, "Their Will Be Done," *Mother Jones* (July 1983), p. 22.

9. Mann and Phillips, "Inside Look," p. 60.

10. D. van Atta, "God and Man at the CIA," *Church and State* (1984), 37:2:13.

11. Ibid.

12. Lee, "Their Will Be Done," p. 21.

13. R. B. Kaiser, "Unholy Wars in the Name of God," *U.S.A. Today* (August 23, 1984), p. 4A.

14. J. McBeth, "The Church Clandestine," *Far Eastern Economic Review* (July 14, 1983), p. 34.

15. Edd Doerr, "Will Religious Liberty Survive the 1980s?" *Religious Humanism* (Spring 1984), p. 53.

16. P. Taubman, "Archbishop Leads Campaign Against Sandinistas," *Raleigh News and Observer* (August 1, 1984), p. 1A.

17. R. C. Brodnick, *The Catholic Encyclopedia* (Nashville: Thomas Nelson, Inc., 1976).

18. *The International Who's Who* (1984).

19. B. Bradley, "International Conference on Population," press release (August 8, 1984), p. 3.

20. P. Blanshard, *American Freedom and Catholic Power* (Boston: The Beacon Press, 1950), p. 259.

21. Editor's note, *Church and State* (1983), 36:7:23.

22. "Catholic, Lutheran School Enrollment Up," *Church and State* (1982), 35:7:20.

23. "Don't Let America Get 'Conned,' " *Church and State* (January 1984), 37:1:18.

24. "AU Bulletin: Con-Con Call Jeopardizes Religious Freedom," *Church and State* (July/August 1983), 36:7:3.

25. J. V. Stevens, Sr., "Tearing Up the Constitution," *Church and State* (March 1983), 36:3:11.

26. J. Tanton, "How Underdeveloped Countries Are Harmed by Uncontrolled Immigration," *Human Survival* (1983), 9:2:4.

27. "The Speaker, On the Border," *New York Times* (September 25, 1983).

28. Gallup Poll, "Hard Line Against Hiring Aliens," *Chapel Hill Newspaper* (November 13, 1983), p. 15A.

29. D. Winston, "Catholic Diocese Is Reaching Out to Area Hispanics," *Raleigh News and Observer* (January 1, 1984), p. 27A.

30. W. Bole, "When Churches Hide Illegal Aliens, They Cite the Concept of Sanctuary," *Church and State* (1983), 36:3:16.

31. G. Fauriol, "U.S. Immigration Policy and the National Interest," *Immigration Policy Paper #2* (December 8, 1983), p. 17.

32. Ibid., p. 19.

33. Tanton, "How Underdeveloped Countries Are Harmed," p. 4.

34. Ibid., p. 4.

35. "The Roybal Bill," *FAIR Immigration Report* (March 1984), 4:6:2.

36. "Texas Governor Blasts Administration—Says Border Patrol Needs More Funds," *FAIR Immigration Report* (December 1983), 4:3:2.

37. Blanshard, *American Freedom and Catholic Power*, p. 138.

38. *Le Monde*, Paris (September 20, 1983).

39. "Vatican on Misuse of Statistics," *Population Today* (1984), 12:2:5.

40. "Vatican Charter Urges Government Support for Parochiaid, Censorship, Population Growth," *Church and State* (1984), 37:1:16.

41. "President Is Urged to Strengthen U.S. Population Resolve," *Popline* (1982), 4:11:1.

42. "Administration Tracking Demographic Trends," *Population Today* (1984), 12:3:3.

43. R. Benedetto, "Vatican Influence," *U.S.A. Today* (June 17, 1983), p. 11A.

44. D. W. Foster, "God and the IRS," *The Humanist* (1984), 44:1:14.

45. S. Salerno, "All This and Heaven Too," *Harper's* (June 1982), p. 54.

46. Blanshard, *American Freedom and Catholic Power*, p. 281.

47. Ibid., p. 29.

48. V. Cohn, "Two Studies Call for Approval of Controversial Birth Control Drug," *Washington Post* (June 3, 1983), p. A2.

49. "Family Planning Doctors Issue Statement on Depo," *IPPF Open File* (May 26, 1983), p. 27.

50. Cohn, "Two Studies Call," p. A2.

51. *The Observer*, London (August 28, 1983).

52. Planned Parenthood-World Population Washington Memo, "Disturbing Trend Continues" (February 8, 1984), p. 3.

53. Planned Parenthood-World Population Washington Memo, "Piecemeal Attacks" (July 13, 1983), p. 5.

54. Ibid.

55. Ibid.

56. Ibid.

57. M. Esherick and A. Bermingham, "Schweicker's Parting Shots," *ZPG Reporter* (1983), 15:1:2.

58. Planned Parenthood-World Population Washington Memo, "Family Planning Transfer" (January 31, 1984), p. 1.

59. R. Connor, "Highlights of Immigration Activites During 1983," Year-end Report to FAIR Members (January 1, 1984).

60. Ibid.

61. Planned Parenthood-World Population Washington Memo, "Demands from Antiabortion Leaders" (February 29, 1984), p. 3.

62. Federation for American Immigration Reform, "Understanding El Salvador" (1984), 4:6:2.

63. Planned Parenthood-World Population Washington Memo, "Foreign Aid Politics a Major Factor" (February 8, 1984), p. 3.

64. United Press International, "U.S. Plans to Boost Military Aid to Turkey," *Raleigh News and Observer* (February 5, 1982), p. 3A.

65. "Pro-Abortion Population Programs Targeted," *Chapel Hill Newspaper* (June 18, 1984), p. 1A.

66. "U.N. Population Conference Opens With Strong Warnings," *Raleigh News and Observer* (August 7, 1984), p. 3.

67. R. J. Meislin, "Free Economies Help Lower Birth Rates, U.S. Envoy Tells Population Conference," *Raleigh News and Observer* (August 9, 1984), p. 1A.

68. R. Watson, J. Contreras, J. Harmes, and P. Chin, "Population Trading Places," *Newsweek* (August 20, 1984), p. 50.

69. Waldo Zimmermann, *Condemned to Live: The Plight of the Unwanted Child* (Vita Press, 2143 Poplar Avenue, Memphis, TN 38104; 1981), p. 36.

70. "Better Health, Better Opportunities," *Popline* (October 1983), p. 2.

71. C. Green, "Voluntary Sterilization: World's Leading Contraceptive Meth-

od," Population Reports #2 (March 1978), p. M42.

72. M. D. Taylor, "The Forgotten Factor in Central America," *Washington Post* (August 30, 1983), p. A19.

73. G. J. MacDonald, "A Fund-Raising Letter Prepared for Conservatives for Illegal Immigration Reform" (1983).

74. Fauriol, "U.S. Immigration Policy and the National Interest," p. 36.

11.

American Conservatism vs. the Radical Religious

> **"If we didn't know the Pope agrees with us, we Catholics in the New Right would have serious conscience problems. I would never work counter to the Church's official position."**[1]
>
> —Paul Weyrich, founder
> Moral Majority
> Christian Voice
> Religious Roundtable

The radical religious in our country, the so-called New Right, religious right, religious conservatives, and the Moral Majority, according to Paul Weyrich, will be guided by policy established in the Vatican.

To ensure that the Moral Majority does not act in ways in which the pope would not approve, the opinion of Weyrich and other Catholics in the organization must bear considerable weight in decision-making by the Moral Majority organization. They must be in positions of leadership. We have discussed earlier the Vatican's control over faithful laypersons, and Weyrich is apparently in this mold. Weyrich and his Catholic colleagues control the Moral Majority. The Vatican controls Weyrich and his colleagues. Thus the Vatican controls the Moral Majority. It is a fact that the American Catholic bishops described the Moral Majority in their 1975 Pastoral Plan of Action (appendix two), four years before Jerry Falwell was asked by the Catholics who named the organization to head it. The importance of this fact must not be underestimated.

A *Washington Post* article revealed that 20 percent of the clergy-men who have joined Christian Voice are Roman Catholic priests (about three hundred).[2] By this means the directions that Christian Voice might take are assured. The Vatican makes certain of its control of the leadership of the organization.

The fundamentalists who purportedly make up the majority of the membership of these two organizations are none the wiser. According to investigative reporter Connie Paige, Falwell serves as the public figure while Catholics Paul and Judie Brown actually organized the fundamentalists into the Catholic-dominated anti-abortion move-ment. The Browns invited the religious fundamentalists leadership to their Catholic-hierarchy-originated and controlled New Right gather-ings. But most important is the fact that the Browns offered to do the fundamentalists' mailings—in the process getting a percentage of the take, keeping an eye on what was being sent, and acquiring a whole new list of names themselves. Few fundamentalists or Protestant Moral Majority members realize that the Catholic Church is writing the fund-raising letters to which they are responding, controls the mailing list and what is sent, and gets dollars they contribute in return. "The grass-roots right-to-life fundamentalists seem a great deal more naive than the Catholics, making them easy game for the sophisticated conserva-tive political operatives who have drawn them in."[4] Paige also quotes Paul Brown, "Jerry Falwell couldn't spell abortion five years ago."[5] The Vatican has been undertaking activities like this for hundreds of years and has developed considerable skill at these kinds of manipula-tions. Fundamentalists cannot mentally accept that there are large numbers of Americans who owe their loyalty to the Vatican in prefer-ence to our country.

That the Catholic Church played the principal role in the crea-tion of the Moral Majority, Christian Voice, Religious Roundtable, and the single-issue groups[6] like U.S. Coalition for Life and Eagle Forum is undeniable. "Almost to a man, their [the New Right] leader-ship can be traced back to a meeting of ninety-three conservatives at the Sharon, Connecticut, estate of William F. Buckley, Jr., in Septem-ber of 1960. The Young Americans for Freedom (YAF) was organized at that meeting."[7] Buckley, who is sometimes referred to as the dean of the YAF, is a member of the secretive Knights of Malta. Accordingly, he has sworn allegiance to the defense of the Holy Mother Church, a necessary condition for membership in the Knights of Malta. In his writings and telecasts, Buckley has almost without exception taken the position of the Vatican on every issue. He apparently owes his first allegiance to the defense of the Church rather than to his country. The YAF grew stronger in the 1970s to the point where its leaders could boast that the Republican platform of 1980 read like a YAF tract from around 1963.[8] It is no coincidence that the Republican platform was consistent with the Vatican agenda (*see,* Table I, page 169). By 1981, the YAF advisory board included President Reagan, six members of his cabinet, nineteen senators, and 102 representatives.[9]

While Richard Viguerie was not invited to the Sharon meeting, he is a devout conservative Catholic and serves as the fundraiser not only for the Moral Majority, Christian Voice, and Religious Roundtable[10] but also for the four New Right political action committees, Conservative Caucus, Committee for the Survival of a Free Congress (Paul Weyrich), the National Conservative Political Action Committee, and the Congressional Club.[11] How much money from the coffers of the Catholic Church finds its way to these organizations cannot be determined because there is no public accountability for either the Vatican's or the American Catholic Church's tens of billions of dollars.

All New Right institutions are tied to the Catholic Church in some way. For example, the Heritage Foundation was founded by Weyrich, and he served as its first president. It was launched with the assistance of a Catholic, Joseph Coors, the beer magnate from Colorado, who put up $250,000.[12] Like Herman Kahn's Hudson Institute, once established, it obtained government monies for research work, no doubt from sympathetic bureaucrats, and invariably findings were consistent with the needs of the Vatican.

Fundamentalists have generally underappreciated the implications of their alliance with the Vatican. The reality of this dual allegiance of some Catholics to the Vatican and America should be of great concern to patriotic Americans. In a *New York Times Magazine* article, Father Andrew Greeley, referring to bishops, stated, "Rarely does the Curia [Vatican] lose in conflicts created by such dual allegiance. . . . Many bishops and archbishops are good men. . . . They would only lie, as the late Jesuit John Courtney Murray put it, for the good of the Church."[13] Unquestionably, the same applies to Catholic laypersons loyal to the Catholic hierarchy. It is a fact that the best interests of the Vatican and the best interests of the United States are not always identical. Fundamentalists who collaborate with the Vatican are used by the Holy See to counter the best interests of the United States when these counter Vatican interests. How can they then consider themselves to be American patriots or American conservatives?

What Is It to Be an American Conservative?

Senator Barry Goldwater is generally recognized as the dean of American conservatism. He does not identify with the New Right, and with good reason. The New Right is not a conservative American political movement; it is a religious one. There is a vast difference between being politically conservative and religiously conservative. Religious conservatism differs from one belief to another and even from one religious leader to the next. American political conservatism essentially remains unchanged.

The New Right has gone to great lengths to be recognized as "conservative." This is nonsense! American conservatives place high value on established rules of procedure, on the orderly conduct of public affairs by the rules, and on the traditional values of institutions. They place great value on the Constitution and on maintaining the restrictive procedural rules, precisely in order to restrain impatient public opinion.

The New Right created the movement for a constitutional convention which can quickly and drastically change our way of life and our government. No American conservative would *ever* propose a constitutional convention. As we have seen, the New Right leadership is mostly Roman Catholic and is solidly behind the admitted items on the Vatican Agenda, such as tuition tax credits for Catholic schools, certainly a radical departure from traditional American values (*see*, Table I, page 169).

Senator Goldwater, in his book *The Conscience of a Conservative*, states, "The enemy of freedom is unrestrained power, and the champions of freedom will fight against the concentration of power wherever they find it."[14] The Catholic Church's power in America is virtually unrestrained. Witness the composition and actions of the Reagan administration. It takes little imagination to foresee the state of affairs with four more Vatican appointments to the Supreme Court like Sandra Day O'Connor and just a little more control in the Senate and House. Political power will then be unlimited. For all practical purposes, the Catholic Church already has unlimited economic power. When an institution, according to Mr. Goldwater, "has gathered unto itself unlimited political and economic power . . . [it will be] able to rule as absolutely as any oriental despot."[15]

Two vast movements that involved millions of non-Catholic Americans set the stage for the rapid acquisition of power in America by the Vatican. The first, which began in earnest more than two decades ago, is the ecumenical movement. This movement has pretty much ceased to make any forward advances. Many of the earlier leaders have dropped out, recognizing that the Protestant groups made virtually all the compromises. Some have dropped out in disappointment, fully recognizing that they have been completely duped by their Catholic counterparts.

The ecumenical movement was exceedingly important, if not

absolutely essential, to the Vatican's march toward unrestrained power in America. It halted, then blocked, criticism of the Catholic Church by all leading Protestant denominations. This no doubt contributed to the Catholic Church's success in silencing all criticism of the hierarchy's actions in the lay press. For the past two decades, all over the country, the call by Protestants has been, "Let's not say anything negative about acts of the Catholic Church. Otherwise, we will jeopardize this important movement of reconciliation among all Christian sects." No doubt, the Vatican carefully nurtured this sentiment and was thereby able to advance its agenda under the cloak of secrecy with the help of Protestants bent on ecumenism.

The second vast movement involved the political mobilization of fundamentalists by the Vatican. According to Paige, the Reverend Edward Bryce, National Conference of Catholic Bishops' director of right-to-life activities, has presided over the transformation of the Church into a right-to-life political machine. Bryce admits that the expenditures on abortion are much larger than the records show and that most of this is buried in bishops' discretionary funds and individual diocesan ledgers.[16] No doubt, much of this "hidden" money of which Father Bryce speaks goes into the election campaigns of both Catholics and non-Catholics who cater to the needs of the Vatican. "The Pastoral Plan was a brilliant blueprint," states Paige.

> The message of the plan was absolutely clear: the Roman Catholic Church was getting into the business of electoral campaigns in a big way. It was as if the bishops had switched on an enormously powerful political engine that then appeared to run on its own. But the perpetual-motion machine is a thing of the imagination. A closer look at the right-to-life machine revealed that fuel and labor costs, maintenance, body work, lubrication, and replacement parts right down to the last screw all remained very much under firm pastoral guidance.
>
> The machine went into high gear, NCHLA organizers created and developed grass-roots right-to-life PACs, which they called "congressional district action committees," in almost half of the country's 435 congressional districts. The CDACs involved thousands of sympathetic Catholics in right-to-life activity, including letter-writing, meeting with elected officials, conducting candidate and voter education projects, and developing efficient phone networks.[17]

The New Right, which is dominated by Catholics such as Richard Viguerie and which answers to the Vatican, drew the fundamentalists in under the guise of religion—but for explicitly political purposes.

"However heartfelt, opposition to abortion was simply part of the plan."[18]

With sufficient wealth at its disposal, the hierarchy of the Church started right-to-life organizations and dominated their early growth, fashioning their philosophy, political base, and strategy and paying their way.[19] In 1975, Roy White, then executive director of the National Right to Life Committee, asserted, "The only reason we have a pro-life movement in this country is because of the Catholic people and the Catholic Church."[20] Connie Paige's extensive investigation led her to state:

> The Roman Catholic Church created the right-to-life movement. Without the Church, the movement would not exist as such today. The Church provided from the start the organizational infrastructure, the communications network, the logistical support, the resources, the ideology, and the people, as well as a ready-made nationwide political machine otherwise impossible to duplicate. Always, the Church contributed money, a great deal of it, either through its own organizations or through direct grants to independent but related groups. . . . What made the Church's right-to-life effort significant was that this was the first time in American history that Catholics had made that kind of all-out bid to influence national policy. In force in almost every state, and everywhere well organized, the Church made it possible for this compelling single issue to dominate for a time the democratic process.[21]

The hierarchy recognized the necessity of the mobilization of fundamentalists prior to the bishops' 1975 pastoral plan. It simply used the abortion issue to accomplish this goal. Now it uses the Moral Majority and other "fundamentalist" organizations to accomplish other items on its agenda, such as breaking down the principle of separation of church and state, enforcing support by taxpayers of the Catholic school system, and the election of obedient Catholics to Congress and state legislatures. Most Americans have the mistaken perception that at least half of the anti-abortion movement is fundamentalist. Nothing could be further from the truth. My own state of North Carolina is Jesse Helms country. The very heart of Moral Majority land, it has a population of six million. Yet, according to the Moral Majority leadership in North Carolina, there are only twenty-five thousand Moral Majority members in this state.[22] That means that only 0.4 percent of the residents of this state belong to the "Majority." Almost ten times this number belong to the Catholic Church, although this is one of the least Catholic states in America. The reason why the Moral Majority membership is so small in North Carolina is because of the small pro-portion of Catholics. In virtually all other states, the ratio of Catholics to fundamentalists is even greater. One can almost invariably dismiss the claim that someone was elected anywhere in America because of "fundamentalist support."

Many New Right non-Catholic senators and congressmen have been big winners in the Vatican's political mobilization efforts set out in the Pastoral Plan of Action. The biggest winner of all has been Senator Jesse Helms of North Carolina, the so-called dean of the New Right. There is little doubt that Helms is the Vatican's most important ally in Congress and, precisely because he is non-Catholic, the most important of all to their agenda. No one has had greater access to the "hidden" money of the Catholic Church of which Father Bryce spoke. Helms is Baptist, but Congressional Club founder and Helms's cam-paign strategist since 1972, Thomas F. Ellis, is Catholic.[23]

Helms gained much of his fame for his ability to tie up the Senate with its own rules. However, it was his legislative aide, James P. Lucier, a Catholic, who "mastered the rules" and devised the strate-gies to accomplish this.[24] The "Helms Amendment," which made him famous, was written by Catholic John Sullivan (see page 118).

Helms spent $8 million in his 1978 campaign, twice the previous all-time Senate campaign record. According to the *Almanac of Ameri-can Politics, 1984*, incumbent Helms spent thirty times as much as his opponent, unknown insurance commissioner John Ingram ($8,123,205 as opposed to $264,088). Yet Helms only won by a margin of 55 per-cent to 45 percent. This extraordinary feat in American politics is a good indication of just how important the New Right and its leader-ship in the Vatican feel Helms is to their political agenda in America.

The Vatican has *unlimited* financial muscle with which to influ-ence political campaigns in America. Attesting to this fact are the Fonzo study of the Vatican, which shows assets of $50 billion to $60 billion, including stock it controls in our stock exchange, and the Foster report, which shows that the Catholic Church in the United States has assets of more than $100 billion (more than ten times the combined wealth of IBM, Exxon, General Motors, and U.S. Steel). The Church can arrange for corporate contributions from corporations it owns, controls, or has a significant voice in. It can call upon parish-ioners to take money from Church funds and give it to political cam-paigns in their name to avoid linkage with the Church. It can also call upon influential Catholic laypersons in corporations to use their influ-ence to direct corporate money to appropriate candidates.

In the 1984 Jesse Helms-Jim Hunt campaign, we are seeing a repeat of 1978 with Helms certain to break his own spending record. More than three-fourths of his contributions are coming from out-of-state.[25] Obviously the Vatican is attaching as much significance to a Helms victory in 1984 as it did in 1978. Jesse Helms has benefited more than any other political candidate (except possibly Mr. Reagan) from the 1975 Bishops Pastoral Plan which specifically says that they are going to elect sympathetic officials (*see*, appendix two). The Vatican is literally buying a senate seat from North Carolinians in which Helms will sit.

Since the leadership of the Moral Majority is almost exclusively comprised of obedient Catholics, it is controlled by the Vatican. The hierarchy has used a relatively small number of Protestants to deceive all of America and to advance their power under the guise of Protestantism.

These Protestants, who are no doubt unwitting participants, could never consider themselves American conservatives. Religious conservatism, yes, but only because religious conservatism, unlike American political conservatism, can only be loosely defined. The intense activity in this country to radically change American ways to fulfill the Vatican agenda means radical changes in our time-proven democratic institutions and their relationships to each other.

True American conservatives must be concerned about a religious institution which is far more political and economic than it is religious and which has a history of repression and tyranny everywhere it has been allowed to establish a political base or a coalition with a political power.

True American conservatives must be troubled by the influx of tens of millions of Catholic illegal aliens who gravely threaten our democratic institutions and our national and personal security. We must be concerned about the forty thousand members of youth gangs, mostly illegal aliens, in Los Angeles who committed more than one thousand murders in the past four years[26] and the eventual spread of this activity to all U.S. cities and towns. We must be alarmed by the 40 million street children in Latin America,[27] millions of whom will be bringing a life-style based on overpopulation and want with them when they migrate here.

Does the Moral Majority express concern for this imminent threat to our national security? No, nor is it likely to do so in any substantive manner, such action being inconsistent with the Vatican's agenda.

True American conservatives must be concerned about overpopulation wherever instability can threaten U.S. security interests. It is no accident that American conservatives Senators Harry Byrd, Jr., Robert Byrd, Goldwater, Jackson, Stennis, and Tower have voted for abortion.[28] Is the Moral Majority concerned about this threat? No, because any response to this threat threatens the Vatican.

True American conservatism must defend freedom of religion.

However, the intolerance of Catholicism threatens this freedom. History has clearly shown that "the accumulation of political power by the churches, in other societies, has led to severe legal restrictions on the churches and often to a denial of religious liberty."[29] While the Catholic Church currently accumulates the political power, in the end, American Protestants and others will pay the price.

True American conservatives must be concerned about our government remaining a truly representative democracy. We must be on guard against Catholic bishops who write to our legislators, saying:

> All major legislative questions are, at root, moral issues. The American people rightly expect that their elected legislators will be profoundly sensitive to the moral dimension of these questions. . . . The bishops should expect a Catholic legislator to have a developed, informed, sensitive sense of what is morally right and wrong. Bishops should expect the Catholic legislator to be even more concerned about the rights and needs of others and to be particularly knowledgeable and effective about moral issues raised in the legislature. We Catholics consider ourselves to have special guidance in matters of faith and morality: the direction that comes from the *objective* official teaching of the Church as expressed by the Pope and the bishops. So, official Catholic teaching on matters confronting legislators is a most helpful guide.[30]

In other words, all legislative issues are moral issues. The pope and the bishops reserve the right to decide on all moral issues. Therefore, as a Catholic legislator, you must vote according to our dictates.

In August 1984, Bishop James Malone, president of the nation's Roman Catholic bishops, was completely clear on this issue. New York Archbishop John O'Connor had sharply criticized Governor Mario Cuomo for taking the position that Catholic politicians should separate their personal moral conviction from the stands they take regarding public policy and lawmaking.[31] Bishop Malone fully supported O'Connor's position, effectively saying that Catholic politicians must vote as their bishops tell them to vote on public policy issues.[32] Roman Catholic Senator Paul Laxalt, Mr. Reagan's campaign chairman and closest confidant in Congress, let his sentiments be known to the 40 million people who watched him nominate Mr. Reagan for a second term by shouting, "Shame on you, Mario Cuomo!"[33]

True American conservatives must be concerned about a pope who instructs Americans to defy democratically established American law, as he did in New York regarding illegal immigration and in Washington regarding abortion in October 1979.[34]

True American conservatives must be concerned about accurately assessing problems that threaten our national and global security. We must recognize that, for every economist-scientist such as Colin Clark, Julian Simon, Roger Reville, and Herman Kahn who takes the Vatican position on whether the world is or will soon be overpopulated, there are a hundred who disagree. We should perceive that these Vatican supporters are usually Catholics themselves (like Clark and Reville) or that they seek the spotlight the Church provides for well-known non-Catholics who support its arguments (like Simon and Kahn). The sentiments of most scientists were expressed in a stinging rebuke to Pope Paul during the 135th meeting of the American Association for the Advancement of Science in Dallas in 1968. About two thousand scientists, including four Nobel laureates, signed the protest which read in part:

> More than half the world is hungry and the environment of the world is deteriorating rapidly because of overpopulation. Any action which impedes efforts to halt the world population growth perpetuates the misery in which millions now live and promotes death by starvation of millions this year and many more millions in the next few decades.
>
> It has been stated by Roman Catholics that the Pope is not evil, but simply unenlightened, and we must agree. But, whatever the motives, the evil consequences of his encyclical are manifest. . . .
>
> The world must quickly come to realize that Pope Paul VI has sanctioned the deaths of countless numbers of human beings with his misguided and immoral encyclical. The fact that this incredible document was put forth in the name of a religious figure whose teachings embodies the highest respect for the value of human dignity and life should serve to make the situation even more repugnant to mankind.[35]

The scientists, in signing the protest, pledged that they "will no longer be impressed by appeals for world peace or compassion for the poor from a man whose deeds help to promote war and make poverty inevitable." Furthermore, more than six hundred Catholic theologians vocally protested Pope Paul VI's ban on birth control.[36]

American conservatives must be concerned about military preparedness for this new national security threat of overpopulation. But I can assure the reader that there is absolutely no preparation being made. In order to begin preparations there must first be an admission that there is a problem of overpopulation. The Vatican is successfully thwarting this admission, even in the military!

The Radical Religious and the American Military

Of all of my concerns, the greatest are the implications of overpopulation for the security of our country. As the two thousand scientists at the 1968 AAAS meeting stated, the pope's "deeds promote war and make poverty inevitable." How is the United States preparing militarily for this new threat and what are the Vatican's activities to thwart those preparations?

In the August 1981 issue of *Military Review*, the U.S. Army's leading military journal, there is an article by LTC John G. Wilcox, study director for International Programs at the U.S. Army Concepts Analysis Agency in Bethesda, Maryland. The article, "Military Implications of the *Global 2000 Report*," was the first ever published in a U.S. military journal on the implications of overpopulation for U.S. military preparedness—*and the last.* It began:

> Despite changing social and scientific trends which indicate a vastly different threat environment in the year 2000, the Army continues to structure and train its forces for conventional war on the plains of Europe. Even "contingency" missions such as those associated with the Rapid Deployment Force are in terms of conventional battle as we knew it in World War II and as we perceive it will be in Central Europe. . . . The war in Vietnam affected the military psyche to such an extent that there has been no serious analysis of the lessons of that war, and what was written of Vietnam has been discreetly purged from the military history books. . . .
>
> The Army has become too inflexible in its rigid adherence to the concepts of fighting a mechanized battle in a sophisticated conventional war of the future. Rather than preparing our Army to defend the United States and our national interests, this fixed strategic model limits U.S. power to apply force in differing situations in differing areas of the world. This article examines some specific demographic trends that indicate a vastly changed world situation in the future in which our Army may be called upon to defend this nation in ways beyond today's comprehension.
>
> The recently published *Global 2000 Report* contains some very stark realities and serious military implications. . . .[37]

I was gratified to see this interest in the military implications of overpopulation because of my conviction that full acknowledgment of the overpopulation problem would come when military analysts became involved.

For more than a decade, I had given much thought to the subjects discussed by Wilcox in his article. So, too, had my colleague, General Dennis Hapugalle, of the Sri Lanka Army. We had discussed our military experiences, which coincided with those predicted by Wilcox, and decided to prepare an article reflecting our views for *Military Review*. The article was entitled "Population Growth and the Security of Nations" and was summarily rejected by the editor-in-chief with the comment that our article "does not fit into subject areas scheduled by the journal." We were astounded. Wilcox's article was probably the most important and relevant ever published by this journal. There were no follow-up articles or discussions whatsoever.

In a letter replying to Malcolm Potts, dated October 21, 1981, Wilcox summed up the reaction to his article:

> The subject of population control requires a great deal of study. I am not sure if the armed forces are willing to acknowledge the implications of current projections. I must tell you that the only feedback I have received has been from the media, politicians, and academics. There has been no official interest expressed by any military official.

Discussion by the U.S. Defense Department of the military implications of overpopulation have been completely suppressed. There is only one reason: such discussion would serious threaten the survival of the Vatican. Catholic Action, Opus Dei, and the Knights of Malta operate in the U.S. military just as they do in all other areas of American life. Military analysts, their superiors, and their publishers are all intimidated by this Vatican-inspired Catholic network.

General Alexander Haig, former secretary of state, experienced what happens even when such a high-ranking person steps forward. During his Senate confirmation hearings, Haig had supported the Carter National Security Council's position:

> I think perhaps the largest, the most pervasive problem by which mankind will be increasingly wrenched is our declining ability to meet human needs in the areas of food, raw materials, and resources, counterpoised against what are clearly rising expectations of growing populations. I think this is the grist from which many of the controversies in the period ahead will evolve.[38]

Haig no doubt infuriated the Vatican with this statement.

According to his own account, he was forced out of the Reagan administration by Catholic colleagues. He maintained his support for the Carter Council position until after his departure from the Reagan administration. Eventually, he realized that he was finished politically unless he recanted. This he did on March 6, 1983. He had become a senior fellow at Herman Kahn's Hudson Institute which produces "research findings" that inevitably agree with the Vatican position on everything. He stated:

> I think the basic approach of Herman Kahn and his colleagues at Hudson, which I share, is that our young people have been plagued with a series of Malthusian assessments for an extended period. This was perhaps exemplified by the Club of Rome report in 1978, and subsequent studies done under President Carter, which suggested to our youth that they're going to inherit a nation that's run out of energy, food, and jobs. But the data suggest precisely the opposite: not an excess of labor and a shortage of jobs, but a shortage of labor as early as 1985 which will be rather severe by 1990. So our young people are going to inherit a nation of great opportunity. . . .[39]

Catholics in the military who seek promotion must similarly respond to the needs of the Vatican. Military officials avoid this new threat to our security because their advancement, like Haig's, depends upon it. After all, pursuit of this line of thinking is "offensive to the Holy See." Instead of facing up to these realities, everything is blamed on "the communists." And our military prepares almost exclusively for a war with the "Russian communists" on the plains of Europe.

In June 1983, former President Carter, in an address to the Global Tomorrow Coalition, sharply criticized the Reagan administration for its handling of overpopulation problems. He also accused Reagan of ignoring poverty and oppression in El Salvador in pursuit of military aid:

> It is tragic indeed for our leaders to ignore these clear warning signals and to allege that they are just the result of ill-advised foreign political decisions or a communist plot against us.[40]

If discussion of the military implications of overpopulation were not suppressed, there would be a deafening clamor rising from the military. As a group, these men and women are the most exposed of any occupational group in America to the effects of overpopulation. It was during my own military experience in Korea in 1969 that I first recognized the obvious serious implications of overpopulation for the security of all nations. Signals abound. For example, in Morocco, more than 240 people were killed in food riots in January 1984.[41] India has announced it will build a barbed wire fence around parts of Bangladesh after four thousand illegal aliens were beaten to death in February 1983.[42] In the United States, refugee settlement organizations (the largest, of course, is Catholic) receive almost four times as much money as *all Immigration and Naturalization Service law enforcement programs combined.*[43] However, all signals are being ignored.

The military role in dealing with the problem of overpopulation is certain to be vast in the future, and an appropriate role has been described in an earlier text.[44] Indonesia, which has the most effective program for a country with a large rural population, other than China, uses its military to assist in providing family planning services. True American conservatives must be concerned about the total lack of such military preparedness in our country.

The Pope as a Leader of True American Conservatives

It is the responsibility, the duty, of the true American conservative to evaluate the pope as a leader since he has usurped this role politically both in the United States and abroad, sometimes in secret. His decisions as a national and international power broker affect all of us in significant ways. After all, President Reagan has repeatedly said that God ought to have a role in the governing of America,[45] and he has called upon the pope to point the way. To evaluate the pope as a leader is an appropriate activity.

There is inordinate attention given by the celibate pope to sex. In October 1980, he stated that "a man might commit adultery in his heart with his own wife." In December 1981, he "ruled out sex in life after death."[46] Subsequently, he announced officially that "virginity and celibacy are spiritually better than marriage but those who marry do no wrong." In December 1983, the Holy See released a thirty-six-page statement on sex education, the preparation of which "required several years of study."[47] Calling nonmarital sex "a grave and selfish disorder," the document praises virginity and describes masturbation as "a deviation reflecting immaturity." It recommends sports for young people as an alternative for sex. The teaching of "artificial" means of contraception can never be a legitimate aspect of sex education. There is a warning against graphic audio-visual teaching materials that "crudely present sexual realities for which the pupil is not prepared and thus create traumatic impressions or raise an unhealthy curiosity which leads to evil."

All of these attempts to paint sexual activity as evil and celibacy as good reveals the pope's own sexual maladjustment. All reinforce *his* decision to be celibate. He obviously views most expressions of human sexuality as terribly evil. Exactly how this affects all of his other decision-making is uncertain, but one must assume that it does. This document also rules out any hope of population growth control.

In a most revealing *New York Times Magazine* article, Kenneth A. Briggs says of the head of the Roman Catholic Church:

> . . . He has become a crusader with an urgency that suggests that time is running out. Underlying this urgency is the Pope's acute awareness of the approaching end of the second Christian millennium. Professor George H. Williams of Harvard's Divinity School, a longtime friend of the Pope who has written a searching book, *The Mind of John Paul II*, says the Pontiff has "more of an eschatological view than anyone would suspect," and that by the year 2000 he "believes something decisive will happen in the world." The substance of eschatology is based on biblical teachings that God will inaugurate His Kingdom through a series of happenings at the close of an age. Such premonitions by the Pope relate to both his mysticism and the business at hand. If he imagines himself as the head of the Church in the final days of the world as we know it, then his pressing desire to purify and unify the Church before that final judgment has its own logic.[48]

According to *Webster's New Collegiate Dictionary*, *eschatological* is defined as "of or relating to the end of the world."

In other words, the pope believes that the world is coming to an end in sixteen years. He is not alone. Mr. Reagan, Mr. Watt, and Jerry Falwell are all on record that they, too, believe that the world is coming to an end about that time. Should true American conservatives accept the leadership of anybody who believes that the world is coming to an end in sixteen years? Do we want these radical religious people to decide on intermediate and long-term policies that affect our nation, as well as ourselves and our children?

Furthermore, Briggs reveals the following:

> Of all the movements in the Church today, none seems closer to the Pope's approach to theology and evangelism than Opus Dei, a semisecret conservative organization of more than seventy-two thousand members in forty nations that fosters piety, obedience to the Church, and commitment to winning influence with people in high places in government and private life. Though liberals regard the movement with suspicion, its favor with the Pope was demonstrated on August 23 when he raised its status from a "secular institute" to a "personal prelature."

Should true American conservatives accept the leadership of a pope whose favorite organization is a "semisecret" organization with seventy-two thousand members that fosters blind obedience to the

Church and that is committed to "winning influence with people in high places in our [democratic] government"?

The pope has repeatedly condemned the arms race but has made it clear that it is correct to maintain and call on armies to protect the Church's interests. He has criticized pacifism in the face of injustice, "The person who truly desires peace rejects any kind of pacifism which is cowardice or the simple preservation of tranquility."[49] It is clear that the pope firmly believes that any amount of armed intervention, including that used in Vietnam, is justified when the existence of the Church in a country is threatened. The Vatican itself no longer has an army to protect its interests. So it avails itself of others'—such as ours. This state of affairs should concern any true American conservative.

Columnist Coleman McCarthy, in pointing out some obvious inconsistencies in the pope's "no politics rule," wrote, "It is known that the pope was tepid in his backing of Archbishop Romero, the slain leader in El Salvador. Romero was a one-time conservative who came late in life to understand the violent effects upon his people of decades of church-state coziness in Latin America."[50] Similarly, columnist Fernando Pinon has stated, "The U.S. Catholic Church realizes that the Church in Latin America . . . and its support of oligarchical power has been a contributing cause to today's rebellions."[51] More recently, Archbishop Obando has been condemned by the Nicaraguan government for "fomenting subversion."[52] The Church is identified with oppression, corruption, and anti-democratic policies in Latin America, though Americans are rarely aware of this. The Church has almost paralyzed population growth control in Latin America.

In February 1984, Pope John Paul II issued an apostolic letter on suffering. He said that "physical, mental, and moral pain pose a mystery that can lead to spiritual growth and salvation."[53] According to this, suffering is good; it is beneficial. In other words, people should accept the suffering caused by overpopulation and the absence of Catholic government response to this problem. They should accept social injustice and oppressive governments. This letter seems to aid oppressive governments.

Is it in our national interest to identify with the Roman Catholic Church in this grossly overpopulated region of 400 million people? True American conservatives must give serious consideration to this question.

In March 1983, Senator Bob Packwood voted against the confirmation of Margaret Heckler as secretary of the Department of Health and Human Services (HHS). In a letter explaining his action, he said, "Difference of opinion is the right of every American. However, the HHS secretary is not just any American. That person is in a pivotal position to advise the president on all matters affecting your right to choose."[54] Heckler's religious views prohibit her from making any decision other than an anti-abortion decision.

It is obvious that the best interests of the United States and the best interests of the Vatican are not always the same. Should Americans place Catholics completely loyal to the hierarchy in certain positions of government leadership where their proven religious views prevent their acting in the best interests of the United States? This may be the most important question facing true American conservatives today.

Notes

1. Maxine Negri, "The Well-Planned Conspiracy," *The Humanist* (1982), 42:3:40.

2. J. Kotkin, "Ready on the Right: Christian Soldiers Are on the March," *Washington Post* (August 25, 1979), A10.

3. Connie Paige, *The Right to Lifers* (New York: Summit Books, 1983), p. 168.

4. Ibid., p. 175.

5. Ibid., p. 225.

6. Negri, "The Well-Planned Conspiracy," p. 41.

7. P. D. Young, "Richard A. Viguerie: The New Right's Power Broker," *Penthouse* (December 1982), p. 146.

8. Ibid., p. 148.

9. Ibid., p.

10. Ibid., p. 210.

11. Ibid., p. 205.

12. J. Conaway, "Righting the Course," *Washington Post* (March 22, 1983), D1.

13. A. M. Greeley, "American Catholics: Going Their Own Way," *New York Times Magazine* (October 10, 1982), p. 74.

14. B. Goldwater, *The Conscience of a Conservative* (Shepherdsville: Victor Publishing Company, 1960), p. 57.

15. Ibid., p. 72.

16. Paige, *The Right to Lifers*, p. 63.

17. Ibid., p. 73.

18. Ibid., p. 156.

19. Ibid., p. 31.

20. Ibid., p. 51.

21. Ibid., p. 51.

22. D. Winston, "Falwell Seeking Voters to Re-elect Helms," *Raleigh News and Observer* (July 7, 1983), 1C.

23. G. Wang, "Ellis Sees End of Role as Helms's Strategist," *Raleigh News and Observer* (February 13, 1984), 7A.

24. R. Whittle, "Top Helms Lieutenants Stay Busy Building New Network of the Right," *Raleigh News and Observer* (November 25, 1979), 9-1.

25. J. Brinkley, "Everyone Has a Stake in This Contest," *Chapel Hill Newspaper*, from *New York Times* News Service (August 14, 1984), p. 5A.

26. W. A. Henry, III., "Journalism Under Fire," *Time* (December 12, 1983), p. 91.

27. "Ragged Army of a Continent," *Population* (1983), 9:9:2.

28. "ZPG Population Action Guide," *ZPG Reporter* (December 1982), 14:6.

29. "Church and Politics: Some Guidelines," *Church and State* (1982), 35:10:4.

30. Bishops of Connecticut, "Pastoral Letter: The Legislator Faces the Abortion Problem," *The Wanderer*, circa U.S. Bishops Pastoral on War and Peace, p. 1.

31. C. T. Rowan, "Fight for Catholic Votes Vital Aspect of '84 Race," *Raleigh News and Observer* (August 16, 1984), p. 5A.

32. "Bishop's Leader Faults Politician's Dual Stances," *Raleigh News and Observer* (August 10, 1984), p. 9A.

33. W. Safire, "The Christian Republican Party?" *Raleigh News and Observer* (August 30, 1984), p. 4A.

34. A. Wlazelek, "Bishop Asks for Pro-Life Measures," *The Morning Call*, Allentown, Oregon (August 15, 1983), p. 81.

35. Waldo Zimmermann, *Condemned to Live: The Plight of the Unwanted Child* (Vita Press, 2143 Poplar Avenue, Memphis, TN 38104; 1981), p. 129.

36. "Pope's Charisma Allays Disputes," *Chapel Hill Newspaper* (October 8, 1979), p. 3A.

37. LTC John G. Wilcox, "Military Implications of the *Global 2000 Report*," *Military Review* (August 1981).

38. From testimony given by Alexander Haig in Senate hearings concerning his confirmation as secretary of state which were held in March 1981.

39. B. Bradlee, Jr., "Al Haig on White House Predators, Lebanon, Foreign Policy, and Carter," *Chapel Hill Newspaper* (March 6, 1983), p. 10.

40. C. Peterson, "Carter Denounces Reagan's Record," *Washington Post* (June 3, 1983), p. A-1.

41. "Food Price Increases Rescinded After 240 Reported Dead in Riots," *Raleigh News and Observer* (January 23, 1984), p. 3A.

42. "India Plans to Fence Out Bangladesh Immigrants," *Raleigh News and Observer* (January 23, 1984), p. 3A.

43. "Refugee Act to be Reauthorized," *FAIR Immigration Report* (1983), 4:10:1.

44. S. D. Mumford, *Population Growth Control: The Next Move Is America's* (New York: Philosophical Library, Inc., 1977).

45. A. Devroy, "Reagan Campaign Themes: Abortion, Tax Cuts, Peace," *U.S.A. Today* (January 31, 1984), p. 7A.

46. P. Nichols, "Pope Rules Out Sex in Life After Death," *The London Times* (December 8, 1981).

47. "Vatican Issues Guidelines on Sex Education," *Raleigh News and Observer* (December 2, 1983), p. 10A.

48. K. A. Briggs, "Using the World as His Pulpit," *New York Times Magazine* (October 10, 1982), p. 25.

49. "Pope Decries War Mentality in Leaders," *Raleigh News and Observer* (December 24, 1983), p. 3A.

50. C. McCarthy, "Church Politics as Usual," *Washington Post* (May 7, 1980), p. A19.

51. F. Pinon, "U.S. Catholic Beliefs Stronger Than Politics," *San Antonio Express News* (September 11, 1983).

52. "Nicaraguan Archbishop Criticizes Sandanista Protestors," *Raleigh News and Observer* (November 11, 1983), p. 3A.

53. "Suffering Spurs Spiritual Growth, Pope Says," *Raleigh News and Observer* (February 12, 1984), p. 9A.

54. B. Packwood, *Senator Bob Packwood's Pro-Choice Report* (March 11, 1983), p. 10.

Conclusion

Whether world population growth is a serious national and global security threat is no longer debatable. It is a reality. It is also true that, if the Roman Catholic Church is not the *only* important opposition to population growth control, it is, at least, the *most* significant opposition.

Overpopulation is not just a biological, resource, or management problem. It is above all a political problem that cannot be considered in isolation from struggles for power, particularly by the Roman Catholic Church.

The fundamental issue is that the best interests of the Vatican are not concurrent with those of the United States or any other country. The institution of the Roman Catholic Church is, above all else, a political one; second, economic in nature; and, only third, a religious organization. As Americans we must judge this arrangement for ourselves. We are not obliged to let the Vatican define itself, though we have in the past.

We have allowed the Vatican to establish the rules which govern our relationship with it. The Vatican rules the communicants of the Roman Church and seeks to control and manipulate governments. Americans must recognize that Catholicism is both a religion and an ambitious, arrogant political institution. To continue to accept it as just another religious institution is to fall into the political trap the Vatican has set. We must no longer play by *its* rules.

The issue of population growth control may be the most obvious example of the serious implications of this arrangement for American democracy. In the collision of the best interests of the Vatican and the best interests of Americans, the Vatican is clearly winning the conflict. The Vatican made the rules and we are blindly following them. As this book shows, American democracy and the very future of Americans are at stake. Patriotic Americans have both a right and an obligation to respond to this totalitarian government in a more appropriate manner. There is a difference between religion and religious tyranny, and the Vatican is using religion to practice tyranny. We must redefine what is acceptable practice for a religious community in the public arena. If we do not, our democracy will take on the characteristics of a Latin American enclave—like El Salvador—in no more than a few decades.

The Church has successfully undertaken this activity in many countries. It is not a new modus operandi for the Vatican. Why should America be treated any differently?

The stage was set for the creation of the population problem more than two centuries ago when Protestant America developed the ethic, "you should never criticize another man's religion." Giving up the freedom to evaluate the impact on our democracy of another person's religion resulted in inhibition regarding criticism of the negative aspects of that religion.

This gave absolute freedom to the Vatican to abuse freedom of religion, in whose name the Church has sought to impose a wall of silence where its actual aims may be in question.

Censorship of the press in this regard is a fact of American life today.

The ecumenical movement was critical to setting the stage for advancement of the Vatican's agenda. For the Vatican, this movement has been a great success and, for everyone else, a colossal failure. Not only did the Vatican step up its abuse of American freedom with the coming of the ecumenical movement, Protestants were standing by to apologize for the Vatican in the name of religion.

The creation of the abortion issue gave the Vatican the oppotunity to politically mobilize in America. The Church's creation of the Moral Majority, the most extensive political lobbying organization America has witnessed, gave it the opportunity to act with impunity under the guise of American Protestantism.

Eric Severeid, in an award acceptance speech at the National Press Club in March 1984, stated that to keep American freedoms they *must* be exercised. We did not exercise the freedom of thought to be critical in appraising certain undesirable aspects of the Vatican's activities, and we are losing the freedom of thought. We are now called upon to accept the religious dogma of the Julian Simons and Herman Kahns as Alexander Haig has done. We did not exercise the freedom of the press to report the negative activities of the Vatican, and it seized on this opportunity to build and impose a far-reaching system of censorship. We have largely lost the freedom of the press regarding the negative activities of the Vatican—but not completely. *Herein lies our hope* both for successfully dealing with the overpopulation problem and reversing the movement of American democracy toward a Latin-style democracy. However, if we do not exercise the freedom of the press, it is clear from current events that we are going to lose it. For this reason, the solution to the world population problem rests, first of all, in the hands of American journalists, editors, and publishers. Only if they first reestablish complete freedom of the press can the population problem be dealt with and the drift of American democracy toward a Latin one be reversed.

It is a fact that the Vatican is anti-democratic and anti-American. It refuses to accept the principal of the separation of church and state which, in fact, threatens its power. The Vatican's refusal to accept this principal makes peaceful coexistence with America impossible.

Vatican manipulation of American government is no longer theory. With the election of Mr. Reagan and the arrival of the Reagan team, this became an undeniable reality. However, it has been evident for years that the Vatican has exercised some influence over both of our major political parties. Neither has discussed vital issues in terms that the Vatican would find unacceptable.

The Vatican's extensive use of secret societies to manipulate American politics is well established. Undertaking secret activities in our democracy as representatives of a foreign power can never be healthy. Their very secrecy suggests that their activities would not be consistent with the open democracy so cherished by patriotic Americans who expect all public issues to be openly debated.

The Vatican is opposed to the freedoms of thought, press, speech, and assembly, which are essential for the survival of American democracy. Because its presence in America is so well established, the Roman Catholic hierarchy is a greater threat to American democracy than communism or any other contemporary political force. Its blatant extensive interference in American efforts to deal with the overpopulation problem, which threatens U.S. security, shows the lengths to which it is willing to go to undermine the American democratic process.

Political realities are not immutable. There are a limited number of Catholic and non-Catholic elected officials who are serving the needs of the Vatican rather than the needs of Americans. They can be voted out of power and the trend reversed. The press must reassert its freedom to expose the Vatican when it behaves in opposition to America's best interests.

To act otherwise would be irresponsible. Other political systems have suffered through repression of speech, assembly, and the press. Realities can be ignored only for so long, as El Salvador has discovered. Rebellion is inevitably a consequence of this repression, which often takes the form of civil war. We must make every effort to avoid this scenario for a "holy civil war," as Bill Moyers called it, by reestablishing our freedom of speech and press regarding *any* church's activities as they reflect on our society.

The Vatican constantly identifies its ambitions with the supposed wishes of its people. It intends to drag down all American Catholics as it goes down. The number of Catholic lives sacrificed by the Vatican to achieve its political ambitions (in Vietnam, El Salvador, Lebanon, and so forth) is incalculable. Therefore each Catholic American has no choice but to take responsibility for the actions of the leadership since he or she is a source of the power being exercised by the Church. American Catholics have a special responsibility for terminating Vatican influence in America.

All Americans, Catholic and non-Catholic, must beware of acting according to rules laid down by the Vatican. Otherwise American democracy will soon be replaced by Latin democracy and America as we know it will disappear.

If Vatican influence in the American democratic process continues to increase, there is certain to be a growing call for an uprising against the Roman Catholic Church in America and its allies, such as the Protestants who belong to the Moral Majority. The threat to U.S. security posed by overpopulation, particularly the threat of massive illegal immigration into our country, the control of which the Vatican now thwarts, will not allow for this confrontation to be postponed for long. Tens of thousands of Vietnamese Catholics lost their lives in a vain attempt by the Vatican to maintain control. Under the present course, American Catholics and non-Catholics are faced with this prospect.

In the long run, non-Catholics who oppose outright confrontation with the Vatican on the serious threat to our national security posed by overpopulation, are doing a great disservice to the entire American community.

Vatican involvement in American policy-making should be of great concern to true conservatives in this country, especially regarding the absence of preparations by the Department of Defense for the consequences of overpopulation relative to national security. Leadership must be forthcoming. The "New Right" approximates a Vatican political party. The "New Right" can best be described as radically religious. Members are radicals, the antithesis of true American conservatives, and they should be thought of as such.

Above all else, people who feel that they must impose the Vatican agenda should not be serving in any capacity in public or in private life in our country. We have a Constitution that we expect people to live by both in spirit and letter. This Constitution must not be changed to fulfill the needs of the Vatican. Americans have every right to demand that all citizens be loyal to our government rather than the Vatican government. The national and global security threat of world over-population cannot be addressed in any significant ways until this confrontation with the Vatican is undertaken and successfully completed. People who state that there can be population growth control in the absence of this confrontation with the Vatican are impractical or charlatans.

The threat to U.S. and global security posed by overpopulation can be successfully addressed and the threat to American democracy posed by the Vatican can be eliminated by reestablishing the freedom of the press regarding the activities of the Vatican in America. This can be done. The fact that *The Humanist* and *Church and State* magazines continue to be published and that articles such as the one cited in *Science* appear clearly show that we have not reached the point of no return.

The challenge rests with the American press. However, it must have the support of all patriotic Americans, of all religious persuasions.

The great success in China shows that the population problem is solvable and the solution affordable. Underdeveloped countries can repeat this success elsewhere if given the chance. We must make that chance possible.

Appendix 1.

From Judge Dooling's Decision

Under date of November 20, 1975, the National Conference of Catholic Bishops promulgated a Pastoral Plan for Pro-Life Activities. . . .

The Pastoral Plan outlined three major efforts: (1) an educational/public information effort, (2) a pastoral effort addressed to the specific needs of women with problems related to pregnancy and abortion, and (3) a public policy effort directed toward the legislative, judicial, and administrative areas so as to insure effective legal protection for the right to life. Then the pamphlet continued:

> This Pastoral Plan is addressed to and calls upon all Church-sponsored or identifiably Catholic national, regional, diocesan, and parochial organizations and agencies to pursue the three-fold effort. This includes ongoing dialogue and cooperation between the NCCB/USCC on the one hand and priests, religious and lay-persons, individually and collectively, on the other hand. In a special way we invite the continued cooperation of national Catholic organizations. . . .

The third major element of the Pastoral Plan is the legislative/public policy. . . .

The abortion decisions of the United States Supreme Court (Jan-

This appendix consists of excerpts from Federal Judge John Dooling's 1980 U.S. District Court, Eastern District of New York, decision in McRae vs. HEW.

uary 22, 1973) violate the moral order, and have disrupted the legal process which previously attempted to safeguard the rights of unborn children. A comprehensive pro-life legislative program must therefore include the following elements:

a) Passage of a constitutional amendment providing protection for the unborn child to the maximum degree possible.

b) Passage of federal and state laws and adoption of administrative policies that will restrict the practice of abortion as much as possible.

c) Continual research into and refinement and precise interpretation of *Roe* and *Doe* and subsequent court decisions.

Noting that well-planned and coordinated political action at national, state, and local levels would be required, the pamphlet states that the activity is not simply the responsibility of Catholics and should not be limited to Catholic groups or agencies. [Author's comment: This is the basis for the formation of the Moral Majority.]

[According to the Pastoral Plan] there is to be in each state a State Coordinating Committee, functioning under the State Conference or its equivalent, which will include bishops' representatives from each diocese in the state and will function: to monitor political trends in the state and their implications for the abortion effort, to coordinate the efforts of the various dioceses and evaluate progress in the dioceses and congressional districts, and to provide counsel regarding specific political relationships within the various parties at the state level.

Diocesan Pro-Life Committees are to coordinate groups and activities within the diocese, particularly efforts to effect passage of a constitutional amendment to protect the unborn child. The diocesan committee is to rely for information and direction on the Bishops' Pro-Life Office and on the National Committee for a Human Life Amendment. The objective of the diocesan committee is: to provide direction and coordination of diocesan and parish education/information efforts and maintain working relationships with all groups involved in congressional district activity, to promote and assist in developing groups involved in pregnancy counseling and those providing alternatives and assistance to women who have problems in pregnancy, to encourage the development of "grass-roots" political action organizations, to maintain communication with National Committee for a Human Life Amendment in regard to federal activity, so as to provide instantaneous information concerning local senators and representatives, to maintain a local public information effort directed to the media, including seeking equal time, etc., and to develop close relationships with each senator or representative.

Parish pro-life committees are to sponsor and conduct intensive education programs, promote and sponsor pregnancy counseling and other alternatives to abortion, general public awareness of the continuing effort to obtain a constitutional amendment (coordinating efforts of parish pro-life groups, Knights of Columbus groups, etc., and seeking ways to cooperate with non-sectarian pro-life groups, including right-to-life organizations; in each congressional district the parishes will provide one basic resource, the clergy having an active role in the overall effort), and prudently convince others—Catholics and non-Catholics—of the necessity of the constitutional amendment to provide a base for legal protection for the unborn.

In each congressional district, a pro-life action group should be formed [Author's comment: now called the Moral Majority]; its task is essentially political, to organize people to help persuade elected representatives, and its range of action limited, focused on passing a constitutional amendment; the action groups should be bi-partisan, nonsectarian, inclined toward political action. The pamphlet states, in italics:

It is not an agency of the Church, nor is it operated, controlled, or financed by the Church.

The congressional district pro-life group is to conduct a continuing public information effort, directed to elected officials and potential candidates, to persuade them that abortion must be legally restricted; to counterbalance propaganda efforts opposing a constitutional amendment; to persuade all residents in the district that permissive abortion is harmful to society and that some restriction is necessary; to persuade all residents that a constitutional amendment is necessary as a first step toward legally restricting abortion; "To convince all elected officials and potential candidates that 'the abortion issue' will not go away and that their position on it will be subject to continuing public scrutiny"; to enlighten sympathetic supporters who will collaborate in persuading others; to enlist those who are generally supportive so they may be called upon when needed to communicate to the elected officials; to elect members of their own group or active sympathizers to specific posts in all local party organizations; to set up a telephone network that will enable the committee to take immediate action when necessary; to maintain an informational file on the pro-life position of every elected official and potential candidate; to work for qualified candidates who will vote for a constitutional amendment and other pro-life issues; and to maintain liaison with all denominational leaders (pastors) and all other pro-life groups in the district.

Appendix 2.

National Conference of Catholic Bishops' Pastoral Plan for Pro-Life Activities

All should be persuaded that human life and the task of transmitting it are not realities bound up with this world alone. Hence they cannot be measured or perceived only in terms of it, but always have a bearing on the eternal destiny of men. . . . For God, the Lord of life, has conferred on men the surpassing ministry of safeguarding life in a manner which is worthy of man. Therefore from the moment of its conception life must be guarded with the greatest care, while abortion and infanticide are unspeakable crimes.

—Constitution on the Church in the Modern World

Respect for human life has been gradually declining in our society during the past decade. To some degree this reflects a secularizing trend and a rejection of moral imperatives based on belief in God and His plan for creation. It also reflects a tendency for individuals to give primary attention to what is personally rewarding and satisfying to them, to the exclusion of responsible concern for the well-being of other persons and society. These trends, along with others, have resulted in laws and judicial decisions which deny or ignore basic human rights and moral responsibilities for the protection and promotion of the common good. In this category are efforts to establish permissive abortion laws, the abortion decisions of the United States Supreme Court in 1973

The Bishops' Pastoral Plan, dated November 20, 1975, was produced by the Publications Office, United States Catholic Conference, 1312 Massachusetts Avenue NW, Washington, DC 20005.

denying any effective legal protection to the unborn child, and the growing attempts to legitimatize positive euthanasia through so-called "death with dignity" laws.

In the Declaration of Independence, our Founding Fathers point to the right to life as the first of the inalienable rights given by the Creator.

In fulfillment of our pastoral responsibilities, the members of the National Conference of Catholic Bishops have repeatedly affirmed that human life is a precious gift from God; that each person who receives this gift has responsibilities toward God, toward self, and toward others; and that society, through its laws and social institutions, must protect and sustain human life at every stage of its existence. Recognition of the dignity of the human person, made in the image of God, lies at the very heart of our individual and social duty to respect human life.

In this Pastoral Plan we hope to focus attention on the pervasive threat to human life arising from the present situation of permissive abortion. Basic human rights are violated in many ways: by abortion and euthanasia, by injustice and the denial of equality to certain groups of persons, by some forms of human experimentation, by neglect of the underprivileged and disadvantaged who deserve the concern and support of the entire society. Indeed, the denial of the God-given right to life is one aspect of a larger problem. But it is unlikely that efforts to protect other rights will be ultimately successful if life itself is continually diminished in value.

In focusing attention on the sanctity of human life, therefore, we hope to generate a greater respect for the life of each person in our society. We are confident that greater respect for human life will result from continuing the public discussion of abortion and from efforts to shape our laws so as to protect the life of all persons, including the unborn.

Thus this Pastoral Plan seeks to activate the pastoral resources of the Church in three major efforts:

1. an educational/public information effort to inform, clarify, and deepen understanding of the basic issues;
2. a pastoral effort addressed to the specific needs of women with problems related to pregnancy and to those who have had or have taken part in an abortion;
3. a public policy effort directed toward the legislative, judicial, and administrative areas so as to insure effective legal protection for the right to life.

This Pastoral Plan is addressed to and calls upon all Church-sponsored or identifiably Catholic national, regional, diocesan, and parochial organizations and agencies to pursue the three-fold effort. This includes ongoing dialogue and cooperation between the NCCB/USCC on the one hand, and priests, religious and laypersons, individually and collectively, on the other hand. In a special way we invite the continued cooperation of national

Catholic organizations.

At the same time, we urge Catholics in various professional fields to discuss these issues with their colleagues and to carry the dialogue into their own professional organizations. In similar fashion, we urge those in research and academic life to present the Church's position on a wide range of topics that visibly express her commitment to respect for life at every stage and in every condition. Society's responsibility to insure and protect human rights demands that the right to life be recognized and protected as antecedent to and the condition of all other rights.

Dialogue is most important—and has already proven highly fruitful— among Churches and religious groups. Efforts should continue at ecumenical consultation and dialogue with Judaism and other Christian bodies, and also with those who have no specific ecclesial allegiance. Dialogue among scholars in the field of ethics is a most important part of this interfaith effort.

The most effective structures for pastoral action are in the diocese and the parish. While recognizing the roles of national, regional, and statewide groupings, this Plan places its primary emphasis on the roles of diocesan organizations and the parish community. Thus, the resources of the diocese and parish become most important in its implementation.

I. Public Information/Education Program

In order to deepen respect for human life and heighten public opposition to permissive abortion, a two-fold educational effort presenting the case for the sanctity of life from conception onwards is required.

The first aspect, a public information effort, is directed to the general public. It creates an awareness of the threats to human dignity inherent in a permissive abortion policy, and the need to correct the present situation by establishing legal safeguards for the right to life. It gives the abortion issue continued visibility and sensitizes the many people who have only general perceptions of the issue but very little by way of firm conviction or commitment. The public information effort is important to inform the public discussion, and it proves that the Church is serious about and committed to its announced long-range pro-life effort. It is accomplished in a variety of ways, such as accurate reporting of newsworthy events, the issuance of public statements, testimony on legislative issues, letters to editors.

The second aspect, an intensive long-range education effort, leads people to a clearer understanding of the issues, to firm conviction, and to commitment. It is part of the Church's essential responsibility that it carry forward such an effort, directed primarily to the Catholic community. Recognizing the value of legal, medical, and sociological arguments, the primary and ultimately most compelling arguments must be theological and moral. Respect for life must be seen in the context of God's love for mankind reflected in creation and redemption and man's relationship to God and to other members of the human family. The Church's opposition to abortion is based on Christian teaching on the dignity of the human person, and the responsibility to proclaim and defend basic human rights, especially the right to life.

This intensive education effort should present the scientific information on the humanity of the unborn child and the continuity of human growth and development throughout the months of fetal existence; the responsibility and necessity for society to safeguard the life of the child at every stage of its existence; the problems that may exist for a woman during pregnancy; and more humane and morally acceptable solutions to these problems.

The more intensive educational effort should be carried on by all who participate in the Church's educational ministry, notably:

- Priests and religious, exercising their teaching responsibility in the pulpit, in other teaching assignments, and through parish programs.
- All Church-sponsored or identifiably Catholic organizations, national, regional, diocesan, and parochial, carrying on continuing education efforts that emphasize the moral prohibition of abortion and the reasons for carrying this teaching into the public policy area.
- Schools, CCD, and other Church-sponsored *educational agencies* providing moral teaching, bolstered by medical, legal, and sociological data, in the schools, etc. The USCC Department of Education might serve as a catalyst and resource for the dioceses.
- Church-related social service and health agencies carrying on continuing education efforts through seminars and other appropriate programs, and by publicizing programs and services offering alternatives to abortion.

Although the primary purpose of the intensive educational program is the development of pro-life attitudes and the determined avoidance of abortion by each person, the program must extend to other issues that involve support of human life: there must be internal consistency in the pro-life commitment.

The annual Respect Life Program sets the abortion problem in the context of other issues where human life is endangered or neglected, such as the problems facing the family, youth, the aging, the mentally retarded, as well as specific issues such as poverty, war, population control, and euthanasia. This program is helpful to parishes in calling attention to specific problems and providing program formats and resources.

II. Pastoral Care

The Church's pastoral effort is rooted in and manifests her faith commitment. Underlying every part of our program is the need for prayer and sacrifice. In building the house of respect for life, we labor in vain without God's merciful help.

Three facets of the Church's program of pastoral care deserve particular attention.

1) *Moral Guidance and Motivation*

   Accurate information regarding the nature of an act and free-dom from coercion are necessary in order to make responsible moral decisions. Choosing what is morally good also requires motivation. The Church has a unique responsibility to trans-mit the teaching of Christ and to provide moral principles consistent with that teaching. In regard to abortion, the Church should provide accurate information regarding the nature of the act, its effects, and far-reaching consequences, and should show that abortion is a violation of God's laws of charity and justice. In many instances, the decision to do what is in conformity with God's law will be the ultimate determi-nant of the moral choice.

2) *Service and care for women and unborn children.*

   Respect for human life motivates individuals and groups to reach out to those with special needs. Programs of service and care should be available to provide women with alternate op-tions to abortion. Specifically, these programs should include:

   - adequate education and material sustenance for women so that they may choose motherhood responsibly and freely in accord with a basic commitment to the sanctity of life;
   - nutritional, pre-natal, childbirth, and post-natal care for the mother, and nutritional and pediatric care for the child throughout the first year of life;
   - intensified scientific investigation into the causes and cures of maternal disease and/or fetal abnormality;
   - continued development of genetic counseling and gene therapy centers and neo-natal intensive care facilities;
   - extension of adoption and foster care facilities to those who need them;
   - pregnancy counseling centers that provide advice, encour-agement, and support for every woman who faces difficulties related to pregnancy;
   - counseling services and opportunities for continuation of education for unwed mothers;
   - special understanding, encouragement, and support for victims of rape;

- continued efforts to remove the social stigma that is visited on the woman who is pregnant out of wedlock and on her child.

Many of these services have been and will continue to be provided by Church-sponsored health care and social service agencies, involving the dedicated efforts of professionals and volunteers. Cooperation with other private agencies and increased support in the quest for government assistance in many of these areas are further extensions of the long-range effort.

3) *Reconciliation*

The Church is both a means and an agent of reconciliation. As a spiritual entity, the Church reconciles men and women to God. As a human community, the Church pursues the task of reconciling men and women with one another and with the entire community. Thus all of the faithful have the duty of promoting reconciliation.

Sacramentally, the Church reconciles the sinner thhough the Sacrament of Penance, thereby restoring the individual to full sacramental participation. The work of reconciliation is also continually accomplished in celebrating and participating in the Eucharist. Finally, the effects of the Church's reconciling efforts are found in the full support of the Christian community and the renewal of Christian life that results from prayer, the pursuit of virtue, and continued sacramental participation.

Granting that the grave sin of abortion is symptomatic of many human problems, which often remain unsolved for the individual woman, it is important that we realize that God's mercy is always available and without limit, that the Christian life can be restored and renewed through the sacraments, and that union with God can be accomplished despite the problems of human existence.

III. Legislative/Public Policy Effort

In recent years there has been a growing realization throughout the world that protecting and promoting the inviolable rights of persons are essential duties of civil authority, and that the maintenance and protection of human rights are primary purposes of law. As Americans, and as religious leaders, we have been committed to governance by a system of law that protects the rights of individuals and maintains the common good. As our founding fathers believed, we hold that all law is ultimately based on Divine Law, and that a just system of law cannot be in conflict with the law of God.

Abortion is a specific issue that highlights the relationship between morality and law. As a human mechanism, law may not be able fully to articulate the moral imperative, but neither can legal philosophy ignore the moral order. The abortion decisions of the United States Supreme Court (January 22, 1973) violate the moral order, and have disrupted the legal process which previously attempted to safeguard the rights of unborn children. A comprehensive pro-life legislative program must therefore include the following elements:

- a) Passage of a constitutional amendment providing protection for the unborn child to the maximum degree possible.
- b) Passage of federal and state laws and adoption of administrative policies that will restrict the practice of abortion as much as possible.
- c) Continual research into and refinement and precise interpretation of *Roe* and *Doe* and subsequent court decisions.
- d) Support for legislation that provides alternatives to abortion.

Accomplishment of this aspect of this Pastoral Plan will undoubtedly require well planned and coordinated political action by citizens at the national, state, and local levels. This activity is not simply the responsibility of Catholics, nor should it be limited to Catholic groups or agencies. It calls for widespread cooperation and collaboration. As citizens of this democracy, we encourage the appropriate political action to achieve these legislative goals. As leaders of a religious institution in this society, we see a moral imperative for such political activity.

Means of Implementation of Program

The challenge to restore respect for human life in our society is a task of the Church that reaches out through all institutions, agencies, and organizations. Diverse tasks and various goals are to be achieved. The following represents a systematic organization and allocation of the Church's resources of people, institutions, and finances which can be activated at various levels to restore respect for human life, and insure protection of the right to life of the unborn.

1. State Coordinating Committee

A. It is assumed that overall coordination in each state will be the responsibility of the State Catholic Conference or its equivalent. Where a State Catholic Conference is in process of formation or does not exist, bishops' representatives from each diocese might be appointed as the core members of the *State Coordinating Committee.*

B. The *State Coordinating Committee* will be comprised of the director of the State Catholic Conference and the diocesan Pro-Life coordinators. At this level it would be valuable to have one or more persons who are knowledgeable about public traditions, mores, and attitudes and are experienced in legislative activity. This might be the Public Affairs Specialist referred to under the Diocesan Pro-Life Committee, or, for example, an individual with prior professional experience in legislative or governmental service. In any case, it should be someone with a practical understanding of contemporary political techniques.

C. The primary purposes of the *State Coordinating Committee* are:

- to monitor the political trends in the state and their implications for the abortion effort;
- to coordinate the efforts of the various dioceses; and to evaluate progress in the dioceses and congressional districts;
- to provide counsel regarding the specific political relationships within the various parties at the state level.

2. The Diocesan Pro-Life Committee

a) *General Purpose*—The purpose of the Committee is to coordinate groups and activities within the diocese (to restore respect for human life), particularly efforts to effect passage of a constitutional amendment to protect the unborn child. In its coordinating role, the Committee will rely on information and direction from the Bishops' Pro-Life Office and the National Committee for a Human Life Amendment. The Committee will act through the diocesan pro-life director, who is appointed by the bishop to direct pro-life efforts in the diocese.

b) *Membership*

- Diocesan Pro-Life Director (Bishop's representative)
- Respect Life Coordinator
- Liaison with State Catholic Conference
- Public Affairs Advisor
- Representatives of Diocesan Agencies (Priests, Religious, Lay Organizations)
- Legal Advisor—Representative of Pro-Life Groups
- Representativis of Parish Pro-Life Committees
- Congressional District Representative(s)

c) *Objectives:*

1. Provide direction and coordination of diocesan and parish education/information efforts and maintain working relationship with all groups involved in congressional district activity.
2. Promote and assist in the development of those groups, particularly voluntary groups involved in pregnancy counseling, which provide alternatives and assistance to women who have problems related to pregnancy.
3. Encourage the development of "grass-roots" political action organizations.
4. Maintain communications with National Committee for a Human Life Amendment in regard to federal activity, so as to provide instantaneous information concerning local senators and representatives.
5. Maintain a local public information effort directed to press and media. Include vigilance in regard to public media, seek "equal time," etc.
6. Develop close relationships with each senator or representative.

3. The Parish Pro-Life Committee

The parish Pro-Life Committee should include a delegate from the Parish Council, representatives of various adult and youth parish organizations, members of local Knights of Columbus Councils, Catholic Daughters of America chapters, and other similar organizations.

Objectives:

a) Sponsor and conduct intensive education programs touching all groups within the parish, including schools and religious education efforts.
b) Promote and sponsor pregnancy counseling units and other alternatives to abortion.
c) Through ongoing public information programs generate public awareness of the continuing effort to obtain a constitutional amendment. The NCCB, the National Committee for a Human Life Amendment, and the State and Diocesan Coordinating Committees should have access to every congressional district for information, consultation, and coordination of action. A chairperson should be designated in each district who will coordinate the efforts of parish pro-life groups, K of C groups, etc., and seek ways of cooperating with nonsectarian pro-life groups, including right-to-life organizations. In each district, the parishes will provide one basic resource, and the

clergy will have an active role in the overall effort.

d) Prudently convince others—Catholics and non-Catholics—of the reasons for the necessity of a constitutional amendment to provide a base for legal protection for the unborn.

4. The Pro-Life Effort in the Congressional District

Passage of a constitutional amendment depends ultimately on persuading members of Congress to vote in favor of such a proposal. This effort at persuasion is part of the democratic process, and is carried on most effectively in the congressional district or state from which the representative is elected. Essentially, this effort demands ongoing public information activity and careful and detailed organization. Thus it is absolutely necessary to encourage the development in each congressional district of an identifiable, tightly knit, and well-organized pro-life unit. This unit can be described as a public interest group or a citizens' lobby. No matter what it is called:

a) its task is essentially political, that is, to *organize people* to help persuade the elected representatives; and

b) its range of action is limited, that is, it is focused on passing a constitutional amendment.

As such, the congressional district pro-life group differs from the diocesan, regional, or parish pro-life coordinator or committee, whose task is pedagogic and motivational, not simply political, and whose range of action includes a variety of efforts calculated to reverse the present atmosphere of permissiveness with respect to abortion. Moreover, it is an agency of the citizens, operated, controlled, and financed by these same citizens. *It is not an agency of the Church, nor is it operated, controlled, or financed by the Church.*

The congressional district pro-life action group should be bi-partisan, nonsectarian, inclined toward political action. It is complementary to denominational efforts, to professional groups, to pregnancy counseling and assistance groups.

Each congressional district should have a chairperson who may serve as liaison with the Diocesan Coordinating Committee. In dioceses with many congressional districts, this may be arranged through a regional representation structure.

Objectives of the Congressional District Pro-Life Group

1. To conduct a continuing public information effort to persuade all elected officials and potential candidates that abortion must be legally restricted.

2. To counterbalance propaganda efforts opposed to a constitutional amendment.

3. To persuade all residents in the congressional district that per-

missive abortion is harmful to society and that some restriction is necessary.

4. To persuade all residents that a constitutional amendment is necessary as a first step toward legally restricting abortion.

5. To convince all elected officials and potential candidates that "the abortion issue" will not go away and that their position on it will be subject to continuing public scrutiny.

6. To enlist sympathetic supporters who will collaborate in persuading others.

7. To enlist those who are generally supportive so that they may be called upon when needed to communicate to the elected officials.

8. To elect members of their own group or active sympathizers to specific posts in all local party organizations.

9. To set up a telephone network that will enable the committee to take immediate action when necessary.

10. To maintain an informational file on the pro-life position of every elected official and potential candidate.

11. To work for qualified cancidates who will vote for a constitutional amendment and other pro-life issues.

12. To maintain liaison with all denominational leaders (pastors) and all other pro-life groups in the district.

This type of activity can be generated and coordinated by a small, dedicated, and politically alert group. It will need some financial support, but its greatest need is the commitment of other groups who realize the importance of its purposes, its potential for achieving those purposes, and the absolute necessity of working with the group to attain the desired goals.

Conclusion

The challenges facing American society as a result of the legislative and judicial endorsement of permissive abortion are enormous. But the Church and individual Catholics must not avoid the challenge. Although the process of restoring respect for human life at every stage of existence may be demanding and prolonged, it is an effort which both requires and merits courage, patience, and determination. In every age the Church has faced unique challenges calling forth faith and courage. In our time and society, restoring respect for human life and establishing a system of justice which protects the most basic human rights are both a challenge and an opportunity whereby the Church proclaims her commitment to Christ's teaching on human dignity and the sanctity of the human person.

Appendix 3.

Policy Statement: International Conference on Population

Introduction

For many years, the United States has supported, and helped to finance, programs of family planning, particularly in developing countries. This administration has continued that support but has placed it within a policy context different from that of the past. It is sufficiently evident that the current exponential growth in global population cannot continue indefinitely. There is no question of the ultimate need to achieve a condition of population equilibrium. The differences that do exist concern the choice of strategies and methods for the achievement of that goal. The experience of the past two decades not only makes possible but requires a sharper focus for our population policy. It requires a more refined approach to problems which appear today in quite a different light than they did twenty years ago.

First and most important, population growth is, of itself, a neutral phenomenon. It is not necessarily good or ill. It becomes an asset or a problem only in conjunction with other factors, such as economic policy, social constraints, need for manpower, and so forth. The relationship between population growth and economic development is not necessarily a negative one. More people do not necessarily mean less growth. Indeed, in the economic history of many nations, population growth has been an essential element in economic progress.

This White House policy statement, prepared for the World Population Conference in Mexico City, August 6, 1984, is little more than a restatement of the Vatican position on abortion, family planning, and population growth control.

Before the advent of governmental population programs, several factors had combined to create an unprecedented surge in population over most of the world. Although population levels in many industrialized nations had reached or were approaching equilibrium in the period before the Second World War, the baby boom that followed in its wake resulted in a dramatic, but temporary, population "tilt" toward youth. The disproportionate number of infants, children, teenagers, and eventually young adults did strain the social infrastructure of schools, health facilities, law enforcement, and so forth. However, it also helped sustain strong economic growth, despite occasionally counterproductive government policies.

Among the developing nations, a coincidental population increase was caused by entirely different factors. A tremendous expansion of health services—from simple innoculations to sophisticated surgery—saved millions of lives every year. Emergency relief, facilitated by modern transport, helped millions to survive flood, famine, and drought. The sharing of technology, the teaching of agriculture and engineering, and improvements in educational standards generally, all helped to reduce mortality rates, especially infant mortality, and to lengthen life spans.

This demonstrated not poor planning or bad policy but human progress in a new era of international assistance, technological advance, and human compassion. The population boom was a challenge; it need not have been a crisis. Seen in its broader context, it required a measured, modulated response. It provoked an overreaction by some, largely because it coincided with two negative factors which, together, hindered families and nations in adapting to their changing circumstances.

The first of these factors was governmental control of economies, a development which effectively constrained economic growth. The post-war experience consistently demonstrated that, as economic decision-making was concentrated in the hands of planners and public officials, the ability of average men and women to work toward a better future was impaired, and sometimes crippled. In many cases, agriculture was devastated by government price fixing that wiped out rewards for labor. Job creation in infant industries was hampered by confiscatory taxes. Personal industry and thrift were penalized, while dependence upon the state was encouraged. Political considerations made it difficult for an economy to adjust to changes in supply and demand or to disruptions in world trade and finance. Under such circumstances, population growth changed from an asset in the development of economic potential to a peril.

One of the consequences of this "economic scatism" was that it disrupted the national mechanism for slowing population growth in problem areas. The world's more affluent nations have reached a population equilibrium without compulsion and, in most cases, even before it was government policy to achieve it. The controlling factor in these cases has been the adjustment, by individual families, of reproductive behavior to economic opportunity and aspiration. Historically, as opportunities and the standard of living rise, the birth rate falls. In many countries, economic freedom has led to economically rational behavior.

That pattern might be well underway in many nations where population growth is today a problem, if counterproductive government policies had not disrupted economic incentives, rewards, and advancement. In this regard, localized crises of population growth are, in part, evidence of too much government control and planning, rather than too little.

The second factor that turned the population boom into a crisis was confined to the Western world. It was an outbreak of anti-intellectualism, which attacked science, technology, and the very concept of material progress. Joined to a commendable and long overdue concern for the environment, it was more a reflection of anxiety about unsettled times and an uncertain future. In its disregard of human experience and scientific sophistication, it was not unlike other waves of cultural anxiety that have swept through Western civilization during times of social stress and scientific exploration.

The combinations of these two factors—counterproductive economic policies in poor and struggling nations, and a pessimism among the more advanced—led to a demographic overreaction in the 1960s and 1970s. Scientific forecasts were required to compete with unsound, extremist scenarios, and too many governments pursued population control measures without sound economic policies that create the rise in living standards historically associated with decline in fertility rates. This approach has not worked, primarily because it has focused on a symptom and neglected the underlying ailments. For the last three years, this administration has sought to reverse that approach. We recognize that, in some cases, immediate population pressures may require short-term efforts to ameliorate them. But population control programs alone cannot substitute for the economic reforms that put a society on the road toward growth and, as an aftereffect, toward slower population increase as well.

Nor can population control substitute for the rapid and responsible development of natural resources. In commenting on the *Global 2000 Report*, this administration in 1981 disagreed with its call "for more governmental supervision and control," stating that:

> Historically, that has tended to restrict the availability of resources and to hamper the development of technology, rather than to assist it. Recognizing the seriousness of environmental and economic problems, and their relationship to social and political pressures, especially in the developing nations, the administration places a priority upon technological advance and economic expansion, which hold out the hope of prosperity and stability of a rapidly changing world. That hope can be realized, of coursi, only to the extent that government's response to prob-

lems, whether economic or ecological, respects and enhances individual freedom, which makes true progress possible and worthwhile.

Those principles underlie this country's approach to the International Conference on Population to be held in Mexico City in August.

Policy Objectives

The world's rapid population growth is a recent phenomenon. Only several decades ago, the population of developing countries was relatively stable, the result of a balance between high fertility and high mortality. There are now 4.5 billion people in the world, and six billion are projected by the year 2000. Such rapid growth places tremendous pressures on governments without concomitant economic growth.

The International Conference on Population offers the United States an opportunity to strengthen the international consensus on the interrelationships between economic development and population which has emerged since the last such conference in Bucharest in 1974. Our primary objective will be to encourage developing countries to adopt sound economic policies and, where appropriate, population policies consistent with respect for human dignity and family values. As President Reagan stated, in his message to the Mexico City Conference:

> We believe *population programs* can and must be truly voluntary, cognizant of the rights and responsibilities of individuals and families, and respectful of religious and cultural values. When they are, such programs *can make an important contribution to economic and social development, to the health of mothers and children, and to the stability of the family and of society.*

U.S. support for family planning programs is based on respect for human life, enhancement of human dignity, and strengthening of the family. Attempts to use abortion, involuntary sterilization, or other coercive measures in family planning must be shunned, whether exercised against families within a society or against nations within the family of man.

The United Nations Declaration of the Rights of the Child (1959) calls for legal protection for children before birth as well as after birth. In keeping with this obligation, the United States does not consider abortion an acceptable element of family planning programs and will no longer contribute to those of which it is a part. Accordingly, when dealing with nations which support abortion with funds not provided by the United States government, the United States will contribute to such nations through segregated accounts which cannot be used for abortion. Moreover, the United States will no longer contribute to separate nongovernmental organizations which perform or actively promote abortion as a method of family planning in other nations. With regard to the United Nations Fund for Population Activities (UNFPA), the United States will insist that no part of its contribution to be used for abortion. The United States will also call for concrete assurances that the UNFPA is not engaged in, or does not provide funding for, abortion or coercive family planning programs; if such assurances are not forthcoming, the United States will redirect the amount of its contribution to other, non-UNFPA family planning programs.

In addition, when efforts to lower population growth are deemed advisable, U.S. policy considers it imperative that such efforts respect the religious beliefs and culture of each society, and the right of couples to determine the size of their own families. Accordingly, the United States will not provide family planning funds to any nation which engages in forcible coercion to achieve population growth objectives.

U.S. government authorities will immediately begin negotiations to implement the above policies with the appropriate governments and organizations.

It is time to put additional emphasis upon those root problems which frequently exacerbate population pressures, but which have too often been given scant attention. By focusing upon real remedies for underdeveloped economies, the International Conference on Population can reduce demographic issues to their proper place. It is an important place, but not the controlling one. It requires our continuing attention within the broader context of economic growth and of the economic freedom that is its prerequisite.

Population, Development, and Economic Policies

Conservative projections indicate that, in the sixty years from 1950 to 2010, many Third World countries will experience four-, five-, or even six-fold increases in the size of their population. Even under the assumption of gradual declines in birth rates, the unusually high proportion of youth in the Third World means that the annual population growth in many of these countries will continue to increase for the next several decades.

Sound economic policies and a market economy are of fundamental importance to the process of economic development. Rising standards of living contributed in a major way to the demographic transition from high to low rates of population growth which occurred in the United States and other industrialized countries over the last century.

The current situation of many developing countries, however, differs in certain ways from conditions in nineteenth century Europe and the United States. The rates and dimensions of population growth are much higher now, the pressures on land, water, and resources are greater, the safety-valve of migration is more restricted, and, perhaps most important, time is not on their side because of the momentum of demographic change.

Rapid population growth compounds already serious problems faced by both public and private sectors in accommodating changing social and economic demands. It diverts resources from needed investment, and increases the costs and difficulties of economic development. Slowing population growth is not a panacea for the problems of social and economic development. It is not offered as a substitute for sound and comprehensive development policies. Without other development efforts and sound economic policies which encourage a vital private sector, it cannot solve problems of hunger, unemployment, crowding, or social disorder.

Population assistance is an ingredient of a comprehensive program that focuses on the root causes of development failures. The U.S. program as a whole, including population assistance, lays the basis for well-grounded, step-by-step initiatives to improve the well-being of people in developing countries and to make their own efforts, particularly through expanded private sector initiatives, a key building block of development programs.

Fortunately, a broad international consensus has emerged since the 1974 Bucharest World Population Conference that economic development and population policies are mutually reinforcing.

By helping developing countries slow their population growth through support for effective voluntary family planning programs, in conjunction with sound economic policies, U.S. population assistance contributes to stronger saving and investment rates, speeds the development of effective markets and related employment opportunities, reduces the potential resource requirements of programs to improve the health and education of the people, and hastens the achievement of each country's graduation from the need for external assistance.

The United States will continue its long-standing commitment to development assistance, of which population programs are a part. We recognize the importance of providing our assistance within the cultural, economic, and political context of the countries we are assisting and in keeping with our own values.

Health and Humanitarian Concerns

Perhaps the most poignant consequence of rapid population growth is its effect on the health of mothers and children. Especially in poor countries, the health and nutrition status of women and children is linked to family size. Maternal and infant mortality rises with the number of births and with births too closely spaced. In countries as different as Turkey, Peru, and Nepal, a child born less than two years after its sibling is twice as likely to die before it reaches the age of five than if there were an interval of at least four years between the births. Complications of pregnancy are more frequent among women who are very young or near the end of their reproductive years. In societies with widespread malnutrition and inadequate health conditions, these problems are reinforced; numerous and closely spaced births lead to even greater malnutrition of mothers and babies.

It is an unfortunate reality that in many countries abortion is used as a means of terminating unwanted pregnancies. This is unnecessary and repugnant; voluntary family assistance programs can provide a humane alternative to abortion for couples who wish to regulate the size of their family [sic], and evidence from some developing countries indicates a decline in abortion as such services become available.

The basic objective of all U.S. assistance, including population programs, is the betterment of the human condition—improving the quality of life of mothers and children, of families, and of communities for generations to come. *For we recognize that people are the ultimate resource—but this means happy and healthy children, growing up with education, finding productive work as young adults,* and able to develop their full mental and physical potential.

U.S. aid is designed to promote economic progress in developing countries through encouraging sound economic policies and freeing of individual initiative. Thus, the United States supports a broad range of activities in various sectors, including agriculture, private enterprise, science and technology, health, population, and education. Population assistance amounts to about 10 percent of total development assistance.

Technology as a Key to Development

The transfer, adaptation, and improvement of modern know-how is central to U.S. development assistance. People with greater know-how are people better able to improve their lives. Population assistance ensures that a wide range of modern demographic technology is made available to developing countries and that technological improvements critical for successful development receive support.

The efficient collection, processing, and analysis of data derived from census, survey, and vital statistics programs contributes to better planning in both the public and private sectors.

The United States at Mexico City

In conjunction with the above statements of policy, the following principles should be drawn upon to guide the U.S. delegation at the International Conference on Population:

1. Respect for human life is basic, and any attempt to use abortion, involuntary sterilization, or other coercive measures in family planning must be

rejected.

2. Population policies and programs should be fully integrated into, and reinforce, appropriate, market-oriented development policies; their objective should be clearly seen as an improvement in the human condition, and not merely an exercise in limiting births.

3. Access to family education and services needs to be broadened, especially in the context of maternal/child health programs, in order to enable couples to exercise responsible parenthood. Consistent with values and customs, the United States favors offering couples a variety of medically approved methods.

4. Though population factors merit serious consideration in development strategy, they are not a substitute for sound economic policies which liberate individual initiative through the market mechanism.

5. There should be higher international priority for biomedical research into safer and better methods of fertility regulation, especially natural family planning, and for operation research into more effective service delivery and program management.

6. Issues of migration should be handled in ways consistent with both human rights and national sovereignty.

7. The United States, in cooperation with other concerned countries, should resist intrusion of polemical or nongermane issues into Conference deliberations.

Appendix 4.

Syllabus of Pope Pius IX
(In the affirmative form)

I. Propositions opposed to the Errors of "Pantheism, Naturalism, and absolute Rationalism."

1. There exists a Divine Power, Supreme Being, Wisdom and Providence, distinct from the universe, and God is another being than nature, and is therefore immutable.

It is false that God, in effect (reapse), is simply produced or developed in man and the world, and that all things are God, and have the very substance of God.

God therefore is not the same being with the world (or matter), and then mind is not the same thing with matter, necessity with liberty, the true with the false, good with evil, justice with injustice.

2. The agency of God in man and the world is not to be denied, but maintained.

3. Only with a due regard to God (or revelation as a guide) is human reason a sufficient arbiter of truth and falsehood, or of good and evil.

4. The truths of religion are not all derived from the inherent strength of human reason, and hence (or because of this exception in the case of religious truth) it is false that reason is the master-rule by which man can or ought to arrive at the knowledge of all truths of every kind.

5. Divine revelation is perfect and, therefore, it is not subject to continual and indefinite progress in order to correspond with the progress of human

---

The syllabus herein quoted is an English translation taken from the Roman Catholic Weekly Register of London, England.

reason.

6. The Christian faith (that is, doctrine) presents no opposition to human reason, and divine revelation not only elevates but also promotes the perfection of man.

7. No prophecies or miracles exhibited and recounted in the Sacred Scriptures are (as represented by the condemned propositions) and fictions of the poets. [sic]

No mystery of the Christian faith is the product of philosophical investigation.

Neither of the books of the two Testaments contain invented myths; nor is Jesus Christ Himself a mythical fiction (a fabulous personage).

II. Propositions opposed to the Errors of "Moderate Rationalism."

8. Since human reason is unequal to (the investigation of) religion, therefore theological questions cannot be treated as philosophical ones.

9. It is false that the dogmas of the Christian religion are all objects (matters of inquiry) of natural science or philosophy; that, such dogmas being proposed as objective to reason, human reason, instructed solely by history, and by its own natural powers and principles, can arrive at the knowledge of even the most abtruse [sic] dogmas.

10. Whereas the philosopher is one thing and philosophy another, not only is it the right and duty of the former to submit himself to that authority which he shall have proved to be true; but philosophy itself both can and ought to be subject to (the same) authority.

11. The Church has a right to occupy herself with philosophy, to refuse to tolerate its errors, and to assume the care of correcting them.

12. It is false that the decrees of the Apostolic See and of the Roman Congregation impede the free progress of society.

13. The method and principles by which the scholastic Doctors of old cultivated theology are not made inapplicable by the demands of this age and the progress of science.

14. Philosophy must not be studied without paying due regard to supernatural revelation.

III. Propositions Opposed to "Indifferentism and Latitudinarianism."

15. **No man is free to embrace and profess that religion which he believes to be true, guided by the light of reason!**

16. Man cannot find the way of eternal salvation, neither obtain eternal salvation in any religion.

17. **The eternal salvation of any out of the true Church of Christ is not even to be hoped for!**

18. Protestantism is not another and diversified form of the one true Christian religion in which it is possible to please God equally as in the Catholic Church.

IV. Propositions opposed to the Errors of "Socialism, Communism, Secret Societies, Bible Societies, Clerico-Liberal Societies."

Pests of this description are frequently condemned in the severest terms in

(1) The Encyc. "Qui Pluribus." Nov. 9, 1846.

(2) Allocution "Quibus quantisque," Aug. 20, 1849.

(3) Encyc. "Nescitis et Noviscum," Dec. 8, 1849.

(4) Allocution "Singulari quadam," Dec. 9, 1854.

(5) Encyc. "Quanto conficiamur moerore," Aug. 10, 1863.

V. Propositions opposed to "Errors concerning the Church and her Rights."

19. The Church is true, perfect, and entirely free association; she enjoys peculiar and perpetual rights conferred upon her by her Divine founder, and it neither belongs to the civil power to define what are these rights of the Church, nor the limits within which she may exercise them.

20. The ecclesiastical power has a right to exercise its authority independent of the toleration or assent of the civil government.

21. **The Church has power to define dogmatically the religion of the Catholic Church to be the only true religion.**

22. The obligation which securely binds Catholic teachers and writers is not limited to those things which are proposed by the infallible judgment of the Church as dogmas of faith for belief by all.

23. **The Roman Pontiffs and ecumenical councils have never exceeded the limits fo their power, or usurped the rights of princes, much less committed errors in defining matters of faith and morals.**

24. **The Church has the power of employing force and (of exercising) direct and indirect temporal power.**

25. The temporal power which is expressly or tacitly conceded by the civil authority as belonging to the Episcopacy, in addition to the power inherent in it, is not revocable at the pleasure of the civil authority.

26. The Church has a natural and legitimate right of acquiring and possessing (property).

27. The ministers of the Holy Church and the Roman Pontiff should be allowed the free exercise of the charge and dominion which the Church claims over temporal interests.

28. Bishops have the right of promulgating (more especially) their apostolic letters without the sanction of the government.

29. Dispensations (or spiritual boons) granted by the Roman Pontiff are to be considered valid even when they have not been solicited by the civil government.

30. Neither the immunities of the Church nor of ecclesiastical persons have their origin in civil law.

31. Ecclesiastical jurisdiction in cases of clerics, and either for civil or criminal offenses, cannot be abolished without the concurrence or against the

consent of the Holy See.

32. The personal immunity by which clerics are exempted from the burden of military service cannot be abrogated without a violation of equity and of natural law; and it is false that this abrogation is verily demanded by civil progress, or in a commonwealth constituted even on the principles of liberal government.

33. It belongs to ecclesiastical jurisdiction, and by a proper and inherent right, to decide upon doctrine in theological questions.

34. The doctrine which equaled the Roman Pontiff to an absolute Prince, acting in the Universal Church, is not a doctrine which prevailed merely in the Middle Ages.

35. Neither by the sentence of a General Council, nor the voice of the universal people, could the Pontifical sovereignty [sic] of the Bishop and city of Rome be transferred to some other bishop and city.

36. The definition of a National Council admits of further discussion, and no civil power can require that things remain as fixed by it.

37. No National Church can be instituted in a state of Division and separation from the authority of the Roman Pontiff.

38. It is false to assert that the extravagant acts of some Roman Pontiffs led to the Eastern and Western divisions of the Church.

VI. Propositions opposed to "The Errors of Civil Society considered both in itself and in its relation to the Church."

39. The government of the commonwealth is neither the origin and source of all rights, nor does it possess power uncircumscribed by limits.

40. The doctrine of the Catholic Church is agreeable to the well-being and interests of society.

41. No indirect or negative (much less direct or positive) power in sacred things belongs to the civil government, even when exercised by a Catholic Sovereign; and it therefore neither possesses the right called Exequatur nor that called Apellatio ab abusu.

42. In legal conflicts between both powers (civil and ecclesiastical) the ecclesiastical law prevails.

43. No lay power has authority to rescind, declare and render null, solemn conventions (commonly called concordats) relative to the use of rights proper to the ecclesiastical community, without the consent of the Apostolic See.

44. No civil authority can interfere in matters relative to religion, morality, and spiritual government; whence it has no control over the instructions which the Pastors of the Church deliver by virtue of their charge, for the regulation of consciences. Further, no civil authority has power to decide in matters pertaining to the Sacraments or to the dispositions necessary for receiving them.

45. The direction of public schools in which the youth of Christian

states are brought up, much less the Episcopal Seminaries partially excepted (in the condemned propositions), neither can nor ought to be assumed by the civil authority alone; or in such a manner that no right shall be recognized on the part of any other authority to interfere in the dispositions of the schools, in the regulation of the studies, in the appointment of degrees, and in the selection and approval of Masters.

46. Much more therefore the method of study to be adopted in clerical schools must be exempted from civil authority.

47. It is false that the best (educational) condition of civil society demands that popular schools open to the children of all classes, or that the generality of public institutions designed for letters and for the superior instruction and more extended cultivation of youth, should be free from all ecclesiastical authority, government, and interference, and should be completely subjected to the civil and political authority in conformity with the will of rulers and the prevalent opinions of the age.

48. **Catholics cannot approve of a system of education for youth apart from the Catholic faith and disjoined from the authority of the Church,** and which regards primarily or prominently the knowledge of natural things, and the ends of social life.

49. No civil authority has power to prevent the chief priests (bishops) of religion and the faithful of the people from communicating freely between each other, and with the Roman Pontiff.

50. No lay authority has in itself the right of appointing bishops, or to require them to take charge of their dioceses before they have received canonical institution and Letters Apostolic from the Holy See.

51. Further, the lay government has not the right of deposing bishops from the exercise of their pastoral duties, and is bound to obey the Roman Pontiff in matters which pertain to bishops and their Sees.

52. **No government possesses the right to change the age prescribed by the Church for religious profession both of men and women, or to prohibit religious establishments to admit persons to solemn engagements without its permission.**

53. Laws which protect religious establishments or secure their rights and duties may not be abrogated by civil government; nay more—

The civil government may not lend its assistance to any who seek to quit the religious life they have undertaken, and to break their vows! also—

Civil government cannot suppress religious orders, collegiate churches, or simple benefices, even though privately endowed; nor subject their goods or revenues to the administration or disposal of the civil power.

54. **Kings and princes are not only not exempt from the jurisdiction of the Church but are subordinate to the Church in litigated questions of jurisdiction!**

55. **The Church ought to be in union with the state, and the state with the Church.**

VII. Propositions opposed to Errors in "Natural and Christian Morality."

56. Moral laws require the Divine sanction, and human laws should both be conformable to the law of nature and receive their obligations from God.

57. **Philosophical principles, moral science, and civil laws may and must be made to bend (declinari) to divine and ecclesiastical authority.**

58. Other forces are to be recognized besides those which reside in matter; and moral and virtuous teaching should not consist in the inculcation of means to be employed (collcari) in the accumulation and increase of riches, or of voluptuous gratification.

59. It is false (to assert) that right consists in the natural fact; that all human obligations are an empty name, and that all human facts have the force of right.

60. It is false that all authority is simply (the power contained in) the sum of material forces and numbers.

61. An injustice in the fact, even although successful, inflicts injury on the sanctity of right.

62. The principle of nonintervention ought neither to be proclaimed nor observed.

63. **Subjects may not refuse obedience to legitimate princes, much less rise in insurrection against them.**

64. The violation of a solumn oath, as well as any vicious and flagitious action repugnant to the eternal law, is not only blameable, but is wholly unlawful, and deserving of the highest censure even when done from a love of country.

VIII. Propositions opposed to "Errors Concerning Matrimony."

65. It is to be maintained it is capable of proof from reason, that Christ has elevated marriage to the dignity of a sacrament.

66. The sacrament of marriage is not merely an adjunct to the contract, and separable from it; and the sacrament itself does not consist merely in the nuptial benediction.

67. The marriage tie is indissoluble by the law of nature; divorce, properly so called, **cannot in any case be pronounced by the civil authority.**

68. The Church has the power of deciding what are diriment (or divorcing) impediments to marriage; **no civil authority possesses such a power, nor can it abolish impediments that may exist to marriage.**

69. In the more backward ages, when the Church laid down certain impediments as diriment to marriage, she did so of her own authority, and not by right borrowed from the civil power.

70. The Canons of the Council of Trent, which invoke the censure of anathema against such as deny the Church the right of determining what are diriment impediments to marriage, are dogmatic, and not to be understood as emanating from such a borrowed power (or power conferred by the state).

71. The form (of solemnizing marriage according to the said Council) of Trent, under penalty of nullity, binds **even in cases where the civil law has appointed another form**, and decrees that this new form shall effectuate a valid marriage.

72. It is false that Boniface VIII (as represented by the condemned propositions) was the first who declared that the vow of chastity pronounced at Ordination annuls marriage (that is, in previously married priests).

73. Marriage among Christians cannot be constituted by any mere civil contract; the marriage-contract among Christians **must always be a sacrament; and the contract is null if the sacrament does not exist.**

74. Matrimonial causes and espousels belong, by their nature, to ecclesiastical jurisdiction.

75. It is false that the children of the Christian and Catholic Church dispute between themselves upon the compatibility of the temporal with the spiritual power!

76. The abrogation of the temporal power upon which the Apostolic See is based would not contribute to either the liberty or the happiness of the Church.

X. Propositions opposed to "Errors referring to Modern Liberalism."

77. **It is necessary even in the present day that the Catholic religion shall be held as the only religion of the state, to the exclusion of all other forms of worship.**

78. **Whence it has been unwisely provided by law, in some countries called Catholic, that persons coming to reside therein shall enjoy the free exercise of their religion.**

79. **The civil liberty of every mode of worship, and full power given to all of openly and publicly manifesting their opinions and their ideas, conduce more easily to corrupt the morals and minds of the people, and to the propagation of the pest of indifferentism.**

80. **The Roman Pontiff cannot and ought not to reconcile himself to, or agree with, progress, liberalism, and modern civilization.**

Appendix 5.

Charter of the Rights of the Family

Presented by the Holy See to All Persons, Institutions, and Authorities Concerned with the Mission of the Family in Today's World

Introduction

The Charter of the Rights of the Family has its origins in the request formulated by the Synod of Bishops held in Rome in 1980 on the theme, "The Role of the Christian Family in the Modern World" (cf. *Propositio* 42). His Holiness Pope John Paul II, in the Apostolic Exhortation *Familiaris Consortio* (No. 46), acceded to the Synod's request and committed the Holy See to prepare a Charter of the Rights of the Family to be presented to the quarters and authorities concerned.

It is important to understand correctly the nature and style of the Charter as it is now presented. The document is not an exposition of the dogmatic or moral theology of marriage and the family, although it reflects the Church's thinking in the matter. Nor is it a code of conduct for persons or institutions concerned with the question. The Charter is also different from a simple declaration of theoretical principles concerning the family. It aims, rather, at presenting to all our contemporaries, be they Christian or not, a formulation —as complete and ordered as possible—of the fundamental rights that are inherent in that natural and universal society which is the family.

The rights enunciated in the Charter are expressed in the conscience of the human being and in the common values of all humanity. The Christian vision is present in this Charter as the light of divine revelation which enlightens the natural reality of the family. These rights arise, in the ultimate

---

The Charter of the Rights of the Family was distributed by the Holy See at the International Conference on Population in Mexico City, August 1984.

analysis, from that law which is inscribed by the Creator in the heart of every human being. Society is called to defend these rights against all violations and to respect and promote them in the entirety of their content.

The rights that are proposed must be understood according to the specific character of a "Charter." In some cases they recall true and proper juridically binding norms; in other cases, they express fundamental postulates and principles for legislation to be implemented and for the development of family policy. In all cases they are a prophetic call in favor of the family institution, which must be respected and defended against all usurpation.

Almost all of these rights are already to be found in other documents of both the Church and the international community. The present Charter attempts to elaborate them further, to define them with greater clarity and to bring them together in an organic, ordered, and systematic presentation. Annexed to the text are indications of "Sources and References" from which some of the formulations have been drawn.

The Charter of the Rights of the Family is now presented by the Holy See, the central and supreme organ of government of the Catholic Church. The document is enriched by a wealth of observations and insights received in response to a wide consultation of the Bishops' Conferences of the entire Church as well as of experts in the matter from various cultures.

The Charter is addressed principally to governments. In reaffirming, for the good of society, the common awareness of the essential rights of the family, the Charter offers to all who share responsibility for the common good a model and a point of reference for the drawing up of legislation and family policy, and guidance for action programs.

At the same time the Holy See confidently proposes this document to the attention of intergovernmental international organizations which, in their competence and care for the defense and promotion of human rights, cannot ignore or permit violations of the fundamental rights of the family.

The Charter is, of course, also directed to the families themselves: it aims at reinforcing among families an awareness of the irreplaceable role and position of the family; it wishes to inspire families to unite in the defense and promotion of their rights; it encourages families to fulfill their duties in such a way that the role of the family will become more clearly appreciated and recognized in today's world.

The Charter is directed, finally, to all men and women, and especially to Christians, that they will commit themselves to do everything possible to ensure that the rights of the family are protected and that the family institution is strengthened for the good of all mankind, today and in the future.

The Holy See, in presenting this Charter, desired by the representatives of the World Episcopate, makes a special appeal to all the Church's members and institutions, to bear clear witness to Christian convictions concerning the irreplaceable mission of the family, and to see that families and parents receive the necessary support and encouragement to carry out their God-given task.

Preamble

Considering that:

A. the rights of the person, even though they are expressed as rights of the individual, have a fundamental social dimension which finds an innate and vital expression in the family;

B. the family is based on marriage, that intimate union of life in complementarity between a man and a woman which is constituted in the freely contracted and publicly expressed indissoluble bond of matrimony, and is open to the transmission of life;

C. marriage is the natural institution to which the mission of transmitting life is exclusively entrusted;

D. the family, a natural society, exists prior to the state or any other community, and possesses inherent rights which are inalienable;

E. the family constitutes, much more than a mere juridical, social, and economic unit, a community of love and solidarity, which is uniquely suited to teach and transmit cultural, ethical, social, spiritual, and religious values, essential for the development and well-being of its own members and of society;

F. the family is the place where different generations come together and help one another to grow in human wisdom and to harmonize the rights of individuals with other demands of social life;

G. the family and society, which are mutually linked by vital and organic bonds, have a complementary function in the defense and advancement of the good of every person and of humanity;

H. the experience of different cultures throughout history has shown the need for society to recognize and defend the institution of the family;

I. society, and in a particular manner the State and International Organizations, must protect the family through measures of a political, economic, social, and juridical character, which aim at consolidating the unity and stability of the family so that it can exercise its specific function;

J. the rights, the fundamental needs, the well-being, and the values of the family, even though they are progressively safeguarded in some cases, are often ignored and not rarely undermined by laws, institutions, and socio-economic programs;

K. many families are forced to live in situations of poverty which prevent them from carrying out their role with dignity;

L. the Catholic Church, aware that the good of the person, of society, and of the Church herself passes by way of the family, has always held in part of her mission to proclaim to all the plan of God instilled in human nature concerning marriage and the family, to promote these two institutions and to defend them against all those who attack them;

M. the Synod of Bishops celebrated in 1980 explicitly recommended that a Charter of the Rights of the Family be drawn up and circulated to all concerned;

the Holy See, having consulted the Bishops' Conference, now presents this Charter of the Rights of the Family and urges all states, international organizations, and all interested institutions and persons to promote respect for these rights, and to secure their effective recognition and observance.

Article 1

All persons have the right to the free choice of their state of life and thus to marry and establish a family or to remain single.

a) Every man and every woman, having reached marriage age and having the necessary capacity, has the right to marry and establish a family without any discrimination whatsoever; legal restrictions to the exercise of this right, whether they be of a permanent or temporary nature, can be introduced only when they are required by grave and objective demands of the institution of marriage itself and its social and public significance; they must respect in all cases the dignity and the fundamental rights of the person.

b) Those who wish to marry and establish a family have the right to expect from society the moral, educational, social, and economic conditions which will enable them to exercise their right to marry in all maturity and responsibility.

c) The institutional value of marriage should be upheld by the public authorities; the situation of nonmarried couples must not be placed on the same level as marriage duly contracted.

Article 2

Marriage cannot be contracted except by the free and full consent of the spouses duly expressed.

a) With due respect for the traditional role of the families in certain cultures in guiding the decision of their children, all pressure which would impede the choice of a specific person as spouse is to be avoided.

b) The future spouses have the right to their religious liberty. Therefore to impose as a prior condition for marriage a denial of faith or a profession of faith which is contrary to conscience constitutes a violation of this right.

c) The spouses, in the natural complementarity which exists between man and woman, enjoy the same dignity and equal rights regarding the marriage.

Article 3

The spouses have the inalienable right to found a family and to decide on the spacings of births and the number of children to be born, taking into full consideration their duties toward themselves, their children already born, the family, and society, in a just hierarchy of values and in accordance with the objective moral order which excludes recourse to contraception, sterilization, and abortion.

a) The activities of public authorities and private organizations which attempt in any way to limit the freedom of couples in deciding about their children constitute a grave offense against human dignity and justice.

b) In international relations, economic aid for the advancement of peoples must not be conditioned on acceptance of programs of contraception, sterilization, or abortion.

c) The family has a right to assistance by society in the bearing and rearing of children. Those married couples who have a large family have a right to adequate aid and should not be subjected to discrimination.

Article 4

Human life must be respected and protected absolutely from the moment of conception.

a) Abortion is a direct violation of the fundamental right to life of the human being.

b) Respect of the dignity of the human being excludes all experimental manipulation or exploitation of the human embryo.

c) All interventions on the genetic heritage of the human person that are not aimed at correcting anomalies constitute a violation of the right to bodily integrity and contradict the good of the family.

d) Children, both before and after birth, have the right to special protection and assistance, as do their mothers during pregnancy and for a reasonable period of time after childbirth.

e) All children, whether born in or out of wedlock, enjoy the same right to social protection, with a view to their integral personal development.

f) Orphans or children who are deprived of the assistance of their parents or guardians must receive particular protection on the part of society. The state, with regard to foster-care or adoption, must provide legislation which assists suitable families to welcome into their home children who are in need of permanent or temporary care. This legislation must, at the same time, respect the natural rights of the parents.

g) Children who are handicapped have the right to find in the home and the school an environment suitable to their human development.

Article 5

Since they have conferred life on their children, parents have the original, primary, and inalienable right to educate them; hence they must be acknowledged as the first and foremost educators of their children.

a) Parents have the right to educate their children in conformity with their moral and religious convictions, taking into account the cultural traditions of the family which favor the good and the dignity of the child; they should also receive from society the necessary aid and assistance to perform their educational role properly.

b) Parents have the right to choose freely schools or other means necessary to educate their children in keeping with their convictions. Public authorities must ensure that public subsidies are so allocated that parents are truly free to exercise this right without incurring unjust burdens. Parents should not have to sustain, directly or indirectly, extra charges which would deny or unjustly limit the exercise of this freedom.

c) Parents have the right to ensure that their children are not compelled to attend classes which are not in agreement with their own moral and religious convictions. In particular, sex education is a basic right of the parents and must always be carried out under their close supervision, whether at home or in educational centers chosen and controlled by them.

d) The rights of parents are violated when a compulsory system of education is imposed by the state from which all religious formation is excluded.

e) The primary right of parents to educate their children must be upheld in all forms of collaboration between parents, teachers, and school authorities, and particularly in forms of participation designed to give citizens a voice in the functioning of schools and in the formulation and implementation of educational policies.

f) The family has the right to expect that the means of social communication will be positive instruments for the building up of society, and will reinforce the fundamental values of the family. At the same time the family has the right to be adequately protected, especially with regard to its youngest members, from the negative effects and misuse of the mass media.

Article 6

The family has the right to exist and to progress as a family.

a) Public authorities must respect and foster the dignity, lawful independence, privacy, integrity, and stability of every family.

b) Divorce attacks the very institution of marriage and of family.

c) The extended family system, where it exists, should be held in esteem and helped to carry out better its traditional role of solidarity and mutual assistance, while at the same time respecting the rights of the nuclear family and the personal dignity of each member.

Article 7

Every family has the right to live freely its own domestic religious life under the guidance of the parents, as well as the right to profess publicly and to propagate the faith, to take part in public worship and in freely chosen programs of religious instruction, without suffering discrimination.

Article 8

The family has the right to exercise its social and political function in the construction of society.

a) Families have the right to form associations with other families and institutions, in order to fulfill the family's role suitably and effectively, as well as to protect the rights, foster the good, and represent the interests of the family.

b) On the economic, social, juridical, and cultural levels, the rightful role of families and family associations must be recognized in the planning and development of programs which touch on family life.

Article 9

Families have the right to be able to rely on an adequate family policy on the part of public authorities in the juridical, economic, social, and fiscal domains, without any discrimination whatsoever.

a) Families have the right to economic conditions which assure them a standard of living appropriate to their dignity and full development. They should not be impeded from acquiring and maintaining private possessions which would favor stable family life; the laws concerning inheritance or transmission of property must respect the needs and rights of family members.

b) Families have the right to measures in the social domain which take into account their needs, especially in the event of the premature death of one or both parents, of the abandonment of one of the spouses, of accident, of sickness or invalidity, in the case of unemployment, or whenever the family has to bear extra burdens on behalf of its members for reasons of old age, physical or mental handicaps or the education of children.

c) The elderly have the right to find within their own family or, when this is not possible, in suitable institutions, an environment which will enable them to live their later years of life in serenity while pursuing those activities which are compatible with their age and which enable them to participate in social life.

d) The rights and necessities of the family, and especially the value of family unity, must be taken into consideration in penal legislation and policy, in such a way that a detainee remains in contact with his or her family and that the family is adequately sustained during the period of detention.

Article 10

Families have a right to a social and economic order in which the organization of work permits the members to live together, and does not hinder the unity, well-being, health, and the stability of the family, while offering also the possibility of wholesome recreation.

a) Remuneration for work must be sufficient for establishing and maintaining a family with dignity, either through a suitable salary, called a "family wage," or through other social measures such as family allowances or the remuneration of the work in the home of one of the parents; it should be such that mothers will not be obliged to work outside the home to the detriment of family life and especially of the education of the children.

b) The work of the mother in the home must be recognized and respected because of its value for the family and for society.

Article 11

The family has the right to decent housing, fitting for family life and commensurate to the number of the members, in a physical environment that provides the basic services for the life of the family and the community.

Article 12

The families of migrants have the right to the same protection as that accorded other families.

a) The families of immigrants have the right to respect for their own culture and to receive support and assistance toward their integration into the community to which they contribute.

b) Emigrant workers have the right to see their family united as soon as possible.

c) Refugees have the right to the assistance of public authorities and international organizations in facilitating the reunion of their families.

Sources and References

Preamble

A. *Rerum Novarum,* 9; *Gaudium et Spes,* 24.

B. *Pacem in Terris,* Part 1; *Gaudium et Spes,* 48 and 50; *Familiaris Consortio,* 19; *Codex Iuris Canonici,* 1056.

C. *Gaudium et Spes,* 50; *Humanae Vitae,* 12; *Familiaris Consortio,* 28.

D. *Rerum Novarum,* 9 and 10; *Familiaris Consortio,* 45.

E. *Familiaris Consortio,* 43.

F. *Gaudium et Spes,* 52; *Familiaris Consortio,* 21.

G. *Gaudium et Spes,* 52; *Familiaris Consortio,* 42 and 45.

I. *Familiaris Consortio,* 45.

J. *Familiaris Consortio,* 46.

K. *Familiaris Consortio,* 6 and 77.

L. *Familiaris Consortio,* 3 and 46.

M. *Familiaris Consortio,* 46.

Article 1

Rerum Novarum, 9; *Pacem in Terris,* Part 1; *Gaudium et Spes,* 26; *Universal Declaration of Human Rights,* 16, 1.

a) *Codex Iuris Canonici,* 1058 and 1077; *Universal Declaration,* 16, 1.

b) *Gaudium et Spes,* 52; *Familiaris Consortio,* 81.

c) *Gaudium et Spes,* 52; *Familiaris Consortio,* 81 and 82.

Article 2

Gaudium et Spes, 52; *Codex Iuris Canonici,* 1057; *Universal Declaration,* 16, 2.

a) *Gaudium et Spes,* 52.

b) *Dignitatis Humanae,* 6.

c) *Gaudium et Spes,* 49; *Familiaris Consortio,* 19 and 22; *Codex Iuris Canonici,* 1125; *Universal Declaration,* 16, 1.

Article 3

Populorum Progressio, 37; *Gaudium et Spex,* 50 and 87; *Humanae Vitae,* 10; *Familiaris Consortio,* 30 and 46.

a) *Familiaris Consortio,* 30.

b) *Familiaris Consortio,* 30.

c) *Gaudium et Spes,* 50.

Article 4

Gaudium et Spes, 51; *Familiaris Consortio,* 26.

a) *Humanae Vitae,* 14; SACRED CONGREGATION FOR THE DOCTRINE OF THE FAITH, *Declaration on Procured Abortion,* November 18, 1974; *Familiaris Consortio,* 30.

b) POPE JOHN PAUL II, *Address to the Pontifical Academy of Sciences,* October 23, 1982.

d) *Universal Declaration,* 25, 2; *Convention on the Rights of the Child,* Preamble and 4.

e) *Universal Declaration,* 25, 2.

f) *Familiaris Consortio,* 41.

g) *Familiaris Consortio,* 77.

Article 5

Divini Illius Magistri, 27–34; *Gravissimum Educationis*, 3; *Familiaris Consortio*, 36; *Codex Iuris Canonici*, 793 and 1136.

a) *Familiaris Consortio*, 46.

b) *Gravissimum Educationis*, 7; *Dignitatis Humanae*, 5; POPE JOHN PAUL II, *Religious Freedom and the Helsinki Final Act* (Letter to the Heads of State of the nations which signed the Helsinki Final Act), 4b; *Familiaris Consortio*, 40; *Codex Iuris Canonici*, 797.

c) *Dignitatis Humanae*, 5; *Familiaris Consortio*, 37 and 40.

d) *Dignitatis Humanae*, 5; *Familiaris Consortio*, 40.

e) *Familiaris Consortio*, 40; *Codex Iuris Canonici*, 796.

f) POPE PAUL VI, *Message for the Third World Communications Day, 1969; Familiaris Consortio*, 76.

Article 6

Familiaris Consortio, 46.

a) *Rerum Novarum*, 10; *Familiaris Consortio*, 46; *International Covenant on Civil and Political Rights*, 17.

b) *Gaudium et Spes*, 48 and 50.

Article 7

Dignitatis Humanae, 5; *Religious Freedom and the Helsinki Final Act*, 4b; *International Covenant on Civil and Political Rights*, 18.

Article 8

Familiaris Consortio, 44 and 48.

a) *Apostolicam Actuositatem*, 11; *Familiaris Consortio*, 46 and 72.

b) *Familiaris Consortio*, 44 and 45.

Article 9

Laborem Exercens, 10 and 19; *Familiaris Consortio*, 45; *Universal Declaration*, 16, 3, and 22; *International Covenant on Economic, Social, and Cultural Rights*, 10, 1.

a) *Mater et Magistra*, Part II; *Laborem Exercens*, 10; *Familiaris Consortio*, 45; *Universal Declaration*, 22 and 25; *International Covenant on Economic, Social, and Cultural Rights*, 7, a, ii.

b) *Familiaris Consortio*, 45 and 46; *Universal Declaration*, 25, 1; *International Covenant on Economic, Social, and Cultural Rights*, 9, 10, 1 and 10, 2.

c) *Gaudium et Spes*, 52; *Familiaris Consortio*, 27.

Article 10

Laborem Exercens, 19; *Familiaris Consortio*, 77; *Universal Declaration*, 23, 3.

a) *Laborem Exercens*, 19; *Familiaris Consortio*, 23 and 81.

b) *Familiaris Consortio*, 23.

Article 11

Apostolicam Actuositatem, 8; *Familiaris Consortio*, 81; *International Covenant on Economic, Social, and Cultural Rights*, 11, 1.

Article 12

Familiaris Consortio, 77; *European Social Charter*, 19.